CAUSES IN COMMON

CAUSES IN COMMON

Welsh Women and the Struggle for Social Democracy

DARYL LEEWORTHY

UNIVERSITY OF WALES PRESS

2022

www.uwp.co.uk

British Library Cataloguing-in-Publication Data
A catalogue record for this book is available from the British Library.

ISBN   978-1-78683-854-4
eISBN   978-1-78683-855-1

The right of Daryl Leeworthy to be identified as author of this work has been
asserted in accordance with sections 77 and 79 of the Copyright, Designs
and Patents Act 1988.

The University of Wales Press acknowledges the financial support of the
Welsh Books Council.

Designed and typeset by Marie Doherty
Printed by CPI Antony Rowe, Melksham, United Kingdom

For Katrina

Contents

Figure

Abbreviations

AL	*Aberdare Leader*
ABTC	*Anti Bread Tax Circular*
ACLC	*Anti Corn Law Circular*
BDN	*Barry Dock News*
BH	*Barry Herald*
BLSA	British Library Sound Archive
CHE	Campaign for Homosexual Equality
CPA	Communist Party Archive
CPGB	Communist Party of Great Britain
CT	*Cardiff Times*
DH	*Daily Herald*
DM	*Daily Mirror*
DW	*Daily Worker*
EEx	*Evening Express*
FCH	*Flintshire County Herald*
GA	*Glamorgan Advertiser*
GG	*Glamorgan Gazette*
GLA	Glamorgan Archives, Cardiff
GLF	Gay Liberation Front
GN	*Gay News*
ILP	Independent Labour Party
IWD	International Women's Day

LHASC	Labour History Archive and Study Centre, Manchester
LL	*Labour Leader*
LP	Labour Party
LSE	London School of Economics
LW	*Labour Woman*
NEC	National Executive Committee
NLW	National Library of Wales
MEx	*Merthyr Express*
MM	*Monmouthshire Merlin*
MP	Member of Parliament
MPn	*Merthyr Pioneer*
MSG	Miners' Support Group
MT	*Merthyr Telegraph*
NG	*Neath Guardian*
NS	*Northern Star*
NWWN	*North Wales Weekly News*
PO	*Pontypridd Observer*
PTG	*Port Talbot Guardian*
RBA	Richard Burton Archives, Swansea University
RDC	Rural District Council
RGASPI	Russian State Archive of Socio-Political History, Moscow
RL	*Rhondda Leader*
RS	*Rhondda Socialist*
SCOLAR	Special Collections and Archives, Cardiff University
SpR	*Spare Rib*
SWCC	South Wales Coalfield Collection
SWDN	*South Wales Daily News*
SWDP	*South Wales Daily Post*

SWE	*South Wales Echo*
SWG	*South Wales Gazette*
SWMF	South Wales Miners' Federation
SWML	South Wales Miners' Library
TNA	The National Archives, Kew, London
TV/TS	Transvestite/Transsexual*
UDC	Urban District Council
WCG	Women's Co-operative Guild
WGA	West Glamorgan Archives, Swansea
WM	*Western Mail*
WLL	Women's Labour League
WLM	Women's Liberation Movement
WWP	W. W. Price Collection, Aberdare Library
WV	*Western Vindicator*

---

* Note that these are legacy terms and appear here only in reference to historic material.

Introduction

Just after six o'clock in the evening on 13 March 1950, Dorothy Mary Rees rose to her feet in the House of Commons. She was 51 years old; the first working-class woman sent by a Welsh electorate to represent them in Westminster. Just over a fortnight earlier, at the general election, she had defeated her Conservative opponent in the Barry constituency by a margin of more than 1,000 votes. Notes in hand, she explained to her colleagues that 'I speak as a housewife'. This was to be her first parliamentary identity. She had intervened in a King's Speech debate on the Labour government's housing policies. 'Women', she said, 'appreciate the fact that the houses [built since 1945] have better accommodation, better fitments, better kitchens, better bathrooms, and better floor finishing'. She then praised the high standards which the minister, Aneurin Bevan, had insisted upon during the 1945–50 government. Eschewing the traditional form of parliamentary maiden speeches, with their renditions of constituency details, Dorothy Rees instead asserted her own knowledge and authority as a politician. She told those in the chamber that she had been a local councillor and heavily involved in the delivery of public housing, and thus, 'I feel that I know something about the problem and the need of people for homes, and about the administrative end of providing those homes'.

The speech was received warmly by commentators, and the following morning newspapers reported both its contents and Dorothy Rees's appointment as parliamentary private secretary to the veteran Labour MP and Minister for National Insurance, Dr Edith Summerskill.[1] In this role, Dorothy Rees joined the British delegation to the Inter-Parliamentary Union conference in Dublin, speaking on recent reforms to child welfare services in the UK – as part of a lengthy debate on a child protection resolution.[2] Other topics discussed during the week-long conference included the teaching of history, how to restore and maintain world peace (the Korean War had recently broken out), and the global response to famine and food supply shortages.[3] However, it was the 'fair sprinkling of women parliamentarians, deputies [and] senators' who were present which caught the imagination of journalists sent to cover proceedings.[4] Alongside Dorothy Rees, who was the only woman in the British delegation, were women from Belgium, Denmark, Finland, Italy, Norway, Sweden, Yugoslavia, Israel and Pakistan, as well as from observers such as the International Labour Organisation. Their participation symbolised the growing influence of women in national parliaments and at the inter-governmental level.

For her second major parliamentary speech, delivered in December 1950, an increasingly confident Dorothy Rees added to the public portrait of her life. 'I am', she told members, 'a docker's daughter and have lived among the dock workers all my life'. Much of what that meant – and the experiences entailed – was left to one side, although the assertion of a working-class identity was plain enough. When parliamentary activities attracted the attention of journalists, a long career in public service and nearly two decades in electoral politics was often minimised; in such portraits Dorothy Rees was merely 'a widow and housewife'.[5] Only rarely was her career as a schoolteacher mentioned.[6] She was born on 29 July 1898 and grew up in a Welsh-speaking household in the shadow of Barry docks, when it was the largest coal port in the world. Her father, Henry Jones, worked as a boilermaker's assistant for one of the port's numerous ship-repair businesses – an industry to which Dorothy made deliberate reference in her parliamentary speeches. Catherine Jones (née Evans), Dorothy's mother, remained at home looking after her daughter and a much younger son, John. As a child, Dorothy proved herself a gifted pupil and progressed, on a scholarship, from Holton Road School to Barry County School for Girls.

In 1916, having completed secondary education, Dorothy Rees went to Barry Training College. She qualified as a schoolteacher just as the First World War entered its final stages. Her career ended abruptly when she married David George Rees (1898–1938), a merchant seaman and Barry native, in 1926. Rees had been decorated with the Conspicuous Gallantry Medal for his service in the Royal Navy during the war.[7] Not yet 30 years old and with no children, Dorothy Rees now devoted herself to public service. She was co-opted on to Barry Education Committee, making use of her practical experience in the classroom to shape local policy; she became steadily more active within the Labour Party, and its women's section in particular, which she joined just after the First World War; and then she began to run for office in the early 1930s.[8] In 1934, she succeeded and was elected on to both Barry Urban District Council (for the central ward) and Glamorgan County Council (for the Barry dock ward).[9] She specialised in education, health and housing, and was a prominent fixture of the respective council committees. During the Second

World War, she was appointed to a post with the Ministry of Food and was subsequently appointed agent for the Barry and Llandaff Constituency Labour Party ahead of the 1945 general election.

After the war, Dorothy Rees resumed her career in local government. Before her eventual retirement, she served on almost every major public body in Wales, from the Welsh Joint Education Committee, to the Welsh Teaching Hospitals Management Board, to the BBC. She was only the second woman to be elected chair of Glamorgan County Council, following in the footsteps of her friend, Rose Davies. In 1964, Dorothy Rees was awarded a CBE for services to local administration. A damehood followed in 1975. No wonder that, in his portrait published in the centenary history of Barry in the 1980s, Peter Stead observed of Dorothy Rees that she 'seemed almost to be the local spokesman of the Welfare State'.[10] For all that, as Deirdre Beddoe has pointed out, Dorothy Rees was 'an "ordinary" woman' whose parents, Henry and Catherine, had once lodged with the historian's own grandparents.[11] Election to parliament was fortuitous but accidental. The Barry and Llandaff constituency, which was created in 1918, was redrawn ahead of the 1950 general election. The sitting Labour MP, Lynn Ungoed-Thomas, who had won the seat for the party in 1945, defeating the incumbent Cyril Lakin, resolved to seek election elsewhere, and Dorothy Rees was seen as the ideal replacement. As secretary of the Constituency Labour Party, a long-serving councillor, and the presumptive electoral agent, she was well-known and popular, 'and as strong as anyone likely to be brought in from outside'.[12]

Remarkably, given her significance to the history of working-class women in Welsh politics, there has never been a full-length biography of Dorothy Rees. Nor, in fact, a single-volume study of either the women's movement (broadly defined, and I shall come on to questions of definition in a moment) or the women's labour movement, which propelled women such as Dorothy Rees into public office. Book chapters, articles and doctoral theses do exist, however.[13] So do discrete studies of specific contexts, such as Sue Bruley's *The Women and Men of 1926* (2010), Matthew Worley's *Labour Inside the Gate* (2005) and Duncan Tanner's consideration of the municipal work of individual women in the interwar years.[14] This absence has led to the attenuation of the collective achievements of working-class women in the fields of politics and public administration; it has further led to the creation of a historical narrative rich in its understanding of the lives of upper- and middle-class women, such as Lady Rhondda, Lady Charlotte Guest, Lady Megan Lloyd George, Amy Dillwyn and even the Ladies of Llangollen, but lacking in a similarly indicative appreciation of those whose lives were neither materially wealthy nor afforded status by title or position.[15] Furthermore, it has resulted in a misrepresentation of the fostering and enabling role played by the Labour Party, which was the largest electoral and representative force for Welsh women throughout the twentieth century.

With the benefit of fuller recovery and revelation, it is clearly insufficient to characterise the emergence of working-class women into elected office, typically on a Labour ticket in the interwar years and afterwards, as indicative of 'an interest to be represented rather than a sex which needed equality'.[16] Such a conclusion, adopted by Neil Evans and Dot Jones, and others who have followed their analysis, does little to underline the profound contribution of Labour women to public administration – as elected and co-opted members of councils and their committees – and plays down the significance of women elected as chairs of education, maternity and child welfare, hospital and housing committees, to say nothing of their election as chairs of council or joint policing committees.[17] Given the relative over-representation in the existing scholarly literature of women members of the Liberal Party in Wales, on the one hand, and the campaign for the vote, on the other; together with an established (if thinly sourced) insistence that nationalism shaped the character of the women's liberation movement; there is an obvious need to better understand those women who were politically active in other ways and who eschewed national identity as the basis for political activity, in favour of material conditions.[18] Those women, exactly like Dorothy Rees, in other words, who were active in the trade unions and their adjunct organisations; who were involved in the co-operative movement or in Chartist activity; who read feminist literature in the miners' institute libraries and other working-class libraries; or who were visible in the women's sections of the Communist and Labour parties.

*

Causes in Common tells the story of these women. It contrasts the diverse struggle for gender equality with the motif of 'Labour Country' and its social democratic ethos. My argument is that these were the essence of the women's movement.[19] This work has not always been straightforward. The absence of archival record for large swathes of the political activities of working-class women can easily amplify the careers of notable individuals and thereby diminish the collective activity of the many thousands of women – if not tens of thousands, if one includes trades unionists and members of allied associations – who were involved in the labour movement. One outcome of this book, I hope, and certainly one aim, is that it draws attention not only to those women who *did* stand out and to the reasons for their prominence, but

also to those pushed to the margins because they did not themselves become councillors, chairs, presidents or secretaries of
branches, or members of parliament. This has involved a recon-
sideration of historical methodology, a close reading of as much
extant evidence as possible, and the use of genealogy to restore as
many names as can be deciphered. I have thus chosen to discuss
Dorothy Rees, rather than either Mrs David George Rees or the
easier variant, Mrs Rees.

Not only does this approach nuance our understanding of
working-class women as political activists and political actors,
but it also adds to our appreciation of the universality of social
democratic ideals and of the influence of different forms of feminism during the nineteenth and twentieth centuries. Readers will
note a deliberate emphasis on local government and local communities. Pamela Graves, following Patricia Hollis, has rightly
concluded that this was 'one area where [women] could assert
their gender identity and serve their class at the same time'.[20] I
would add, considering women such as Barry's Elvira Gwenllian
Payne (née Hinds), the first black woman councillor in Wales,
and Butetown's Gaynor Legall, that local government was also an
arena to express other identities and the intersectionality of class,
gender and race. Intersectionality prompts a necessary extension
of the thematic coverage of women's political activism from those
which were common to every period – material status, political
status, reproductive rights, civil rights, and self-determination
– to those which emerged generationally, such as the call for
lesbian liberation and for recognition of the trans community.
The latter was not always comfortably integrated, either into the
women's liberation movement or the male-dominated gay civil
rights movement, although historically there was never any deliberate attempt to exclude trans experiences.

Moreover, there was greater synergy, politically and philosophically, between lesbian feminism and women's liberation than often there was between lesbian feminism and gay men's liberation, especially on matters of gender equality. Almost as soon as the civil rights movement was established in Wales in the early 1970s, organisation of gays and lesbians experienced fractures along gender lines. These continued into the 1980s. Nor was the Welsh LGBTQ+ civil rights movement unique. Across Britain, even in the most radical and avowedly anti-sexist groups, such as the Gay Left Collective, there were fierce debates and demands to 'contain *within it and reflect*, a knowledge of women's oppression and of female sexual experience'.[21] Trans groups themselves were initially divided between members who were heterosexual and those who fell somewhere on the queer spectrum. Consequently, what might otherwise be set out as a positive, even progressive narrative of continuous advance in equality and representation is necessarily qualified by the continuing struggle of those pushed to the margins and who have fought back from that position of marginality. That struggle took place within the women's movement as much as within wider society and became apparent over the course of the twentieth century as activists gained the language, and the platform, through which to campaign.

Here I am particularly interested in the roots of those social democratic ideas, organisations, and individual and collective actions which were absolutely at the core of twentieth-century politics, and in the responses of working-class women (in the main) to moments that are familiar to audiences but not always explored in this way: Chartism, the rise of the Labour Party, the economic and social turmoil between the wars, post-war affluence, and the remaking of Britain at the end of the twentieth century. In each generation women responded to – and sought to alter – the material circumstances in which they found themselves, and in so doing created and re-created a movement. These generations of activists and campaigners, politicians and trade unionists, did not always speak to each other, and some of the work undertaken or the possibilities created were forgotten, diminished or fell into neglect as time went on. To convey this historical rhythm and its implications, I have constructed the narrative of each chapter around individual life stories, and it is through these life stories that the links between the collective activity of women, the organisations they joined, and the significance of what they did, are made apparent.

My approach in this book, as elsewhere in my work, follows the methodological instincts of historical recovery, with appropriate nods to the theoretical dimensions of other cognate forms of historiography. Writing the history of women in the Welsh labour movement has been an outstanding and urgent task for decades. Without such a history, our collective understanding of the labour movement – and of social democracy – has been lopsided and our appreciation of the diversity of modern society appreciably diminished. This provides the principal caveat: my emphasis is on those women who formed part of the labour movement or were aligned with one of the political parties to which it gave rise. I have not, by contrast, focused much attention on members of the Liberal or Conservative parties or on those involved in nationalism, except (for reasons of coherence) where they were involved in the liberation movements of the 1970s and 1980s or appeared as antagonists of the labour movement. Those alternative political forces deserve to (and must) be recovered on their own terms, possibly (though not necessarily) by those sympathetic to their aims, before being integrated into historical synthesis.[22]

Given that social democracy was the mainstream of political life throughout the twentieth century – for men and for women – it makes absolute sense to seek to understand the organisation of women within the broad sphere of social democratic politics. That means, ultimately, focusing attention on the Labour Party and the wider labour movement, and women's agency within both elements. By the interwar years, the women's movement was itself built on the same platform. It means asking questions such as 'To what extent did women shape social democratic politics and political language in Wales?', or 'To what extent were women responsible for some of the policy outcomes – birth control clinics and nursery schools amongst them?', or 'What happened when women rejected the Liberal Party and moved into the Labour Party or, less frequently but no less fervently, into the Communist Party?' What happened, then, when women became active in material concerns and widening democratic participation? This is not to suggest e.g. that national identity was never important – the career of Annie Powell, Rhondda's Welsh-speaking communist mayor, is a clear indication that it was, at times – but that a political commitment to nationalism was a minnow compared with the battle for an eight-hour day, improved wages and conditions, or the spectrum of civil rights, including the ability to vote, to own property, to not have to give up one's job on marriage, and to seek an abortion on demand.

Language and geography provide certain complications and clarifications of these themes, albeit contingent themselves on the ever-present realities of regional variation. Political culture in the north-western and western counties retained its connection with liberalism and the Liberal Party for much longer than that of the south-east or north-east. That connection ultimately translated into popular support for Plaid Cymru – although that was assured only in the last quarter of the twentieth century. In a different vein, the space given to women's voices in southern newspapers and magazines, such as the *Rhondda Socialist*, the *Merthyr Pioneer*, or the *Colliery Worker's Magazine*, the official journal of the South Wales Miners' Federation, was much less apparent in northern equivalents – in either language. Assessing those variances, and accepting that they existed, is essential to creating a plurality and inclusive historiography of the Welsh. Likewise, if we are to avoid over-romanticising the past, we must also be aware of the rampant sexism which sat alongside more progressive views. The National Union of Mineworkers, for example, had 'page three girls' in magazines it published in the 1960s and 1970s; at the same time, the union campaigned for the end of apartheid in South Africa and intervened in the international peace movement. Such was the contradictory attitude towards equality.

*

In making the case for the social democratic roots of the women's movement, I have deliberately sought to show the peaks and troughs of progress rather than flatten historical experience by asserting a linear development. I have also tended to avoid focusing the narrative on the campaign for the vote, since this is already a well-considered theme, even in the Welsh setting, and for the sake of clarity in the text, I have removed appropriate historiographical discussion to the accompanying endnotes. Chapter 1 covers the sixty years or so between the advent of women's sections of the Chartist movement in the 1830s and the establishment of the Independent Labour Party and the first Welsh branches of the Women's Co-operative Guild in the 1890s. Chapter 2 carries the story through to the end of the First World

War, focusing its attention primarily on the Women's Labour League. Chapter 3 utilises the bookends of the Representation of the People Acts of 1918 and 1928 to chart the rise of women's sections within the Labour Party, whilst Chapter 4 adds the women's sections of the Communist Party into the mix, concluding with peace in 1945. Chapter 5 offers a revisionist perspective on the post-war decades and argues, contrary to existing literature, that this was not a fallow period for women's activism but rather one of steady consolidation, as women moved, in ever greater numbers, into positions of administrative authority. Chapter 6 tackles the liberation movements of the 1970s and 1980s and brings the story to the advent of devolution.

Such a chronology, for all its structural convenience, demonstrates only the unfolding of organised activity and cannot fully convey the construction and transmission of feminist knowledge from one generation to the next. Nor does a focus on political activity entirely capture the absorption of feminist ideas in society – particularly amongst the working class. This juncture is where the benefits of a multifaceted methodology become apparent, as well as a willingness to tackle the mistakes of earlier historians. On the shelves of the Maindy and Eastern Workmen's Institute in Ton Pentre there was once a copy of Mary Wollstonecraft's 1792 treatise, *A Vindication of the Rights of Women* – the volume now resides in the South Wales Miners' Library. It was published by the Newcastle-based Walter Scott as a centenary edition in 1892 and carried a foreword by the American feminist writer and Wollstonecraft biographer Elizabeth Robins Pennell. Of her biographical subject, Pennell concluded that

> [Wollstonecraft] may have written from impulse; she may often have sacrificed logic to rhetoric, but sincere

partisanship never made her lose her common sense. She was always an enthusiast, never a fanatic, and this, in our age of sentimental fanaticism, is not the least of her merits.[23]

But who amongst the readers of a workmen's institute in 1890s Rhondda was engaging with the intellectual legacy of early feminism? Historians have traditionally assumed that women were, in the words of Angela John, 'effectively barred from miners' institutes' and could not even 'go along and borrow books themselves'. As a result, women were not 'part of a public collective autodidactic tradition'.[24] This analysis was wrong, although it has been influential. Women were members of several miners' institutes and could, in fact, borrow books at their leisure, with sections of many libraries devoted to women readers of varying ages. By 1918, as many as a quarter of the borrowers from the library at Abergorki institute in the Rhondda were women.[25] Nor was this a recent development. Aberaman Workmen's Hall, which was opened by Keir Hardie in 1909, had a 'ladies' reading room and library', provision sustained by a separate rate of subscription.[26] The workmen's hall in Ystrad in the Rhondda, which was more than a decade older, made similar provision, as did the institutes in Maerdy and Tredegar.[27]

The remnants of these women's reading rooms – in both languages, although mostly in English, and almost completely unstudied – are now held at the South Wales Miners' Library. On the shelves originally, as one correspondent of the *Pontypridd Observer* recalled in 1949, were 'the many essentials necessary to home making [and] mothercraft'.[28] Indeed, before the First World War, Bargoed Institute had a copy of Phyllis Browne's *Practical Housekeeping* (1911) and Eduard Wagner's *Recipes for the Preserving of Fruit, Meat and Vegetables* (1908); Blaengarw Workmen's Hall had *Cassell's Book of the Household* (1891); and Mountain Ash a copy of Thomas Thomas's *Llyfr Coginio a Chadw Tŷ*, published in Wrexham in 1880. Given the unlikelihood of Victorian and Edwardian men reading books of 'domestic science', a key component of the late-nineteenth-century ideology of domesticity, there was only one likely audience for this material: women.[29] In the interwar years, Bargoed added to its collection by purchasing Mrs Peel's *The Art of Modern Housekeeping* (1935) and Thelma Benjamin's *Everyday in My Home* (1936). In addition to guides to cooking and cleaning, institute libraries bought material linked to family planning and birth control, such as Marie Stopes's *Radiant Motherhood* (1925) and *Sex and the Young* (1926) – copies of which survive from the institutes at Glynneath and Bargoed (respectively).

Personal book collections also reveal items catalogued as belonging to men alone, although obviously available (and in several cases almost certainly belonging) to women in the household – and thus are indicative of the intellectual life of working-class women. George Daggar, the Labour member of parliament for Abertillery between 1929 and 1950, owned everything from a copy of Mrs Beeton's *Book of Household Management*, to Marie Stopes's *Wise Parenthood* (1918), to Edward Carpenter's *Love's Coming of Age* (1913). D. J. Williams, the Labour member of parliament for Neath from 1945 until 1964, had a copy of Fanny Herbert's *Sex-Lore: A Primer on Courtship, Marriage and Parenthood* (1918) and of Auguste Forel's *The Sexual Question* (1931). Abel Morgan, a Labour councillor from Ynysybwl, owned Norah March's *Sex Knowledge* (1920) and Marie Stopes's *Radiant Motherhood*, amongst numerous books on local government and the co-operative movement. There are similar indications in the collections donated by S. O. Davies, the Labour member of parliament for Merthyr Tydfil (1934–72), whose younger (second) wife Sephora was a noted political activist in her own right, and the schoolteacher Brinley Griffiths, who, in the words of Hywel Francis and Sian Williams 'built up an impressive socialist library' with his wife Tillie.

Yet, as the survival of Mary Wollstonecraft's writing suggests, the literary environment available to women in the coalfield was not limited to domestic science textbooks or uniquely in service of an underlying social ideology. On the shelves of the institutes were copies of those novels which the women's liberation movement of the 1970s recovered through initiatives such as the Virago Modern Classics series, a hint at the continuity of feminist knowledge and understanding. Of the first three authors republished by Virago – the Catholic convert Antonia White (1899–1980), the communist Sylvia Townsend Warner (1893–1978) and the Australian Marxist Christina Stead (1902–83) – only the latter is absent from extant collections. The two novels by Sylvia Townsend Warner, *Mr Fortune's Maggot* (1927) and *Summer Will Show* (1936), which survive from Abercraf and Abergorki respectively, are instructive, however.[30] Set in revolutionary Paris in 1848, *Summer Will Show* is rich in its portrait not only of radical politics but also of same-sex desire: the novel's protagonist, the aristocratic Sophia Willoughby, falls in love with her husband's Russian mistress, Minna.[31] *Mr Fortune's Maggot* is similarly infused with same-sex desire, although in this case between the middle-aged Christian missionary Timothy Fortune and the only person he manages to convert in three years, a younger man called Lueli.[32]

Mary Webb (1881–1927), the fourth novelist republished by Virago, who wrote in a romantic style and set much of her work in the Shropshire countryside, was widely available in the institute network by the 1930s, particularly in the Rhondda. Abergorki Institute used some of a fifty-pound grant from the Carnegie Trust to buy much of Mary Webb's writing in 1930, joining in with a wave of popular enthusiasm for the writer which began a couple of years earlier. Webb's popularity, which had declined in the 1920s to the extent that she was an obscure figure at her death in 1927, was recovered by the Conservative Prime Minister Stanley Baldwin. At a speech to the Royal Literary Fund in April 1928, he described Webb as a neglected genius. 'Now that the Premier has praised Mary Webb', commented the *Daily Mirror* afterwards, 'it is hoped that the public will read her work'.[33] Within six months, much of her writing had been reprinted by publisher Jonathan Cape, some with additional forewords by popular contemporaries such as G. K. Chesterton, and sales stood at 50,000 copies.[34] This continued through much of the mid-twentieth century. After the Second World War, Ferndale Workmen's Hall acquired a set of Webb's novels, perhaps in response to the release of the film adaptation of *Gone to Earth* (1917) in 1950.[35]

These intellectual lineaments, set alongside a narrative of unfolding political activity, afford a sophisticated image of working-class women; one removed from the prevailing impression of lives lived in domestic service with little opportunity for engagement with the public sphere – and little appetite for such, in any case. This is not to soften, unduly, the harsh experiences endured. Working-class women bore the brunt of bad housing and overcrowding, state provision of education which stopped at a young age, poor healthcare, and the lack of an independent income, which restricted leisure and curtailed standards of living. 'The unremitting toil of childbirth and domestic labour', wrote Dot Jones, indicatively, 'killed and debilitated Rhondda women as much as accident and conditions in the mining industry killed and maimed Rhondda men'.[36] It was to those conditions of economic, material and physical hardship that politics, intellectual life and consumer culture responded. Weaving these themes into an otherwise chronological narrative of a movement is essential to reach an understanding of life lived in its entirety. Moreover, this approach seems to me to be the best one if the aim is to make a real impact on assumptions about the past, to recover the experiences of cis- and trans women, as well as of those who sought romantic relationships or sexual partnerships with other women.

*

All of which brings me back to Dorothy Rees and to her hometown of Barry. It is a profound irony that a historiographical tradition which prides itself on examining the past from the bottom up – and has largely succeeded in that ambition when discussing men's experiences – has tended to explore women's history from the opposite direction. 'A society whose dependence on female labour, at the work-place as well as in the home, has been lengthy and complex', argued Dai Smith, 'needs an analysis of the social culture erected, often with calculation, around this more real biological divide'. Women, he added, 'were never "outside" the actual history of Wales'.[37] That actual history was one of work – a world of labour, to borrow an apt phrase from Eric Hobsbawm – and of a material society built around, and in response to, that gendered core.[38] One of the organisations which stands out as indicative of a labouring milieu, and with which Dorothy Rees was almost certainly familiar from her life in Barry docks, was the Railway Women's Guild (RWG). Formed as an 'auxiliary' to the Amalgamated Society of Railway Servants (the forerunner of the National Union of Railwaymen) in 1900, it had a strong presence in Barry, Cardiff, Newport and Swansea, the latter being one of the earliest established branches in Britain.

The RWG brought together the wives and daughters of unionised railwaymen and those women who worked for railway companies, it fostered harmony amongst the 'railway family', and it provided grassroots education in trade union and labour matters, and the politics and purpose of social democracy. Members were encouraged to read the women's column in the *Railway Review*, the NUR's national magazine, and to debate matters of policy and politics – ranging from peace to housing shortages – all from the point of view of railway women.[39] For some members, such as Siniah Bannister of Aberdare, the RWG was just one of several workplace organisations which shaped her life outside the home – others included the local branch of the Great Western Railway's Temperance Union, which her husband, Joseph, chaired for several years.[40] Historians miss the point, it seems to me, if they contain the life of someone such as Siniah Bannister solely within the home: indeed, they rather miss the life actually lived by their subject. Yes, she laboured domestically, she cooked, she cleaned, she ensured the household was 'kept'; but her life was richer than that and lived outside the home as well as inside. It was a life fulfilled: in the social terms understood by working-class women of her generation.

The great value of a kaleidoscopic approach to women's organisation and activism in the nineteenth and twentieth centuries lies, of course, in recognising the diversity of feminism in discrete historical moments and over time. In her recent study of global feminisms, Lucy Delap has shown persuasively that each successive generation of feminists was motivated by both the 'specific concerns of their historical moment' and their immediate context.[41] Those changed over time. Social class, race, sexuality and material inequality were, however, issues of long lasting salience. That, I suggest, is why the women's movement, over the course of two centuries, was built on a platform of social democratic politics, social democratic ideas and social democratic ideals – even as those three things were themselves being constructed and moving from the margins to the centre of public life. It is why the women's movement and the labour movement, for all the battles over policy and representation, came together as they did. Why, ultimately, a docker's daughter from Barry was the first working-class Welsh woman to be elected to and to speak in parliament.

Notes

1. *WM*, 14 March 1950.
2. *Irish Independent*, 14 September 1950.
3. James Douglas, *Parliaments Across Frontiers: A Short History of the Inter-Parliamentary Union* (London, 1976), p. 55.
4. *Irish Independent*, 8 September 1950.
5. *Yorkshire Post*, 25 February 1950.
6. *DH*, 24 April 1950.
7. *BDN*, 14 June 1918, 6 September 1918, 25 October 1918. According to his merchant sailor's registration card, by 1922 he was working as a quartermaster. The National Archives, Kew, Merchant Seamen Registration Documents, 1918–41, BT349: David George Rees, Barry, 31 October 1922.
8. *WM*, 26 March 1932, 4 April 1932.
9. *WM*, 22 February, 28 February, 6 March, 13 April 1934.
10. Peter Stead, 'Barry since 1939', in Donald Moore (ed.), *Barry: The Centenary Book* (Barry, 1985), pp. 455–6.
11. Deirdre Beddoe, *Out of the Shadows* (Cardiff, 2000), p. 6.
12. *PO*, 15 January 1949.
13. Lowri Newman, '"Providing an opportunity to exercise their energies": the role of the Labour Women's Sections in shaping political identities, South Wales, 1918–1939', in Esther Breitenbach and Pat Thane (eds), *Women and*

Citizenship in Britain and Ireland in the Twentieth Century: What Difference Did the Vote Make? (London, 2010); Lowri Newman, 'A Distinctive Brand of Politics: Women in the South Wales Labour Party, 1918–1939' (unpublished MPhil thesis, University of Glamorgan, 2003); Ursula Masson, '"Political conditions in Wales are quite different..." Party politics and votes for women in Wales, 1912–15', *Women's History Review*, 9/2 (2000).

14. Duncan Tanner, 'Gender, Civic Culture and Politics in South Wales: Explaining Labour Municipal Policy, 1918–39', in Matthew Worley (ed.), *Labour's Grass Roots: Essays on the Activities of Local Labour Parties and Members, 1918–45* (Aldershot, 2005), pp. 170–93.

15. Angela John, *Turning the Tide: The Life of Lady Rhondda* (Cardigan, 2013); Angela John, *Rocking the Boat: Welsh Women Who Championed Equality, 1840–1990* (Cardigan, 2017); Angela John and Revel Guest, *Lady Charlotte Guest: An Extraordinary Life* (London, 2007 [1989]); Victoria Owens, *Lady Charlotte Guest: The Exceptional Life of a Female Industrialist* (London, 2020); Elizabeth Major, *The Ladies of Llangollen: A Study in Romantic Friendship* (London, 2011); Fiona Brideoake, *The Ladies of Llangollen: Desire, Indeterminacy and the Legacies of Criticism* (London, 2017); David Painting, *Amy Dillwyn* (Cardiff, 2013); Mervyn Jones, *A Radical Life: A Biography of Megan Lloyd George* (London, 1991).

16. Neil Evans and Dot Jones, 'Women in the Labour Party', in Duncan Tanner, Chris Williams and Deian Hopkin (eds), *The Labour Party in Wales, 1900–2000* (Cardiff, 2000), p. 226.

17. Here I follow Pat Thane's positive assessment of the relationship between women and the Labour Party. Pat Thane, 'Women in the British Labour Party and the Construction of State Welfare, 1906–1939', in Seth Koven and Sonya Michel (eds), *Mothers of a New World: Maternalist Politics and the Origins of Welfare States* (London, 1993); Pat Thane, 'The Women of the British Labour Party and Feminism', in H. L. Smith (ed.), *British Feminism in the Twentieth Century* (Aldershot, 1990).

18. Ursula Masson, *For Women, For Wales and For Liberalism: Women in Liberal Politics in Wales, 1880–1914* (Cardiff, 2010); Ursula Masson (ed.), *Women's Rights and Womanly Duties: The Aberdare Women's Liberal Association, 1891–1910* (Cardiff, 2005); Ryland Wallace, *The Women's Suffrage Movement in Wales, 1868–1928* (Cardiff, 2009); Lisa Tippings, *Women's Suffrage in Wales* (Barnsley, 2019); Jane Aaron and Ursula Masson (eds), *The Very Salt of Life: Welsh Women's Political Writings from Chartism to Suffrage* (Dinas Powys, 2007). The relationship between Welsh nationalism and women's

liberation was asserted by Avril Rolph, 'A movement of its own: the Women's Liberation Movement in south Wales', in Helen Graham, Ann Kaloski, Ali Neilson and Emma Robertson (eds), *The Feminist Seventies* (York, 2003), p. 44.

19. The motif is, of course, my own. Daryl Leeworthy, *Labour Country: Political Radicalism and Social Democracy in South Wales, 1831–1985* (Cardigan, 2018).

20. Pamela M. Graves, *Labour Women: Women in British Working-Class Politics, 1918–1939* (Cambridge), p. 224; Patricia Hollis, *Ladies Elect: Women in English Local Government, 1865–1914* (Oxford, 1987).

21. Sue Bruley, 'Women in Gay Left', *Gay Left*, 3 (Autumn 1976). Italics in original.

22. Charlotte Aull Davies, 'Women, Nationalism and Feminism', in Jane Aaron and Angela V. John (eds), *Our Sisters' Land* (Cardiff, 1994); Laura McAllister, 'Gender, Nation and Party: an uneasy alliance for Welsh nationalism', *Women's History Review*, 10/1 (2001), 51–70; Sam Blaxland, 'Women in the organisation of the Conservative Party in Wales, 1945–1979', *Women's History Review*, 28/2 (2019).

23. Elizabeth Robins Pennell, 'Introduction', in Mary Wollstonecraft, *A Vindication of the Rights of Woman* (London, 1892), xxiv.

24. Angela John, 'A Miner Struggle? Women's Protests in Welsh Mining History', *Llafur*, 4/1 (1986), p. 76.

25. Richard Burton Archives, South Wales Coalfield Collection, Abergorki Workmen's Hall Records, D20: List of Members, 1918–1920.

26. *CT*, 19 June 1909.

27. *Pontypridd Chronicle*, 7 February 1896.

28. *PO*, 3 September 1949.

29. Kay Boardman, 'The Ideology of Domesticity: The Regulation of the Household Economy in Victorian Women's Magazines', *Victorian Periodicals Review*, 33/2 (Summer 2000), 150–64.

30. Warner's fiction has been widely examined, particularly in relation to its politics and homosexual thematics. The best biography of the writer is Claire Harman, *Sylvia Townsend Warner: A Biography* (London, 2015 [1989]).

31. Thomas Foster, *Transformations of Domesticity in Modern Women's Writing: Homelessness at Home* (Basingstoke, 2002), considers the revolutionary tone of the novel and argues that it 'launches a double critique' of both traditional Marxist and modernist literature, providing a historical context for same-sex desire (pp. 115–36).

32. This portrait has been subject to a degree of debate. Nigel Rigby suggests that the homosexuality present in the novel is a metaphor for a critique of British imperialism. Rigby, '"Not a good place for deacons": the South Seas, sexuality and modernism in Sylvia Townsend Warner's *Mr Fortune's Maggot*', in Howard J. Booth and Nigel Rigby (eds), *Modernism and Empire* (Manchester, 2000), pp. 224–48. Jane Garrity, by contrast, stresses the feminised character of Timothy Fortune and Lueli and suggests that this is an 'inverted binary' of what otherwise rests as a portrait of lesbian desire. Garrity, *Step-Daughters of England: British Women Modernists and the National Imaginary* (Manchester, 2003). 'Inverted binary' is discussed on p. 145.

33. *DM*, 27 April 1928.

34. *Western Times* (Exeter), 19 October 1928.

35. Other surviving examples derive from the libraries at Bargoed and Glynneath.

36. Dot Jones, 'Counting the Cost of Coal: Women in the Rhondda, 1881–1911', in Angela V. John (ed.), *Our Mothers' Land* (Cardiff, 2011 [1991]), p. 124.

37. Dai Smith, 'Introduction', in Dai Smith (ed.), *A People and a Proletariat: Essays in the History of Wales, 1780–1980* (London, 1980).

38. Eric J. Hobsbawm, *Worlds of Labour: Further Studies in the History of Labour* (London, 1984).

39. *CT*, 21 October 1905; *BDN*, 21 November 1913, 23 January 1914.

40. *AL*, 4 November 1905.

41. Lucy Delap, *Feminisms: A Global History* (London, 2020).

1

Before the Vote

M uch of what women did in the public sphere in the nineteenth century was forgotten in the twentieth. Or, it was
understood only through the campaign for the vote. 'In the early
days', recalled Elizabeth Andrews, the Labour Party's women's
organiser for Wales in the interwar years, in her memoir published in 1957, 'women were very new in politics, and were afraid
of being called suffragettes. Much educational work had to be
done in simple language and made interesting'. As influential
as this memory has proven itself to be, the reality of women's
involvement in the politics of the industrial age was far more complex. Women were active as campaigners long before a wave of
violence and suffrage organisation shook Edwardian Britain, saw
individuals spied upon, imprisoned and force-fed, and provided
newspaper editors with sensation to sell copy and even invent
the term 'suffragette'. Eighty years earlier, in fact, during the anti-
slavery campaigns, anti-corn law activism, and Chartist agitation,
women responded to the shock of industrialisation, to punitive
legislation such as the New Poor Law of 1834, and to the campaign
for democratic rights, by forming their own independent radical
associations and penning their own reform-minded manifestos.[1]

Out of this multifaceted wave of activity, which involved working-class and middle-class activists and campaigners, emerged liberal and social democratic ideas about the relationship between women and contemporary politics. There was not inconsiderable cross-over, in personnel and aim, between the repeal and abolitionist movements which, although by no means lacking support in the industrial countries of southern Wales, were chiefly the preserve of middle-class liberals and those living in northern counties.[2] One campaigner observed in 1842, for instance, that 'the colliers of North Wales ... would make efficient auxiliaries to the Chartists of Glamorgan and Monmouth in extending the faith of democracy'.[3] They failed to be. Wrexham and Caernarfon were, instead, organisational hubs for the Anti Corn Law League, the focus of the repeal movement. Chartism, through which the working class tended to organise itself, was often suspicious of the repeal movement and Chartists could be found heckling at tariff reform meetings, e.g. in Swansea.[4] Even in Llanidloes, where Chartists 'behaved themselves well' at gatherings, there was fear in advance that there would be unrest. 'It would be well', concluded the ACLL's newspaper, with such behaviour in mind, 'if some of our Lancashire bigots who assume the name Chartists could take a lesson of toleration from their Welch brethren'.[5] This mutual antagonism, which mirrored later tension between advocates of independent labour representation and those persuaded that the Liberal Party should remain a 'big tent force', was material in nature rather than moral. Chartists were themselves opposed to slavery and in favour of free trade, and all three campaigns were rooted in Protestant nonconformity and anti-establishmentarianism.

The involvement of Welsh women in the repeal movement was not frequently recorded. It was formally organised only in Wrexham, although there is evidence of participation in Carmarthen and Caernarfon.[6] In January 1842, a meeting at Caernarfon Guildhall concluded with the circulation of a repeal petition to parliament and a separate memorial to be sent to Queen Victoria, which was signed by the 'wives and female relatives of the petitioners'.[7] Following similar meetings, which were held across Denbighshire and Flintshire, almost 2,500 Welsh women had added their names to the national memorial, which itself was signed by more than 250,000.[8] Much of the work of gathering signatures was undertaken by the Wrexham women's section, which comprised individuals such as Sarah Thornley, wife of wealthy hat manufacturer Robert Thornley; Mary Rawson, wife of the Leeds-born solicitor and hymnist George Rawson, who lived at Pickhill Hall; Martha Lewis (née Kenrick, of Wynne Hall, Ruabon), wife of Dr George Lewis, the town's surgeon; and the railway investor Sarah Hilditch.[9] These women were linked together both by their work on behalf of the repeal movement and by their membership of the congregation at Wrexham's Penybryn Chapel.[10]

A figure such as Sarah Hilditch, who was born in Oswestry in Shropshire (where her father, Thomas, was the town's mayor) in the first decade of the nineteenth century, but who came to reside for a period in Wrexham's King Street, has typically been understood through her abolitionist work.[11] Together with her younger sister, Blanche, who was born deaf and dumb, Sarah Hilditch met with American abolitionists such as William Lloyd Garrison (1805–79), editor of *The Liberator*, and a founder member of the American Anti-Slavery Society; she met with memoirist and activist Frederick Douglass (1817–95), himself a former slave; and corresponded with Maria Weston Chapman (1806–85), editor of the anti-slavery journal, *The Non-Resistant*, which was based in Boston, Massachusetts. During the American Civil War and its aftermath, Hilditch also provided funds, via the Edinburgh Ladies' Emancipation Society (of which she was a member), to support emancipated former slaves in the United States.[12] As befitted the entanglement of repeal and abolitionism in the 1830s and 1840s, Sarah Hilditch was equally prominent in the campaign against the corn laws, serving on various committees, signing petitions, organising the Wrexham women's group, and becoming closely identified with the women's section of the national repeal movement.[13]

Anti-corn law campaigners undoubtedly recognised the appeal of repeal to working-class families and pressed the case in industrial areas, partly in an effort to win over those who had joined the Chartist movement.[14] As one meeting in Monmouthshire concluded,

> the corn laws are highly injurious to the nation at large, but more particularly to the industrious classes ... [and we] consider that nothing short of their total repeal will remove the present suffering which prevails among the working men of this county.[15]

Working-class consumers were affected by high bread prices and by the worst effects of industrialisation: low wages, the rent book, unfair credit systems, and the malfeasance of businesses and industrialists.[16] Activism and debate entailed a moral commentary on contemporary politics, the absence of those rights associated with full citizenship, and the economic misfortunes of the poor – those trapped in a system of wage labour which extracted an enormous personal price for little material reward, or who were enslaved.[17] Women were most especially marginalised, their earning potential as low as twelve shillings a week – less than half the wage earned by men in unskilled work. Thus, in her wide-ranging study of the Victorian economy and its domestic implications, *Bread Winner*, Emma Griffin notes that

> the highly gendered nature of the pre-1914 labour market has often been acknowledged but its full implications have not. As highly marginalised members of the workforce, adult women did not take a direct share in the wealth created by industrialisation. Instead, their share reached them through the hands of their husbands and older children, for whom they, in returned, performed the unpaid work of the house.[18]

The result was a life of permanent precarity, of constant struggle to maintain a household on an income shared with other people. 'Finding a suitable husband', Griffin adds, 'persuading him to spend his wages on his family and agreeing how best to allocate food at the dinner table', all determined the health and wellbeing of adult women. Unsurprising, then, that working-class women found in Chartism a platform to bring about potential reform of their own situation, as well as that of their social class.

More than a hundred women's Chartist groups were established across Britain in the late 1830s. At least a dozen of them were formed by those who lived in the industrialising valleys of Glamorgan and Monmouthshire, in Newport, and in the industrial crucible of Merthyr Tydfil.[19] Members adopted a diverse nomenclature, reflecting the breadth of their ideas and their organisational purpose. There was the Female Patriotic Association of Blackwood, a title akin to that of the women's lodges established in Bristol and Newport. In Abersychan and Merthyr Tydfil members chose to call themselves a Female

Radical Association, evoking similar groups in the north of England.[20] These societies met in sympathetic public houses or in the private homes of activists and agitated publicly for universal suffrage – for men and women. Members campaigned, too, for improvements to material conditions. They listened to lectures, read pamphlets, sang songs, debated ideas, wrote letters, signed petitions, made and presented banners, marched in the great processions, usually at the head of the column, and raised their consciousness as women.[21] In the passive legalese of Mr Thomas, the defence solicitor at the trial held in the aftermath of the 1839 Chartist march on Newport, 'the bands of female Chartists were not thought unformidable'.[22]

And yet, by the time Elizabeth Andrews sat down to write her memoir, these remarkable women, the first who set out to create a working-class women's movement, and their activities in support of the People's Charter, were forgotten. The same fate was not afforded to male Chartists, whose memory was faithfully recorded by historians of the labour movement from the outset.[23] Only as professional study of the Chartist movement gathered pace in the 1960s, with the innovations of social history, women's history and labour history, has the fuller history of Chartism, a movement which included women and people of colour, come to light. However, most of those women (and people of colour) who joined associations or marched in processions remain anonymous, as hidden from history to us as they were to Elizabeth Andrews more than six decades ago. Even the more prominent activists, such as Mary Frost or Joan Williams (who organised the Blaina Female Chartist Association), have faded into the background, compared with their husbands John and Zephaniah. One woman Chartist about whom contemporaries wrote a great deal was Jane Dickenson of Newport. Her mother,

Sarah, was a prominent Chartist, as was her father, John, who was a butcher by trade.

Jane Dickenson regularly chaired meetings at the Bush Inn in Commercial Street, where the Newport Working Men's Association gathered. On 20 March 1839, for instance, she presided over a lecture given by Henry Vincent (1813–78), amongst the most prominent of Chartist leaders in the south-west of England and himself a supporter of women's suffrage. Earlier in the day, Vincent had addressed an open-air rally attended by hundreds of supporters, including a significant number of women. 'I found', he reported in a column for the *Western Vindicator*, a Chartist newspaper, that 'from four to five hundred people assembled, three hundred of whom were ladies'.[24] The crowd listened attentively as Vincent explained the purpose of the People's Charter, the necessity of the campaign for the vote, and, most importantly of all, heard the orator's direct appeal 'to the ladies for assistance, encouragement, and support'. At the Bush Inn that evening, Vincent reiterated his call for women's collective involvement in the campaign for the People's Charter. Proceedings concluded with a rendition of the popular hymn 'The Democrat', with Jane Dickenson accompanying on the piano. The meeting then moved outside and joined a gathering procession 'four abreast'. Women at the front, men following behind.

'The Newport ladies', Vincent observed later, 'are progressing with great spirit to the terror of the Aristocrats of the town and neighbourhood'. He believed it was true across the Monmouthshire valleys. In each of the communities Vincent travelled to and spoke in, women formed a substantial contingent of those who came to listen. Oftentimes, women were in the majority. Vincent's speeches addressed them directly. Women, he said, 'were more interested in a good state of government

and society than men'. It was a fact, he explained to readers of
the *Western Vindicator*, 'of which they seemed fully convinced'.
At Pontllanfraith, for instance, speaking to a crowd of around
1,000 people outside the Greyhound public house, Vincent
sought to prove to those women present 'their intimate connection with the political interests of their country'.[25] Having put his
case, the Chartist Petition was then passed around for signature,
with dedicated sheets for gathering the signatures of the women
who were present. By the time the National Petition was submit-
ted to parliament on 14 June 1839, more than 1,250,000 people
had signed, a fifth of them women. A thousand of the women's
signatures were from Monmouthshire alone, a testament to the
efficacy of the local associations.

Material inequality mattered fundamentally to women active
in the Chartist movement and they were to be found at the forefront of campaigns to create co-operative shops, co-operative
farms, and other mutualised forms of consumption; they were
also those keenest in directing pressure to deal only with those
shopkeepers and traders who subscribed to the shared ideals of
the movement.[26] Chartist women thus laid the foundations of
the co-operative movement, which emerged formally in the mid-
Victorian period. Moreover, out of the involvement of women in
Chartism came, in effect, the organisational and thematic cues of
the social democratic wing of the women's movement: material
inequality, equal rights of citizenship, and the struggle for the
franchise. It is also possible to observe the emergence of single-
sex associational culture rooted in working-class music, drama,
poetry, autodidactic education and patterns of consumption.[27]
Newspapers such as the *Northern Star* and the *Western Vindicator*
contained short stories, poems and songs written by women,
including the 'Lion of Freedom' by an otherwise anonymous

'Welsh female Chartist'.[28] A handful of activists, typically those from middle-class backgrounds, even wrote novels, setting down the political ethos of the Chartist movement for wealthier members of society so that they might understand its existence and be less obviously hostile to its aims.[29]

Across many of the short stories and several of the Chartist novels, working women (often seamstresses or dressmakers) featured as representatives of the 'hardships and possible social repercussions of industrialization'.[30] From working-class women themselves there was a record of autobiography, poetry and other writing, which set down lives as they lived them – this body of writing has only relatively recently been explored.[31] When working-class autobiography was first recognised as a potentially rich source of first-hand information about the industrial revolution, via material collected by John Burnett, David Mayall and David Vincent, women provided only a fragment of the total in the archive.[32] As the three noted in 1984, the 'most obvious distortion in the main body of autobiographies is the small number written by women'.[33] Their total was seventy works out of more than 2,000 collected. Two years earlier Vincent had established a figure from his own research of less than five per cent of nineteenth-century working-class autobiographical writing being by women authors.[34] Determined study in more recent years has identified an additional thirty narratives, providing, as Florence Boos suggests, for the possibility that 'the ratio was presumably somewhat better than has previously been assumed'.[35] But not in the Welsh context, where such writing (at least in English) was, if survival is taken as a meaningful measure, practically non-existent.[36]

What remained was the novel, in particular retrospective works, such as Amy Dillwyn's *The Rebecca Rioter*, which was first published in 1880, and Irene Saunderson's *A Welsh Heroine*,

published in 1910.[37] Neither Dillwyn, a liberal Swansea businesswoman and industrialist, nor Saunderson, the wife of a Swansea
doctor, who regularly wrote for the *South Wales Daily Post*, were
working-class.[38] Although they wrote about working-class people
with a degree of sympathy and, in Saunderson's case, awareness
of the tensions between labour and capital, their perspective was
ultimately that of the middle classes. Striking miners were por-
trayed as 'poor, deluded creatures', for example, and the solution
to the battle between workers and employers was compromise
rather than any sort of proletarian revolution.[39] A compromise moreover led by the titular heroine, Morfydd Llewellyn,
rather than by trades unions or any representative of the labour
movement. Amy Dillwyn's writing, which was endowed with a
sense of economic and social justice – at least from the point
of view of contemporary liberalism; her father, Lewis Llewelyn
Dillwyn (1814–92), was the Liberal member of parliament for
Swansea from 1855 until his death – was perhaps more notable
for nuanced awareness of gender and female sexuality (including
homosexuality) ahead of its time.[40]

*

By the 1850s, Chartism and other forms of industrial protest had
faded, but the material reasons for the movement's existence and
the waves of unrest in the 1830s and 1840s did not simply evapo-
rate.[41] Nor did the corn law repeal enacted in 1846 immediately
improve the quality of food available to working-class consumers. Producers widely adulterated their produce to turn a profit.
So common was the practice that newspapers offered readers
tips on its detection. Plunge a knife 'heated sufficiently to melt
wax ... into the middle of a suspected loaf', advised the *Cambrian*
in 1819, 'and if there be alum, it will encrust the knife with a

paste, after remaining in the bread ten minutes'.[42] More than a decade later, the *Carmarthen Journal* reminded its readers that 'potatoes are often used by bakers in making bread, and a great popular clamour has been raised against the practice'.[43] In the middle of the nineteenth century, adulteration of food and drink encompassed everything from bread and milk to beer and coffee. 'We are told', observed the *North Wales Chronicle* sardonically, 'that a good-looking compound is made up of a small portion of genuine coffee, a good deal of chicory, refuse ship-biscuit, damaged bean-flour, rope-yards, raddle, and soot to deepen the colour'. As for milk,

> [it] has very little indeed to do with cows; it is made of bull-ocks' brains, soft water, whiting, and the scraping of raw hides coloured (if you will insist on cream) with a little of the thing called annatto: the thicker your cream, the more bullocks' brains are you treated to.[44]

As the paper rightly concluded: 'Filthy stuff'.

Fortunately, adulteration of milk with pureed cattle brains was a relatively rare occurrence. Producers preferred instead to water it down and then add food colouring to restore appearance: initially, colouring comprised carrot juice, chalk and flour, with synthetic dyes being used later on.[45] Watered-down milk was common across much of Wales, with western and midland counties showing particularly high instances from the 1870s through to the First World War. Production quality was at its best in Glamorgan and Monmouthshire, partly because wages were highest in those counties and partly because of the influence of the co-operative movement. In 1914, Cardiff's food standards officers analysed more than 500 samples of milk and recorded adulteration in just thirty-six (some six per cent of the total).[46] In Monmouthshire, in 1920, officers found that the rate of adulteration was under five per cent.[47] But in Cardiganshire, even into the mid-1920s, almost a third of samples were found to have been tampered with.[48] The response of working-class consumers was evident in the emergence of the co-operative store, a Chartist innovation, which, with its guiding principles of honesty, fair pricing and high quality, stood as a bulwark against rampant adulteration of food and drink, and extended lines of consumer credit in ways which served members rather than private profiteering.

The success of co-operatives owed much to working-class women, especially married women. They controlled the domestic economy and were the major participants in matters of working-class consumption. A 'distinctive universe of values', which was engendered by retail co-operatives in the nineteenth and early twentieth centuries, was thus built by women.[49] Although independent organisation within the co-operative movement was not achieved until 1883, with the founding of the Women's Co-operative Guild (WCG), and there remained a constant struggle, as Peter Gurney notes, 'against prejudice from male co-operators who commonly believed women's involvement should be confined to shopping at the stores and helping at social events', women gained a presence not only as shoppers but also as members, employees and, ultimately, administrators of co-operative societies.[50] By the beginning of the twentieth century, there was at least one woman serving on the management committee of a Welsh co-operative, namely Mrs Thomas, the branch president of the Cardiff WCG. She had been elected by members of the Glamorgan Co-operative Society. The *Co-operative News* noted that women members in that society were given 'great encouragement from the men'. In Pembroke Dock, there were supportive utterings from local co-operative officials, who made it known to members at large that they 'would like to see a woman on the management committee'.[51] This remained an aspiration rather than a reality for many years thereafter, however.

As with women's involvement in politics, much of what was traditionally known about the early development of the WCG in Wales relied on the impressionistic and partial account provided by Elizabeth Andrews in her memoir. Therein she remarked on establishing the first WCG branch in the Rhondda, at Ton Pentre, in 1914, and her own role as its secretary. 'The Guild', concluded Deirdre Beddoe on this evidence, 'took off rather late in Wales'.[52] Thanks in large part to the pioneering research of Helen Thomas, which I have followed and supplemented here, this conclusion and the account on which it was based are now known to be incorrect.[53] The first Rhondda branch was indeed formed in Ton Pentre, but it was established by an entirely different group almost fifteen years earlier.[54] Moreover, the first Welsh branches of the WCG were created within a decade of the national movement's foundation: in Newport and Swansea in 1891, in Cardiff in 1892, and in Abertillery and Risca in 1893.[55] Yet it was a fragile presence. Of the branches formed in the early 1890s, only Newport survived – and that was despite regular difficulties and diminishing membership. The forty members tallied in 1894 had halved by the end of the decade.

Part of the challenge facing the women who organised the Newport WCG – and who attempted to establish a regional presence for the movement – was the organisational structure of the Guild itself. England and Wales were divided into various sections, which were themselves partitioned into districts. Newport was a member of the Gloucester and Monmouth District (established in 1897), part of the Western and South Western Section. With most branches in the district located around Gloucester, and with the section largely governed by members based in Plymouth, Newport found itself on the periphery in both and without much support. A district committee for southern Wales was eventually formed in 1900, to accommodate and to sustain the growing number of branches and almost 300 members located in the region – this in turn led to a rapid expansion of the Women's Co-operative Guild.[56] In the north, branches formed after 1900, such as Brymbo and Queensferry, joined the Cheshire and North Wales District.[57] The branches which came together to form the South Wales and Monmouthshire District were (in approximate order of creation) Newport, Pembroke Dock, Cardiff, Ton Pentre, Newtown, Llanelli, Cross Keys, Splott and Canton. Barry Dock followed in January 1902.[58] The most influential were Newport, Cardiff and Llanelli, the branches which provided the district's senior officers.[59]

Only one of the women involved in the Newport branch in the mid-1890s can now be identified with a strong degree of certainty, thanks chiefly to her unusual surname: Alice van der Plank (née Turner). Born in London in the late 1850s, she lived on Risca Road, Newport, with her husband, William, a coachman, and their two children: Gertrude (a shop assistant) and Harold (a schoolteacher). Two things are apparent about Alice van der Plank's activities: she served for a time as treasurer for the Bristol and Somerset District, out of which the Gloucester and Monmouth District was formed, and she spoke at WCG conferences on matters such as 'the dividend: what it is and how it is made'. It also appears that, in the early part of the twentieth century, she drifted away from the Women's Co-operative Guild and became more closely associated with the Conservative

Party.[60] She joined the Primrose League, the Conservative Party's women's organisation, and was prominent in the women's section of the Newport branch of the British Legion after the First World War.[61] It is difficult to know exactly the reason for the break, of course, but political affiliation, to say nothing of the war itself, may have had something to do with it.

Alice van der Plank was by no means the wife of an industrial labourer, but this did not necessarily make her unusual as a co-operator in the early part of the WCG's existence: organised consumer co-operation appealed first to the upper echelons of the working class before becoming a mass movement. The most readily identifiable member of the inaugural Ton Pentre branch, for instance, was Mrs J. B. Price. That is, Annie Price (née John), who was, at the time, headmistress of Gelli Infants' School.[62] Her husband, John Bowen Price, was a clerk with the Ocean Coal Company.[63] Unfortunately, other names published in newspaper accounts of the branch – Mrs Lewis, Mrs Richards, Miss Price, Mrs Morgan, Mrs Bebb, Mrs Ingram and Mrs Pierce – are now largely anonymous, so a precise social composition is more difficult to arrive at. Cumulatively, they subscribed to a movement which, in the words of the *Rhondda Leader*, had the object of 'giving women members of the Co-operative Society special opportunities for gaining a knowledge of co-operation, by which the working class may become more prosperous, better educated, and more valuable as citizens'. Together they organised classes and lectures on cooking, dressmaking, domestic medicine, housekeeping and the tenets of co-operation, and built an autodidactic system of adult education under the national umbrella of the Co-operative Educational Association.

The Women's Co-operative Guild, which sought to alter the terms of consumption, education and administrative representation, as well as politics, provided obvious continuity with Chartism, but there remains a considerable gap (some forty years, almost) between the decline of the latter and the rise of the former. As a supplier of healthcare and personal insurance, as well as high quality foodstuffs and learning, the co-operative movement was an advanced form of the friendly society, which had offered homosocial organisation, culture and meeting space to working-class men and women since the late eighteenth century. Amongst the earliest known women's friendly society in Wales was the one registered at Llangynwyd near Maesteg in 1812. Many persisted into the second half of the nineteenth century, entering significant decline at around the same time as alternative organisations – including the Women's Co-operative Guild – were being established. By the late 1850s, Merthyr Tydfil alone had more than a dozen registered women's friendly societies – and probably at least as many which were not officially recognised by the government registrar.[64] Nicola Reader has estimated that around sixty per cent of women's societies did not register, twice the figure for men's.[65] Like the Chartist associations, they were typically headquartered at public houses and provided platforms for class consciousness, industrial relations, working-class independence, mutuality and co-operation, as well as forms of philanthropy and deference.

*

The importance of the friendly society to the women's movement in the nineteenth century cannot be over-stated: as a women-only environment – for the most part, some societies employing male secretaries or medical advisers – the friendly society established the organisational principles of sisterhood, as well as the language and customs of first-wave feminism as received and developed by working-class women. Amongst some societies, such as Tongwynlais Female Friendly Society – also known as Castell Coch Female Friendly Society – which was founded in 1807, there was a self-conscious use of terms such as 'the sisterhood'.[66] The female friendly society was a model of mutualism and collective endeavour of far greater significance than the ritualistic outbursts such as the Rebecca rioters, the *Ceffyl Pren* or the later 'white shirting', all of which have more readily attracted the attention of historians. In her research, Dot Jones noted that of the total number of registered friendly societies for Glamorgan between 1794 and 1832, as many as one in six (or thirty of the 180) were for women. That was in line with the contemporary tally for London, as Anna Clarke has established, but was somewhat lower than the ratio of one in five apparent for the same period in Lancashire.

Overall, the number of women involved in friendly societies likely ran into the tens of thousands – if, as Dot Jones concluded, 'at least half of the adult male population of Glamorgan contributed to friendly societies' during the nineteenth century, a number running itself into the hundreds of thousands. As so often, the names of those very many women who joined societies are now lost and only the ephemeral discussion of meetings published in newspapers and other sources fill the gaps left in the official registers – and then, of course, only in part. There was not inconsiderable diversity. In Merthyr Tydfil women's friendly societies organised under a variety of names, from the Faithful Female Friendly Society, which met at the Dynevor Arms, to the New Union Sisters' Society, which met at the Miners' Arms, to the Friendly Sisters' Society, which met at the Bridge Inn. Even those meeting in the same place, such as the three societies which gathered at the Globe Inn, each had a distinctive nomenclature. There was the New Union Society of Women, the Society of Women and the Queen Anne Female Benevolent Society.[67] Despite occasionally grand titles, these were local groups operating independently of the large, national friendly societies and quasi-secret orders.

The latter, which included organisations such as the Ancient Order of Foresters (AOF), the Wrexham-based Philanthropic Order of True Ivorites (the only organisation to conduct its business entirely in Welsh), the temperance-focused Independent Order of Rechabites, the Loyal Order of Shepherds, and the Independent Order of Odd Fellows, Manchester Unity, all excluded women at various points. However, towards the end of the nineteenth century several established their own official women's sections, long after unofficial sections had come into being. The Ivorites, for instance, had women's lodges in Aberavon, Aberkenfig, Cardiff, Denbigh, Harlech, Hirwaun, Rhymney, Tredegar and Kenfig Hill by the mid-1870s.[68] There were women's sections of the AOF in Newport from the 1850s.[69] There were lodges of Oddwomen, too, from Llandeilo in the west to Pontypool and Blaenavon in the east, with a notable concentration in the Cynon and Taff valleys. This mirrored the overall focus of the Oddfellows in Glamorgan and in the Rhondda Cynon Taff area. Of the 50,000 male members of the Oddfellows in Wales by 1880, almost half were situated in Glamorgan, with a third of them resident in the valleys north of Pontypridd. The overall number of Oddwomen by 1880 was probably in the hundreds, rather than the thousands; however, given the absence of exact records, it is difficult to be precise.

One of those who joined the Ancient Order of Foresters in the 1890s was Amy Dillwyn. In a letter to the *South Wales Daily Post*, published in October 1894, she remarked on the recent creation of an official women's lodge in Belfast under the AOF banner – the AOF began to formally admit women as independent members in the early part of the decade. 'This is, I believe', she wrote, 'the first female friendly lodge in existence, and perhaps, when Swansea women know that such a thing is possible, they may care to consider the expediency of imitating the example'.[70] She formally joined the order a few weeks later.[71] A women's branch named for her was established in Swansea at around the same time.[72] It was, in fact, the town's second women's branch of the AOF; the first, named after Elizabeth Daniel, wife of the industrialist and politician Edward Rice Daniel, had formed in December 1893.[73] Despite its administrative and financial association with the well off in Swansea society, the branch was composed of, in the words of the secretary Gertrude Grenfell, 'school teachers, dressmakers, and working men's wives'. Grenfell was herself a schoolteacher and lived in the Waun Wen area, a mile north of the town centre.[74]

For her part, Amy Dillwyn used her AOF membership to tackle some of the order's internal culture. She pushed back against what she perceived to be misogyny and inequality and strove to secure uniform life insurance payments regardless of gender. The AOF's funeral fund valued a woman at half of a man.[75] But this was unusual. For the most part, the official women's sections simply copied the scarves, iconography, phraseology, hand gestures and modes of address used by the men's lodges, and did not instinctively challenge the financial arrangements of the orders. Even Amy Dillwyn's female foresters gave themselves titles such as Chief Ranger, Senior Woodward and Beadle. The titles were drawn from the medieval courts which had administered justice in the royal forests and maintained forest law. The Oddwomen were more distinctive and used the beehive emblem – a nod to the order's origins in Manchester – and marching banner mottos such as 'sisterly love' and 'peace and plenty to all'. All of which conveyed the ethos of organised sisterhood as they understood it.[76] This was effective at attracting women to take part: the Blaenavon Odd Sisters, for instance, saw 'upwards of 200 members and friends' attend their social gatherings in the mid-1860s.

The involvement of Amy Dillwyn in the Ancient Order of Foresters in the 1890s points to another misperception of women's organisation in the nineteenth century. In their analysis of the rise and fall of women's friendly societies in that period, many historians have noted that the movement decayed after 1830, whereas men's organisations continued to thrive. Writing in the *Journal of Women's History* in 2012, Andrea Rusnock and Vivien Dietz suggested that in England this disparity was due

> to new notions of the household economy, female domestic-
> ity, and the male breadwinner wage, ideas which ultimately
> informed legislation such as the New Poor Law (1834) ... lim-
> ited opportunities for female employment ... [and] in such an
> environment, there was less scope for organizations intended
> to protect labouring women's income from the disruptions
> of illness and reproduction.[77]

In her study of Scottish women's friendly societies, Jane Randall has argued that by the middle of the Victorian age, organisations were declining 'partly for financial reasons, but also as a result of the rise and appeal of the more assertively masculine affiliated orders and the growing promotion of male breadwinning as a familial model'. Dot Jones made much the same point in her study of Welsh societies, too, noting that they 'faded away at the same time as women's participation in industrial employment declined'. However, mass digitisation of newspapers and other sources, which reveals the survival of women's friendly societies into the last quarter of the nineteenth century, suggests a different chronology and conclusion. In short, it was not male breadwinning which forced a decline but remodelling of women's activism and the emergence of alternatives: co-operative societies which offered mutualised insurance, medical aid societies, the women's suffrage campaign, and the women's sections or auxiliaries of political parties and trade unions. After all, if women's friendly societies had been defunct by the 1890s, why would Amy Dillwyn have made such a pointed and public intervention?

*

By the end of the nineteenth century, the disparate elements of the women's movement had brought into public consciousness the idea of women's rights. As political discourse, an intellectual framework, and a popular struggle, the campaign to achieve equality for women – in its broadest sense – opened fault lines throughout society. The intellectual construction of women's rights, as conceived by the feminist first wave, focused initially on the achievement of legal rights and was endowed with a liberal sense of citizenship. Commentators wrote, not always enthusiastically, about the rise of professional women in the United States and considered the possibility of the same trend happening in Britain. In 1886, for example, the *Aberdare Times* observed, in the aftermath of a resolution disapproving of the appointment of women preachers, that 'the Calvinistic Methodists of East

Glamorgan are evidently not advocates of Women's Rights' and added that, from the newspaper's point view,

> we do not see any harm in women becoming doctors ... women have a perfect right to become scholars if they are inclined that way ... we may even yet look with composure upon women as civil engineers, architects, and so on. But for them to invade our pulpits, our lawcourts, and even our House of Commons, is certainly going too far.[78]

More than two decades later, the *Carmarthen Journal* lamented in similar terms that 'there is nothing left to a "mere man" except his vote, and the poor, clinging dears are trying to grab that just now'.[79]

As the nineteenth century wore on, feminists became 'increasingly self-confident about women's potential', as Kathryn Gleadle has put it, and 'trumpeted the unique female qualities which women might bring to the "public world"'. In so doing, the most radical elements of the women's movement 'cohered around far-reaching visions to challenge the nature of sexual relations'.[80] They found allies in the radical wings of the labour movement, which were beginning to look beyond even advanced liberalism as the basis of a politics of social justice. The Cardiff Fabians, founded in 1890, steadily attracted women to its ranks with a swathe of progressive policies, including the provision of nursery schools, day crèches, free school meals, smaller class sizes, free evening continuation classes for adults, free secondary education, and even the recognition of, and teaching in, the Welsh language in elementary schools.[81] Socialist groups in Swansea and Barry were no less successful in gaining women members.[82] Fabian and ILP branches were especially successful in appealing to women as members, organisers and lecturers through the auspices of the Labour Church. Its aim was the examination and development of 'the human side of labour' and activities followed along those lines.[83]

Amongst those who preached at the Cardiff Labour Church held in St John's Hall were prominent national lecturers, such as Enid Stacy and Katherine Conway, and local women, such as Anne Gaunt (1855–1914), secretary of the Cardiff Women's Liberal Association, who spoke about 'Women as Poor Law Guardians', and Henrietta Louisa Trimnell (1876–1929), who focused her attention on 'The Work of the Labour Church and the New Movement'. Behind the scenes, the Cardiff Labour Church was sustained by several activists, including the branch organist, Miss Griffiths, and Harriet Robinson, wife of the branch secretary, Edwin. On at least one occasion 'the arrangements and conduct of the service' were place 'into the hands of the women'.[84] Of the Cardiff-based lecturers, Henrietta Trimnell was probably the most interesting. She was born and educated locally but in 1893 won a Drapers' Company scholarship to study science at university, attending the University College of South Wales and Monmouthshire. On graduation, she worked as a schoolteacher – including for a period in Llandrindod Wells – before returning to university to train as a doctor. Active in the Cardiff branch of the Women's Social and Political Union, as well as in the labour movement, she was part of the Cardiff contingent who joined the women's crusade to London in 1908.[85]

For women involved in either the labour movement or the women's suffrage campaign or both, achieving the vote, which moved to the 'heart of the movement for female emancipation' after the Second Reform Act in 1867, was a means to a much more significant end – the revision of whole swathes of public life to take account of the distinctions of gender and to provide an equal platform for women. 'Every-day life proved', argued Gertrude Jenner (1835–1904) of Wenvoe Cottage, secretary of the Cardiff branch of the National Society for Women's Suffrage, 'that widows and spinsters who contributed to the taxes and rates of our country were all too often the victims of tyranny and oppression, and they were simply anxious to secure any protection they could'.[86] Jenner spent much of her life fighting to regain an inheritance from the Wenvoe Castle estate, from which she felt she had been excluded by her brother, Robert.[87] Thirty years later, speaking at the Unitarian Church in Swansea in 1908, Amy Dillwyn similarly lamented the 'injustice of withholding the Parliamentary vote from women with business interests at stake', adding that 'she, with many other business women, bitterly felt the ignoring of her position'.[88]

Although a focus on inheritance and business was indicative of Dillwyn and Jenner's middle-class origins, it was part of a portfolio of ideas which included changes to educational opportunities. At the height of her activism, Jenner was amongst the most prominent Welsh campaigners for advances in education.[89] 'High schools', she argued in 1880, 'were urgently needed ... for with the exception of Howell's Charity at Cardiff, they had not a single girls' school in the whole of South Wales'.[90] The point was iterated, too, by Emily Higginson, the founding secretary of the Swansea Women's Suffrage Society.[91] At an enquiry into the provision of secondary education, held in 1880, Higginson called for day colleges for girls with an all-female teaching staff. A faculty who all had degrees.[92] Her own interest in education led her to stand, successfully, as a candidate for Swansea's school board, promising electors that she would 'put my long experience as a mother and teacher of the young at your service'.[93]

One local newspaper recorded that 'no school board should be without the presence of a lady experienced in the education of children'.[94] Emily Higginson had replaced fellow suffrage campaigner Emma Brock (1848–1913), who was herself the first woman elected on to Swansea School Board.[95]

The involvement of Amy Dillwyn and Gertrude Jenner in the suffrage campaign drew attention to another *fin-de-siècle* anxiety: the female masculinity of the 'New Woman'. Photographed in middle age with shortened hair and often with a cigar, Dillwyn conveyed a tomboyish, gender-nonconforming persona long before Radclyffe Hall seemed, as Laura Doan has put it, to 'fashion sapphism'.[96] In her diaries, Amy Dillwyn famously referred to her friend Olive Talbot as her 'wife' and declared herself 'romantically, passionately, foolishly' in love. Unfortunately for Dillwyn, Talbot failed to reciprocate, and the businesswoman spent much of her life depressed by 'unrequited' feelings.[97] She used her own desires, however, to endow her novels, such as the 'quasi-autobiographical' *Jill* (1884), and the *Rebecca Rioter* (1880), with same-sex coding rare in Welsh literature in either language in the nineteenth century.[98] Like their author, and women she knew, including Gertrude Jenner, many of Dillwyn's fictional women were tomboyish and independently minded – characters who struggled against the iniquities of a patriarchal and heteronormative society. As a writer, and someone who left behind clear signals of her own feelings in her private papers, Amy Dillwyn is easily interpreted as a woman who desired other women.

She was not alone in those feelings, even if clear identification of such 'other women' in the nineteenth century – particularly from poorer backgrounds – is much more difficult. Throughout Victorian society, women who desired other women, or women who presented in a perceptively 'masculine' or gender-nonconforming manner, were clearly spoken of in conversation and discussed in the press, albeit in a code which has now to be interpreted. Fortunately, there are some indications as to the terminology, particularly for words such as 'tomboy'. In 1907, the philologist John Jones completed his survey of the dialect of Caernarfonshire and published it under the title *Gwerin-Eiriau* ('Folk Words'). The local word for tomboy, Jones recorded, was *ysgaflog*.[99] In use in Caernarfonshire and western parts of Meirionnydd, *ysgaflog* (or sometimes simply *sgaflog*) meant a 'rough, masculine girl' or an ugly woman.[100] Elsewhere, people spoke of a *cadi fachgen* (in the south) or *cadi bechgyn* (in the north), all with the same approximate meaning and implication. The literary equivalents of *rhampen* and *hoeden*, which had a much broader and longer usage, including 'bold woman', 'harlot' and 'whore', little reflected anxiety about female masculinity. *Hoeden* had been present in Welsh for several centuries, mirroring its English equivalent *hoyden* and likely borrowed from the same Dutch antecedent, *heiden*, meaning boisterous, rude and uncivilised, and was largely divorced from nineteenth-century gender conceptualisation. Indeed, such feelings – and descriptions of behaviour – did not manifest themselves into a movement until late in the twentieth century.

*

When the publisher Walter Scott launched his 'Scott Library' series in the spring of 1892 with a cheap edition of *A Vindication of the Rights of Women*, one Welsh newspaper responded by telling readers that 'advocates will find in it many strong arguments for the object they have so near their heart'.[101] The struggle for gender equality, which had evolved steadily in the century since Mary Wollstonecraft first wrote her pamphlet, from Chartism through friendly societies and co-operatives to socialism and the suffrage campaign, was no longer marginal to mainstream discussion. As women's activism became more diverse over the course of the nineteenth century, so did the language used to express feminist ideas and purpose. Sisterhood moved from pamphlet to reality, although there was a limit to what could be achieved on the outside. As working-class men began to debate in the 1890s whether the Liberal Party was the right platform for advancement of their interests, and sought to elect the labour interest to parliament, so too did working-class women. With liberalism seemingly having failed to achieve equality, the more radical political edges began to focus their efforts on organising within the growing, but still nascent, socialist movement.

The Independent Labour Party, which was founded in 1893, instinctively placed women's suffrage on its platform, as did the Labour Party, following its creation early in the twentieth century. Labour's election manifesto in 1910, for instance, insisted that 'restrictions upon the franchise, including the sex bar, must be swept away'. Yet for all the inclusive optimism of those statements, women active in political movements, whether liberal or socialist, still faced the issue of having to work 'against the grain', as Karen Hunt has put it, because the 'assumptions of many of their male comrades were still tied to the existing sexual division of labour and a restricted vision of women's capacities and potential'.[102] For all the diversity of campaigning evident across the nineteenth century, from abolitionism to friendly societies and co-operatives, women remained either auxiliaries, rather than equals or leaders in a male-dominated movement, or created their own separate sections – and these were liable to be led by middle-class women. 'What is needed', argued the *Rhondda Socialist* of politics and political activism in 1912, 'is one or more women of the working class, whose interest is not the result of pity from a distance, but the effect of life's contact with working-class conditions'[103]. The women of the working class, the newspaper concluded, must be brought into the labour movement, and the Labour Party, not the Liberal Party, made the most suitable platform for women. It is to that process that we turn in the next chapter.

Notes

1. The literature on women's political activism across Britain, once a very small component of the literature on nineteenth century politics, is now substantial – although relatively few titles tease out Welsh concerns or experiences. Indicative studies include Jutta Schwarzkopf, *Women in the Chartist Movement* (Basingstoke, 1991); Anna Clark, *The Struggle for the Breeches: Gender and the Making of the British Working Class* (Berkeley, 1995); Barbara Taylor, *Eve and the New Jerusalem: Socialism and Feminism in the Nineteenth Century* (London, 1983); Claire Midgley, *Women Against Slavery: The British Campaigns, 1780–1870* (London, 1992).

2. Ryland Wallace, 'The Anti Corn Law League in Wales', *Welsh History Review*, 13/1 (June 1986), 1–23; also I. G. Jones, 'The Anti Corn Law Letters of Walter Griffith', *Bulletin of the Board of Celtic Studies*, 28/1 (1978), 95–128. Appointed in the spring of 1840, Griffith served as the ACLL lecturer for Wales. For a fuller sense of the ACLL across Britain, see Paul A. Pickering and Alex Tyrrell, *The People's Bread: A History of the Anti-Corn Law League* (Leicester, 2000).

3. *NS*, 28 May 1842, 4.

4. *ACLC*, 8 October 1840.

5. *ACLC*, 10 September 1840.

6. For Carmarthen, see *ABTC*, 3 November 1842. The wider history of women in the League is considered by Simon Morgan, 'Domestic Economy and Political Agitation: Women and the Anti Corn Law League, 1839–46', in Kathryn Gleadle and Sarah Richardson (eds), *Women in British Politics, 1760–1860: The Power of the Petticoat* (Basingstoke, 2000), pp. 115–33.

7. *The Welshman*, 14 January 1842, 2.

8. *ABTC*, 21 April 1842.

9. *ABTC*, 24 January 1843.

10. Alfred Neobard Palmer, *A History of the Older Nonconformity of Wrexham and its Neighbourhood* (Wrexham, 1888).

11. For instance, in Daniel G. Williams, *Black Skin, Blue Books: African-Americans and Wales, 1845–1945* (Cardiff, 2012). For a sense of the wider relationship between Wales and chattel slavery see: Chris Evans, *Slave Wales: The Welsh and Atlantic Slavery, 1660–1850* (Cardiff, 2010).

12. Edinburgh Ladies' Emancipation Society, *Annual Report* (Edinburgh, 1862), p. 25; Edinburgh Ladies' Emancipation Society, *Annual Report* (Edinburgh, 1864), p. 34; Edinburgh Ladies' Emancipation Society, *Annual Report* (Edinburgh, 1867), p. 22.

13. *ABTC*, 13 January 1842.

14. Wallace, 'Anti Corn Law', 17.

15. *The Cambrian*, 26 March 1842, 3.

16. Without entering into the debate here, this is the essence of Eric Hobsbawm's influential – but much considered – discussion of working-class standards of living in the industrial revolution. E. J. Hobsbawm, 'The Standard of Living during the Industrial Revolution: A Discussion', *Economic History Review*, 16/1 (August 1963), 119–46, covers the debate from Hobsbawm's original entry ('The British Standard of Living, 1790–1850', *Economic History Review*, 10/1), published in 1957–63. For a recent (albeit partisan) discussion see Emma Griffin, 'Diets, Hunger and Living Standards During the British Industrial Revolution', *Past and Present*, 239/1 (May 2018), 71–111.

17. Jane Humphries, *Childhood and Child Labour in the British Industrial Revolution* (Cambridge University Press, 2011); Emma Griffin, *Liberty's Dawn* (Yale University Press, 2013).

18. Emma Griffin, *Bread Winner: An Intimate History of the Victorian Economy* (Yale University Press, 2020).

19. Malcolm Chase, *Chartism: A New History* (Manchester, 2007), p. 42; Joe England, *Merthyr: The Crucible of Modern Wales* (Cardigan, 2017).

20. *WV*, 27 July 1839, 31 August 1839; *NS*, 4 January 1840; *The Silurian*, 27 April 1839.

21. Dorothy Thompson, 'Women and Nineteenth-Century Radical Politics: A Lost Dimension', in her *Outsiders: Class, Gender and Nation* (London, 1993), pp. 77–192.

22. *MM*, 18 January 1840.

23. In the Welsh setting, the Chartist movement was incorporated into Ness Edwards's studies published in the 1920s, including his *John Frost*

and the Chartist Movement in Wales (Abertillery, n.d. but c.1926); *The Industrial Revolution in South Wales* (London, 1924); and *The History of the South Wales Miners* (London, 1926). Mark Hovell (1888–1916), a lecturer at Manchester University and a tutor for the Workers' Educational Association, who was killed in action during the First World War, did note the early commitment of the Chartists to women's suffrage in his posthumously published *The Chartist Movement* (Manchester, 1918).

24. Henry Vincent, 'Life and Rambles', *WV*, 7 (6 April 1839), 3.

25. All references to Vincent's reminiscences in this paragraph are from Henry Vincent, 'Life and Rambles', *WV*, 7 (6 April 1839), 3.

26. David J. V. Jones, 'Woman and Chartism', *History*, 68/222 (1983), 16.

27. Chase, *Chartism*, pp. 143–4; Kate Brown and Paul Pickering, '"Songs of the Millions: Chartist Music and Popular Aural Tradition', *Labour History Review*, 74/1 (2009), 44–63; Michael Sanders, '"God is our Guide! Our Cause is Just!" The National Chartist Hymn Book and Victorian Hymnody', *Victorian Studies*, 54/4 (2012), 679–705; Andrew Davies, *Other Theatres* (London: Macmillan, 1987).

28. Robert George Gammage, *The History of the Chartist Movement* (London, 1854), p. 446.

29. These include Thomas Doubleday, *The Political Pilgrim's Progress* (London, 1839); Ernest Jones, *Woman's Wrongs* (London, 1852); and George Reynolds, *The Seamstress* (London, 1853).

30. Lynn M. Alexander, 'Creating a Symbol: The Seamstress in Victorian Literature', *Tulsa Studies in Women's Literature*, 18/1 (1999), 29–38; Michael Sanders, *The Poetry of Chartism: Aesthetics, Politics, History* (Cambridge, 2009).

31. For instance, in Regenia Gagnier, *Subjectivities: A History of Self-Representation in Britain, 1832–1920* (Oxford, 1991) and Emma Griffin, *Liberty's Dawn: A People's History of the Industrial Revolution* (New Haven, 2013).

32. John Burnett, David Mayall and David Vincent (eds), *The Autobiography of the Working Class: An Annotated Critical Bibliography* (Brighton, 3 vols, 1984–9).

33. John Burnett, David Mayall and David Vincent (eds), *The Autobiography of the Working Class: An Annotated Critical Bibliography, Volume One* (Brighton, 1984), xviii.

34. David Vincent, *Bread, Knowledge and Freedom: A Study of Working-Class Autobiography* (London, 1982).

35. Florence S. Boos, *Memoirs of Working-Class Women: The Hard Way Up* (Basingstoke, 2017), p. 2.

36. In her study of nineteenth-century working-class poetry, Boos notes that writing from Scotland is much better preserved than that from Wales. Florence S. Boos, *Working-Class Women Poets in Victorian Britain: An Anthology* (Toronto, 2008), p. 16. Similarly, the autobiographies included in her book *The Hard Way Up* (see the map on p. 3) include examples from Scotland, England and Ireland, but not from Wales.

37. Kirsti Bohata and Alexandra Jones, 'Welsh Women's Industrial Fiction, 1880–1910', in *Women's Writing*, 24/4 (2017), 499–516.

38. *SWDP*, 30 June 1910, 11 August 1910.

39. Irene Saunderson, *A Welsh Heroine* (London, 1910), p. 162.

40. Kirsti Bohata, '"A Queer Looking Lot of Women": Cross-Dressing, Transgender Ventriloquism and Same-Sex Desire in the Fiction of Amy Dillwyn', *Victorian Review*, 44/1 (Spring 2018), 113–30.

41. Keith Flett, *Chartism After 1848: The Working Class and the Politics of Radical Education* (Pontypool, 2006).

42. *The Cambrian*, 16 October 1819.

43. *Carmarthen Journal*, 19 February 1830.

44. *North Wales Chronicle*, 15 June 1850.

45. P. J. Atkins, 'Sophistication Detected: Or, the Adulteration of the Milk Supply, 1850–1914', *Social History*, 16/3 (1991), 320–1.

46. Cardiff County Borough Council, *Report of the Medical Officer of Health for 1914* (Cardiff, 1915), p. 66.

47. Monmouthshire County Council, *Report of the Medical Officer of Health for 1920* (Newport, 1921), p. 63.

48. Cardiganshire County Council, *Report of the Medical Officer of Health for the Years 1920 to 1926* (Aberystwyth, 1927), p. 9.

49. Peter Gurney, *Co-operative Culture and the Politics of Consumption in England, 1870–1930* (Manchester, 1996), p. 61; Peter Gurney, 'Labor's great arch: Co-operation and cultural revolution in Britain, 1795–1926', in Ellen Furlough and Carl Strikwerda (eds), *Consumers Against Capitalism? Consumer Co-operation in Europe, North America and Japan, 1840–1990* (Lanham, MD, 1999), pp. 135–71.

50. Gurney, 'Labor's great arch', pp. 135–71.

51. *Co-operative News*, 3 February 1900; cited in Helen Thomas, '"A Democracy of Working Women": The Women's Co-operative Guild in South Wales, 1891–1939', *Llafur*, 11/1 (2012), 152.

52. Beddoe, *Out of the Shadows*, p. 38.

53. Thomas, '"A Democracy of Working Women"', 149–69.

54. *RL*, 4 August 1900. The formation of the 1914 branch is recorded *RL*, 7 November 1914.

55. J. C. Gray (ed.), *The Twenty-Fourth Annual Co-operative Congress* (Manchester, 1892), pp. 61, 108; J. C. Gray (ed.), *Report of the Twenty-Fifth Annual Co-operative Congress* (Manchester, 1893), p. 108; J. C. Gray (ed.), *Report of the Twenty-Sixth Annual Co-operative Congress* (Manchester, 1894), pp. 119–20.

56. Compared with a national membership of 13,000 and almost 300 branches. *SWDN*, 3 September 1900.

57. *Wrexham Advertiser*, 2 June 1900; *Cheshire Observer*, 23 May 1908.

58. *BDN*, 3 January 1902.

59. The founding president, Mrs A. M. Morris, came from Newport; the early secretaries Mrs Fry and Mrs Hitchings came from Cardiff, and Mrs Nicholas from Llanelli.

60. *Star of Gwent*, 9 May 1902.

61. *WM*, 23 June 1923.

62. *RL*, 24 October 1908, 13 November 1915.

63. *CT*, 27 February 1904.

64. *MT*, 26 September 1857.

65. Nicola Reader, 'Female Friendly Societies in Industrialising England, 1780–1850' (unpublished PhD thesis, University of Leeds, 2005).

66. *CT*, 2 July 1870.

67. *MT*, 26 September 1857.

68. *GG*, 21 November 1840; *The Cambrian*, 23 October 1841, 16 July 1842, 30 July 1842; *CT*, 20 September 1873, 21 August 1875.

69. *MM*, 15 August 1857, 13 October 1876. Dot Jones also noted 'one Court of Female Foresters in the Ogmore Valley' in the 1850s. Dot Jones, 'Self-Help in Nineteenth Century Wales: The Rise and Fall of the Female Friendly Society', *Llafur*, 4/1 (1984), 19.

70. *SWDP*, 26 October 1894.

71. *SWDN*, 28 January 1895.

72. *SWDP*, 26 January 1895, 21 February 1895; *The Cambrian*, 1 February 1895.

73. *SWDP*, 16 December 1893. Gertrude Grenfell wrote to the *SWDP* pointing out the existence of the earlier branch. Her letter was published on 29 October 1894.

74. *SWDP*, 2 November 1894.

75. *SWDP*, 13 August 1896, 14 August 1896.

76. *Illustrated Usk Observer*, 19 July 1856.

77. Andrea A. Rusnock and Vivien E. Dietz, 'Defining women's sickness and work: Female friendly societies in England, 1780–1830', *Journal of Women's History*, 24/1 (2012), 60–85.

78. *Aberdare Times*, 27 November 1886.

79. *Carmarthen Journal*, 18 September 1908.

80. Kathryn Gleadle, *British Women in the Nineteenth Century* (Basingstoke, 2001), p. 163.

81. *Evening Express*, 5 January 1893.

82. Martin Wright, *Wales and Socialism: Political Culture and National Identity Before the Great War* (Cardiff, 2016), p. 125; *BDN*, 5 January 1900, 21 November 1913.

83. *SWDN*, 6 February 1893.

84. Wright, *Wales and Socialism*, p. 126; *SWDN*, 1 February 1894.

85. *SWDN*, 1 February 1894; *CT*, 15 December 1894; *EEx*, 20 August 1894. Enid Stacy was also a graduate of University College of South Wales and Monmouthshire (*BDN*, 11 September 1896). *EEx*, 24 February 1892; 16 September 1892; 18 May 1907; *CT*, 6 June 1903; 7 October 1893; 27 June 1908; *SWDN*, 14 August 1896.

86. *SWDN*, 26 February 1881. Cited in Ryland Wallace, *Organise! Organise! Organise! A Study of Reform Agitations in Wales, 1840–1866* (Cardiff, 1991), p. 165; Jenner's role as secretary was reported in National Society for Women's Suffrage, *Annual Report for 1873* (London, 1873), p. 16; National Society for Women's Suffrage, *Annual Report for 1875* (London, 1875), pp. 5–6.

87. *BDN*, 22 April 1904; *CT*, 23 April 1904.

88. *Women's Franchise*, 16 January 1908.

89. *Women's Suffrage Journal*, 1 August 1879.

90. *Women's Suffrage Journal*, 1 April 1880.

91. *Women's Suffrage Journal*, 1 February 1874, 1 June 1874, 1 January 1877.

92. *The Cambrian*, 10 December 1880.

93. *The Cambrian*, 28 November 1879.

94. *Swansea Journal*, 29 November 1879.

95. Brock was elected in 1876. She retired before her marriage to the unitarian minister John Edmondson Manning. *The Cambrian*, 16 January 1880.

96. Laura Doan, *Fashioning Sapphism: The Origins of a Modern English Lesbian Culture* (New York, 2001).

97. Kirsti Bohata, 'Foreword to the New Edition', in David Painting, *Amy Dillwyn* (Cardiff, 2013).

98. Kirsti Bohata, 'Mistress and Maid: Homoeroticism, Cross-Class Desire, and Disguise in Nineteenth-Century Fiction', *Victorian Literature and Culture*, 45/2 (June 2017), 341–59; Bohata, '"A Queer-Looking Lot of Women"', 113–30; Bohata, '"A Queer Kind of Fancy": Same-Sex Desire, Women and Nation in Welsh Literature', in Huw Osborne (ed.), *Queer Wales: The History, Culture and Politics of Queer Life in Wales* (Cardiff, 2016), pp. 91–114.

99. John Jones, *Gwerin-Eiriau Sir Gaernarfon* (Pwllheli, 1907), p. 59.

100. Ioan Brothen, 'Llafar Gwald Gorllewin Meirionydd', *Cymru*, 62/370 (May 1922), 179; Osbert Henry Fynes-Clinton, *The Welsh Vocabulary of the Bangor District* (London, 1913), p. 481.

101. *Montgomeryshire Express*, 19 April 1892.

102. Karen Hunt, *Equivocal Feminists: The Social Democratic Federation and the Woman Question, 1884–1911* (Cambridge, 1996), p. 249.

103. *Rhondda Socialist*, 21 December 1912.

2

A Women's Labour Party

Grace Metcalfe, who would emerge as the most important woman activist in the South Wales Federation of the Independent Labour Party (ILP) before the First World War, was born in Halifax, in the West Riding of Yorkshire, in 1863. Her father, Robert, was a police sergeant looking for an escape from the county constabulary. A few years after his daughter was born, he got a job as the relieving officer for the Board of Guardians, but then the family was thrown into uncertainty when Ann Metcalfe, Grace's mother, died suddenly. To supplement the family income, Grace left school at the age of twelve and went to work in a cigar factory. Sometime around her twentieth year she met Nathan William Scholefield, a commercial traveller and the son of Halifax publicans. Grace married Nathan in the summer of 1886 and the pair moved to Keighley, where they started a family of their own. For a few years, Nathan carried on with his commercial travelling work and Grace looked after their young children. Early in 1893, Grace and Nathan heard about the formation of the ILP in Bradford and joined the Keighley branch almost soon as it was founded. They were founder members of the Keighley Labour Church when it came into existence that December, and the following year Grace was elected to the executive of Keighley ILP – one of the first women to gain such a position anywhere in Britain.[1]

As an itinerant commercial traveller, Nathan Scholefield was frequently drawn to developing industrial towns, since these communities were regarded as ready-made but novel markets for the worsted and woollen products of Yorkshire's textile mills. As the result of one such journey, which Nathan made in the mid-1890s, the Scholefield family moved south to Glamorgan. Nathan had been taken on at Stoddart's hosiery mill in Glebeland Street, Merthyr Tydfil.[2] To supplement his income, Nathan taught swimming and diving at the town's Gwaunfarren Baths; he had been a champion swimmer as a young man.[3] The Scholefields were not in Merthyr for very long when they realised the absence of the ILP. They joined with Oliver Jenkins and Martin Hamson and began organising a local branch. 'One soon discovers', wrote Keir Hardie in the *Labour Leader* in early October 1896, that 'the people are ready for change, provided the way can be shown them whereby effective action may be taken to bring the change about'. He added that in Merthyr, 'the miners are the head and front of the movement. Two Yorkshire lads – [Nathan] Scholefield and [F. W.] Smithson – well known to the movement round Halifax and Keighley way, are actively if quietly lending their influence and experience.'[4] Five years later, with Keir Hardie elected as member of parliament for Merthyr Tydfil and the town established as a rallying point for the Labour Party, Nathan Scholefield became the organising secretary of the entire South Wales ILP Federation.[5]

But what of Grace? Her absence from the record of the ILP in the second half of the 1890s is one of presentation rather than reality. Given her role in fostering the party in Keighley, it is certain that she was at the heart of the South Wales ILP Federation, along with her husband. Indeed, in September 1896, Keir Hardie visited the Merthyr branch and spoke to an audience where, in his words, 'a number of ladies' were present.[6] Grace was undoubtedly amongst them. The *Labour Leader* was later to record that 'Mrs Scholefield and other Labour women were toiling night and day for Mr Keir Hardie's candidature among the miners of Mountain Ash, Aberdare and Merthyr. And they made no song about their efforts and never had time to think about fatigue'.[7] That was during the 1906 general election, but it is impossible to imagine that it was any different in 1900, when Hardie was first returned to the House of Commons for Merthyr Boroughs, or in either election of 1910, when Hardie was re-elected. As for the influence of Grace Scholefield and the other women Hardie identified, the commitment of the Dowlais branch of the ILP (and doubtless the Merthyr branch, too, although the records are not extant) to women's suffrage and to equality of civil rights was as much an indication of that influence, as it was a nod to the national policy platform.[8]

What brought Grace's political work back into public view was the growing size and importance of the ILP, together with the formal creation of the Labour Party in 1906, and the greater interest shown in both organisations by the mainstream press, which was otherwise divided in its support for the Liberal or Conservative parties. By then, the Scholefields had moved to Cardiff, the result of Nathan's work for the South Wales ILP Federation. Grace herself was one of those 'lady members' involved in the preparations for Cardiff to host the annual ILP conference in 1904. From then on, her position was sufficiently senior, locally, to take the chair at the Women's Social and Political Union (WSPU) meetings at the Cory Hall, itself a sign of Grace's personal commitment to women's suffrage as well as that of the ILP, to chair public gatherings of the Cardiff branch of the ILP, and to be part of delegations which went into communities with a view to establishing new sections.[9] In September 1907, for instance, she spoke at the workmen's hall in Abercynon ahead of the formation of the local ILP.[10] This was hardly the activity of someone who was not an important figure, and in her own right, in the organisation and function of the South Wales ILP Federation.

Grace Scholefield was by no means alone in her combination of work for the ILP (and subsequently the Labour Party) and on behalf of the women's suffrage campaign. Mary Keating-Hill (1863–1929), who was born into a working-class, immigrant Irish family in Mountain Ash, was a very well-known contemporary; she was a member of the WSPU and one of the founders of the Cardiff branch of the Women's Freedom League in 1909. As the branch secretary for a period before the First World War, she was to be its most prominent member.[11] In December 1906, she would be the first Welsh woman to be imprisoned for her suffrage campaigning – long before Lady Rhondda attacked a postbox. Together with her younger brother, the miner turned journalist and novelist Joseph Keating, who served as a Labour councillor on Mountain Ash Urban District Council after the First World War, she was active on behalf of the ILP and the Labour Party and was much in demand as a public speaker. In July 1907, for example, she joined the Clarion Van on its tour of the coalfield; she spoke at ILP branch meetings in Barry, Cardiff, Pontypridd, Newport and the Rhondda; and in 1912, on the eve of the national coal strike, became the inaugural president of the Cardiff ILP's women's guild.[12]

In Swansea, the twin role of labour activism and suffrage campaigning was undertaken by Emily Phipps (1865–1943), then headmistress at Swansea Municipal Secondary School for Girls. She established the Women's Freedom League branch in the town in 1909 and was a key figure in the National Union of Women Teachers, rising to become the union's president between 1915 and 1917.[13] She spoke regularly to the ILP branches in and around Swansea, encouraging members to support the struggle for the franchise – support indicated by the passing of a motion in favour at public meetings, often unanimously.[14] Particular advantage was taken of industrial unrest shortly before the First World War, which focused attention on the need for a more radical political solution than was being offered by either the governing Liberal Party or the opposition Conservatives. In November 1910, the WFL national newspaper, *The Vote*, noted of meetings 'composed of the coal-strikers and their women folk' in Aberdare and Aberaman, that 'we had two of our best ... [the audience] showed both sympathy and interest'.[15] This was hardly surprising. Indeed, as Ryland Wallace has observed, there was a close synergy between the ILP and the women's suffrage movement (whether the WSPU or the WFL), at least in the southern counties of Wales.[16]

In one sense, such a collaboration between the radical elements of Edwardian British (and thus Welsh) politics was an obvious one. The ILP and the Labour Party were both committed to extending and equalising the franchise, and the organisations which pushed the most progressive case – universal suffrage for men and women – were formed within a few years of each other at the start of the twentieth century and from within much the same cohort of activists.[17] The Women's Social and Political Union came into being in 1903, the Women's Labour League in

1906, and the Women's Freedom League in 1907. Collaboration was also about ensuring that the labour movement and its political wing did not end up emulating the perceived failures of the existing two-party system, particularly of the Liberal Party, and that the Labour Party would be a different and more democratic force. 'Our aim', declared the members of the Cardiff ILP Women's Guild indicatively in 1913, 'is to bring to bear upon the labour movement of our country the point of view of woman as well as man'.[18] Thus, Mary Keating-Hill spoke of 'the need of socialism for the workers' and the 'power of labour united', as well as about 'women in politics' and the 'New Democracy'.[19]

The intervention of the labour movement in the suffrage debate in these years provided some outlet for women frustrated by the failure of the Liberal Party to act and the debacle over the series of Conciliation Bills presented to parliament between 1910 and 1912. One consequence was the creation of the Election Fighting Fund (EFF) by the National Union of Women's Suffrage Societies in May 1912, which provided material support to Labour candidates in by-elections where they were opposed by a Liberal, and to Labour candidates who stood against incumbent anti-suffrage members of cabinet. Some of the money raised was also spent on training NUWSS organisers to work closely with Labour. In effect, the EFF brought about an alliance between the NUWSS and Labour, which the former regarded as 'the best friends of Women's Suffrage'.[20] As Ursula Masson has noted, there was a degree of nuanced hostility within the Liberal-dominated suffrage movement in Wales to the EFF policy, with some members fearing that the 'support of the Labour MPs was not to be relied on', and others concerned about the likely impact on the political balance within their individual groups. Branches and the district committee came round belatedly to the NUWSS policy in 1913.[21] There were similar qualms about the policy evident in Liverpool, too, perhaps unsurprisingly, given the strength of Liberal (and indeed Welsh nonconformist) traditions in the city, with members from Manchester, the north-east of England, and Edinburgh leading the support for the EFF.[22]

One source of disquiet in the background of largely Liberal opposition to the EFF was the failure of the Labour MPs from coalfield areas – miners' leaders from the South Wales Miners' Federation, such as William Abraham, William Brace and John Williams, for instance – to vote for any of the Conciliation Bills. Their absence was noted with obvious disappointment, although the industrial tumult evident in the coalfields, stretching from the Cambrian Combine Dispute in 1910–11 through to the National Coal Strike in the spring of 1912, provided some mitigation of their actions. South Wales members of the NUWSS believed Abraham 'not quite reliable', Brace and Williams 'sound', and Keir Hardie 'perfectly sound', on the question of suffrage.[23] Indeed, Brace and Williams often joined Hardie on platforms at suffrage rallies – Abraham was more conspicuously and regularly absent.[24] The ILP asserted its suffragist position at its annual conference in Merthyr Tydfil in May 1912, with the Labour Party's own annual conference in London in January 1913 further consolidating the stance. The next generation of miners' leaders, long-term ILP and Labour activists, such as Vernon Hartshorn, who entered parliament in 1918, were much more consistent in their support for universal suffrage. As, it seems, were many miners themselves. In a letter to the Liberal MP for Mid Glamorgan, Samuel Thomas Evans (1859–1918), sent after the 1906 general election, at which Evans was unopposed, Hartshorn proffered the advice that 'as far as I have been able to gauge the opinion of the miners of Maesteg ... there is a preponderance in favour'.[25]

Miners in Maesteg were not only led on this issue by male suffragists, such as Hartshorn, but also given concrete examples of the independent efficacy and validity of women working from within the labour movement to effect wholesale change. To the fore was Vernon's wife Mary Hartshorn, an indefatigable campaigner for pithead baths, state provision for maternity and child welfare, healthcare services, and education.[26] When the Maesteg branch of the Women's Labour League was founded in the summer of 1912, she became its campaigning president, 'breaking down the prejudices of the miners and their wives', as the *Labour Leader* enthusiastically reported.[27] In these efforts she was supported by her friend Henrietta Hodges, wife of the miners' agent for the Garw valley, Frank Hodges.[28] Mrs Hodges was herself closely involved in the activities of at least two branches of the Women's Labour League in this period: those at Ogmore Vale and at Tondu.[29] She was not, however, an identifiable 'leader' of a branch in the same way as Mary Hartshorn, preferring instead to focus her efforts on the pithead baths campaign. A similar stance was taken by Nellie Brace, who had previously tended to appear 'in support' of her husband, William, rather than as an activist in her own right.

*

The Women's Labour League (WLL) worked to turn women into Labour Party activists, as well as to obtain the representation of and for women in parliament and in local government under the Labour banner, to secure the full rights of citizenship for all women and men, and to improve the social and industrial conditions of women in local communities.[30] The distribution of the League in Wales mirrored those areas of ILP strength: notably Barry, Cardiff, Newport, Swansea and the larger coalfield communities. Initially, there was a degree of hesitancy amongst male organisers. John A. Kelly, secretary of the Barry Labour Representation Committee, explained in a letter to the WLL's headquarters in London that the branch 'discussed [the] circular on 19 November [1906]. Much doubt [was] expressed at the possibility of forming a local branch although the majority recognised that the existence of such a branch would be a source of strength to the labour movement here.'[31] This uncertainty was slowly overcome – the result of months of activism and the promotion of Labour Party meetings in the town as being open to 'all working men and women' – and the Barry branch of the WLL, the first of its kind in Wales, was established in September 1909.[32] The impact was immediate, and officials registered a sharp rise in the number of women active in the local labour movement.[33] Eleven months earlier, the *South Wales Daily News*, the most prominent Liberal newspaper in the region, had noted the creation of the Women's Labour League and remarked that it was beginning to combat the idea that 'women are indifferent to politics'. Wryly, the paper looked forward to the creation of a 'Female Labour Party'.[34]

Alongside the WLL branches were a handful of women's sections of the ILP, the most significant of which (and one of the best documented at a national level) appears to have been formed in Aberdare in the spring of 1906.[35] Cardiff and Swansea ILP branches had organised women members, as did Newport ILP, and there was also a women's section in Taibach near Port Talbot.[36] The origins of the Aberdare women's section lay in the visit of Annie Kenney (1879–1953), the Oldham-born suffrage campaigner and WSPU activist, in January 1906. A group of women who attended a meeting with Kenney at a house in Trecynon, just outside the centre of Aberdare, formed a WSPU branch and simultaneously joined the local ILP as an autono-mous women's section.[37] Both the WLL and the ILP women's sections (and in many areas of Britain it should be acknowledged there was considerable overlap in membership) were an attempt to develop left-wing political organisation amongst women, although the absence of a national ILP women's movement or a national framework, constitution, newspaper, or platform of propaganda, proved advantageous to the WLL as an institution (which had all of those things), and in Wales it proved to be the dominant organisation as a result.[38] Although some men tended to view the League and the ILP sections as auxiliaries, nice to have but not necessary for the growth of the labour movement, others were agreed that the entry of women into Labour Party politics was an important step forward.[39] Writing in April 1908, the *Aberdare Leader* enthused that,

> If the Labour Party in Aberdare and Mountain Ash wish to win a few more wards, let them take my tip and enlist the ladies to fight for them. The I.L.Peers have been wise in their generation in establishing a feminine auxiliary force in con-nection with their Aberdare Branch. At the last election the Labour Amazons rendered yeoman service. In fact, they won the Blaengwawr citadel for Labour. I would advise the Labour Party to plant a battalion of this Territorial Force in each con-tested ward at the next election. The ladies, once they begin to fight in earnest, are invincible. Let them earmark any seat, and it is a safe cop.[40]

Overall, women's involvement has tended to be viewed by histori-ans as an auxiliary of the otherwise male-dominated Labour Party and ILP of the Edwardian period. Martin Wright, for example, concludes that 'what is clear is that women were a small minority within the movement' and that there is 'no record of a woman taking an official executive role in any of the south Wales socialist organisations'.[41] This is not entirely accurate. Elizabeth Maude Orlidge (née Roden, 1879–1956), a member of Newport ILP, was elected the assistant financial secretary of the branch in 1906.[42] This was a role which gave her a degree of importance during (the future South Wales Miners' Federation president) James Winstone's attempt to win the Monmouth Boroughs seat for the ILP in that year's general election. Subsequently, Elizabeth Orlidge became the financial secretary of the Newport branch of the WLL, on its foundation in the autumn of 1909, and served a similar function on the Labour Party annual conference organising committee, when it came to Newport in 1910.[43] These positions within the organisational constellation of Newport Labour Party almost certainly reflected Elizabeth Orlidge's background, which was in shopkeeping. Together with her husband, Ernest, she ran a small business in Newport town centre specialising in glassware, china and children's toys.

By the time Labour's annual conference was held in Newport, the Women's Labour League had established a presence in each of the five principal towns of southern Wales: Barry, Cardiff, Merthyr Tydfil, Newport and Swansea – the result of a spate of organisational activity since the autumn of 1909.[44] In the same period, the national WLL had grown from thirty-seven branches to sixty-nine, with the Welsh branches accounting for almost a fifth of the new ventures. The Cardiff branch of the Women's Labour League came into being with Grace Scholefield as its leading figure. Its reported activities were indicative of an organisation which hit the ground running – in part thanks to the work of the ILP in previous years. During the first year of its existence, the Cardiff WLL branch held nearly forty meetings, including a public rally in the city centre. Members had even run for election to the Board of Guardians, all despite apparently aspiring to 'steady plodding work' from which 'good results are sure to follow'.[45] The guest for the public rally was Margaret Bondfield (1873–1953), who was later to serve as Labour MP for Northampton (1923–4) and Wallsend (1926–31), and who was the first woman in cabinet, as Minister of Labour in the 1929–31 Labour government.

Bondfield returned to Cardiff the following year amidst the strikes which shook the city in 1911. Grace Scholefield and her colleagues stepped in to provide leadership and guidance to the cigar workers, shop assistants and other women, who were often taking industrial action for the first time. A lengthy report, published in the *Labour Leader* in August, captured the scene:

> The great strike wave which swept over the district with dramatic suddenness and force called out women and girl workers as well as men. They were to be seen walking about in terrified leaderless groups, and in singing groups, equally without direction, until our League women took hold. The president of the branch, with Mrs Scholefield, the secretary, and some half-dozen other members made it known that they would meet at the Ruskin Institute to help and advise the girls. The president took charge inside while Mrs Scholefield and I [Margaret Bondfield] went into the highways and parks, holding odd meetings in odd places for cigar girls, bottling girls, and laundry workers. Then came the great march of Monday night, with its long procession of women under the banner of the Workers' Union. Their battle-cry was 'Fall in and follow me'.[46]

Margaret Bondfield and Grace Scholefield were busy unionising women at the Freeman's cigar factory and in the city's laundries. At a packed meeting at the Cory Hall on 2 August 1911, delegates charged a small committee to draft a 'Laundry Workers' Charter': a list of demands aimed at not only settling the strike but also improving pay and working conditions. A second outcome of that rally was the establishment of a women's branch of the Workers' Union in Cardiff, with Grace Scholefield appointed as organiser.[47] Little more than a week later, a further march through the city, involving 120 women from the Freeman's factory, ended in a major rally at Cathays Park.[48] As Margaret Bondfield noted in her own column that week, 'On Wednesday [9 August] I went back to Cardiff, where I had promised to give them a meeting ... but I found them still so busy with the strike that they had not been able to make arrangements'.[49] This work amplified the status of the WLL, which grew steadily from 1910 until the outbreak of the First World War, adding branches across the coalfield from east to west, and propelled Grace Scholefield to the forefront of women's labour activism in Wales.[50]

Other identifiable members of the WLL in this period include women who served successively as president and branch secretary in Newport. The chief member of the branch on its foundation was Minnie Wagstaff (née Gibson, 1883–1962), who, as president, welcomed delegates to the WLL national conference held at Newport's Central Hall in 1910.[51] She was succeeded in the office in 1912 by the founding secretary, Susan Milward.[52] Originally from Manchester, by 1910 Susan Milward was living on the eastern edge of Newport with her husband, Albert, who was himself from Staffordshire. Albert was a foreman at the Orb Iron Mill – owned and operated by W. R. Lysaght. Susan Milward was succeeded as branch secretary by Mary Morrish (1881–1918), who used the platform provided by the Women's Labour League to become active in public administration. Following the creation of the Newport Insurance Committee in 1912, which oversaw the local implementation of the 1911 National Insurance Act, she was appointed as a member.[53] 'Congratulations', remarked the *Labour Leader* when news reached the paper's offices, 'the Newport members are bestirring themselves'.[54] The Morrish family were linked to the railway – Mary's husband, Thomas (1884–1946), was an engine fitter for the GWR – and lived in the Malpas area of the town.[55]

The variety of backgrounds – familial and personal – of women involved in the Labour Party in Edwardian Newport suggests that this was not a fringe interest in the town's labour movement or one tied to very specific circumstances, such as the dominance of the railway trade unions. Minnie Wagstaff's family were in the building trade – her husband was a brick-layer – Susan Milward provided a link to heavy industry, Mary Morrish to the railway, and Elizabeth Orlidge to small business. This diversity was mirrored in other branches in the region, not least in Barry. There, the branch was guided by its president, Elizabeth Henson, and secretary, Beatrice Lewis, and was the centrepiece of women's political organisation in the town – along with the Women's Co-operative Guild and the Railway Women's Guild.[56] Elizabeth Henson was originally from Jarrow but had moved to Barry with her husband, James, who was the district secretary of the Seamen's Union. Beatrice Lewis's husband, William Jenkin Lewis, on the other hand, was a coal trimmer in the docks. Given the importance of James Henson's position in the trade union movement, Elizabeth Henson was readily put forward as a Labour candidate in local elections. In 1910, she was nominated for, and elected to, the Board of Guardians – running for re-election in 1913 alongside her husband, who was standing for the district council.[57]

It would be wrong to see Elizabeth Henson's political activities through the lens of her husband – although this undoubtedly added to her status within the labour movement in Barry. She was active in the ILP and Women's Co-operative Guild several years before the creation of the local branch of the WLL, and maintained an active schedule of public engagement up to, and after, her election as a Guardian.[58] She joined the Worker's Educational Association and took part in the work of the Barry branch, including the 'home problems' circle, which debated matters perceived to be of direct relevance to house-wives.[59] Beatrice Lewis enjoyed a similar career trajectory: in 1919, she was the only woman to stand for election to Barry Urban District Council and ultimately topped the poll in the Castleland ward when voters went to the polls in early April.[60] She had previously been a founding member of the town's Naval and Military War Pensions Committee.[61] Her own activity within the ILP ranged from moving motions protesting events in Dublin during the 1913 lockout to involvement with the Barry branch's performance of plays by George Bernard Shaw and Henrik Ibsen.[62]

Given the interest taken in the organisation of the labour movement in Barry by the town's press, the *Barry Dock News* and the *Barry Herald*, quite a lot can be discerned about the local activities of the WLL – more so than in many other parts of Wales. In 1910, for instance, the branch debated suffrage, child welfare, employment, anti-militarism and peace; it endorsed William Brace's general election campaign in the South Glamorgan constituency; and it welcomed speakers such as Mary Keating-Hill and Margaret Bondfield. As Beatrice Lewis concluded, the year's efforts showed that the WLL was 'not a handy-man league; it was not a movement that would degrade man but was intended to give woman her rightful place in the body politic'.[63] Branch members had also helped to organised the first WLL regional conference in Wales.[64] Held at Barry's Co-operative Hall, the conference saw a 'large number of delegates' arrive to discuss the work of the League and to debate issues such as the safety of women working in seamen's hostels and the need for women's hostels and lodging houses in dock towns. These were issues of clear relevance to those from Barry, Cardiff, Newport and Swansea who attended, but were also part of a wider, national policy platform being developed by League members and by the women's suffrage movement.[65]

*

There was one place where the Women's Labour League was conspicuously absent, however: the Rhondda. The industrial unrest and political radicalism resulting from the Cambrian Combine Dispute of 1910–11 proved advantageous not only to the politicisation of male trade unionists, but also for women. In December 1911, the *Rhondda Socialist*, the organ of the Rhondda Socialist Society (an amalgam of the local ILP and SDF branches), published its women's column for the first time.[66] It was written anonymously by an activist using the nom de plume, 'Matron'. They have never been confidently identified. The column began by focusing on infant mortality. It had a deliberately punchy style: '770 babies under 1 year old died in the Rhondda area during the year 1910', wrote 'Matron'. 'Herod slew a score or so, but who "slew all these?"'[67] Poverty was the direct answer. 'The social condition of the mothers in the Rhondda is far from ideal', the writer added, the pinch of poverty is felt in most homes where there is a young family. Poverty and high rent meant that the mother, in order to keep the home going, must meet part of the expense by keeping lodgers, or sharing the house with another family.

In several parts of the Rhondda, not least in Maerdy, where houses had as many as fifteen residents, it was widely known that beds never got cold.

Who exactly was the woman behind the column? Ursula Masson proposed two probable candidates: Elizabeth Andrews and Gwen Ray. The former was resident in Ton Pentre, at that time, where her husband, Thomas, had been a founding member of the local branch of the ILP. Elizabeth herself was secretary of the recently revitalised Ton Pentre Women's Co-operative Guild. As evidence of Elizabeth Andrews's possible involvement in the column, Masson noted that 'Andrews and Matron shared characteristics as writers: a liking for quotation, especially from the bible, a positive relish for statistics and hard data to support arguments.'[68] But Elizabeth Andrews was almost certainly not 'Matron' – her subsequent prominence has tended to amplify her earlier career beyond its original, limited terms. Moreover, her politics were not those of the *Rhondda Socialist*, which was linked to the Unofficial Reform Committee and the authors of the *Miners' Next Step* (1912). The real 'Matron' was Gwen Ray. The column had likely been prompted, as Ursula Masson rightly noted, by a call from the Penygraig ILP, published in the newspaper in November 1911, to take the organisation of women in the labour movement more seriously.[69] This link with Penygraig is the key to identifying 'Matron'.

At that time, Gwen Ray was living in Williamstown,

immediately to the south of Penygraig, and teaching at Trealaw Girls' School. She was involved in the Wesleyan Church in Williamstown, the Rhondda branch of the National Federation of Class Teachers, the Mid Rhondda Workers' Suffrage Federation, and was honorary secretary of the Mid Rhondda Women's Suffrage Society. Most importantly for the newspaper, she was also active in Penygraig ILP. Thus, if the *Rhondda Socialist* was likely to describe anyone as 'one of the ablest and best-known women in the Rhondda', it would be her. Indeed, the feminist and class-orientated language employed in the columns by 'Matron' reflected Gwen Ray's long-term political allegiances and was not all that different from her columns in the communist *Daily Worker*, written more than two decades later. 'The sight of a woman on her knees', she wrote, indicatively, in June 1912, 'fills one with disgust. Where does the dignity and glory of womanhood come in here? Why should we waste precious life on insensate paving stones?'[70] Gwen Ray's syndicalism revealed itself in a column published six months later, in which she diagnosed the problems of women in the labour movement and asserted the need for a class solution, not one that relied on middle-class leadership and a led working class. She wrote,

> The Women's Labour League founded to benefit working women, is a case of the women of the middle class bending to help women of the working class. All the names of women prominent in the Labour Movement are women who have come into the movement out of sympathy, and not out of a real experience of the working woman's needs and struggles. They are not women of the working class.[71]

In her portrait, Gwen Ray drew on proto-socialist feminist ideas and added that,

> There is something to account for this difference between the Labour Movement as evolved by men and the Labour Movement as evolved by women. The lower economic position of the working women partly accounts for the position. These women cannot afford to pay secretaries, agents and leaders to give their time to organisation. These upper-class women step in; they have money and leisure to bestow, and they do the work gratuitously. But if working-class women are to be anything else but a subject class, they must work out their own social and political salvation from within. This is particularly true with regard to the wives of working men.

The column by 'Matron' continued to be published in the *Rhondda Socialist* until the spring of 1913, when the newspaper was absorbed into the *South Wales Worker* and production shifted to Merthyr Tydfil. Although the latter occasionally reprinted syndicated columns by Marion Phillips, the national Women's Labour League secretary, under the heading 'the working woman in politics', its direct link to ideas and politics on the ground in the Rhondda was lost.[72] Gwen Ray herself would go on to lead the 1919 Rhondda teachers' strike and, in its aftermath, be the first woman to chair Mid Rhondda Trades and Labour Council.

A flavour of the sort of column that Elizabeth Andrews would probably have written for the *Rhondda Socialist* can be found in the pages of the *Worker's Journal*, the organ of the Edwardian labour movement in Swansea. Written by Ruth Chalk, the secretary of the Swansea Women's Labour League, using the abbreviated nom de plume 'R.C.', the *Worker's Journal*'s women's column was considerably less pointed than that of the *Rhondda Socialist* and much less influenced by syndicalism. If, indeed, at all. Ruth Chalk began her first column, published in April 1912, with the following words. Note the absence of class analysis.

> The Editor has very kindly placed a column of the 'Journal' at our disposal and has asked me – by way of an introduc- tion – to explain why we want the wives and daughters of the men of the Labour Movement to join the Labour League. We are frequently told that a woman's place is in the home, that she should stay at home and mind the baby or darn her husband's socks, and that, therefore, the Women's Labour League and such like bodies are not necessary. The persons who reason in this way never stop to consider whether all women have homes, or whether all homes are fit places for the women and the children to stay in.[73]

Whether politically radical in tone, or more moderate, the space afforded to women's voices in the newspapers of the South Walian labour movement is surely notable. It was essential to the forging of a local image of the Labour Party as one committed to equality and to full representation of women. The columns reveal to readers, past and present, the distinctive characteristics and points of emphasis of women's activism and, in the con- trast between Gwen Ray and Ruth Chalk alone, the spectrum of diverse positions available to members. For would-be readers, the local women's columns were mirrored by similar initiatives in the national labour press, including in the *Labour Leader* and *Justice*, and were supplemented by the creation of the *League Leaflet* – the forerunner of the *Labour Woman*, the national maga- zine of the Women's Labour League – in 1911. It was for the latter, as part of her duties as women's organiser for the Labour Party in Wales, that Elizabeth Andrews wrote from the 1919 onwards.

*

One of the central problems of the labour movement which Gwen Ray identified in her columns for the *Rhondda Socialist* was the relative lack of women elected or co-opted on to public bodies. The existence of the Women's Labour League and ILP women's sections in parts of Glamorgan and Monmouthshire had certainly made election and co-option possible. By the spring of 1913, Labour women had been elected to the Boards of Guardians in Abertillery and Barry, with candidates run in Bargoed, Griffithstown, Ogmore Vale and Swansea that year, too.[74] Others had been appointed or co-opted on to insurance committees, nursing committees and education committees. Ruth Chalk even ran for election to Swansea Council, although she was easily defeated, coming bottom of the poll in the St Helen's ward.[75] A modest electoral presence, to be sure, but it was still an impressive achievement, given that even the most senior WLL branches in the region were not more than four years old. In the case of the Bargoed branch, which succeeded in getting its president, Hetty Jones, elected to the Monmouthshire county insurance committee in 1913, it had been in existence for just twelve months. As women members in Swansea boasted, 'we are doing the work that ought to have been done by the men years ago'.[76]

Certainly, women who were organised and active in the labour movement on the eve of the First World War appear to have been hopeful for the future. The WLL's presence had expended to almost a dozen active branches in the region, from Ystalyfera in the west to Newport in the east. But there were limits. There had been little success in the attempt to build a women's labour movement outside of Glamorgan and Monmouthshire, and the southern industrial fringes of Breconshire. Hopes in the north were pinned on Wrexham ILP, which was the most substantive force outside of the industrial heartlands of the south. In May 1913, the *Labour Leader* reported a visit of the WLL's regional organiser, Agnes Brown, hosted by the Wrexham ILP. The meeting 'which was packed out' was intended as the spur for the League in the town.[77] Agnes Brown returned again in August and expressed hopes of being able 'to open a strong branch'.[78] A similar optimism was expressed in the pages of the *Labour Leader* in early September.[79] However, there is no indication that it did in fact form, and the proposed branch was not mentioned on lists compiled by the national headquarters and published in the *Labour Woman* early in 1914.

Failure to establish a branch in Wrexham contrasted with the success of efforts in Ystalyfera, where the local branch was established on 22 December 1913. On that date, a 'goodly number' of women gathered at the town's ILP institute to hear an address by Ruth Chalk, who travelled up from Swansea. She explained to those present the importance and necessity of women joining the labour movement and becoming political activists independent of their husbands, brothers, fathers, and sons. At the end of the meeting, the Ystalyfera branch of the Women's Labour League was created. Elsie King (1891–1980), an elementary school teacher and an already active member of the ILP, was elected general secretary.[80] She was to be the branch's most important activist and the key to the WLL's presence in the upper Swansea valley.[81] But she was not alone. By the time of the branch's first annual general meeting, in early 1915, membership had grown to more than twenty. They were active in selling copies of the

Labour Woman, hosted a range of speakers, including Katherine Bruce Glasier and Marion Phillips, and debated and discussed topics as various as the history of women in the ILP, Christianity and democracy, the campaign for pithead baths, better housing, the water supply, and public transportation.[82]

Sarah Ann Moore, the branch president, told the 1915 annual general meeting that, although they were 'only a small band of women ... they were very enthusiastic and were hoping to make further progress'. She added, 'They wanted the women of the neighbourhood to rally round them ... helping [to] forward the movement ... let them do their part in saying there shall be no more wars for the sake of the women and children.'[83] The war context provided for some achievement of those aims, not least with the co-option of prominent members on to public committees dealing with women's employment, education, war pensions, maternity and child welfare, and agricultural wages; involvement of members in the Union of Democratic Control, the No Conscription Fellowship and the Women's Peace Crusade; and the continued growth of the Women's Labour League.[84] Several new branches were established, including at Pontypool, Gorseinon and Blackwood, and district conferences took place every six months.[85] At one such conference, held in December 1916, delegates passed a resolution in favour of 'limiting families so long as they were denied the right to live under fair conditions'.[86] A materialist basis for birth control, in other words. Perhaps most importantly, the Women's Labour League appointed Grace Scholefield as its regional organiser for South Wales in the summer of 1916, a post which she held until the dissolution of the League in 1918.[87] Her appointment, now entirely forgotten, pre-dated Elizabeth Andrews's work as organiser for the whole of Wales by nearly three years and illustrated the extent to which the Women's Labour League had grown, and was likely to continue to grow, in Glamorgan and Monmouthshire.

Grace Scholefield joined another unsung figure of the Welsh ILP, whose work organising the Labour Party and women members began in earnest during the First World War: Minnie Pallister (1885–1960). Born in Cornwall, educated in Pembrokeshire and at the University College of South Wales and Monmouthshire in Cardiff, she became a schoolteacher and settled in Brynmawr. There, she became active in the ILP – serving as lecture secretary for Monmouthshire from 1912 – and later the No Conscription Fellowship, of which she was the south Wales regional secretary.[88] In the summer of 1914, Pallister was elected president of the Monmouthshire ILP, from which platform she then moved to become the regional organiser of the South Wales and Monmouthshire ILP Federation in 1916.[89] She replaced the recently deceased Nathan Scholefield, who had died suddenly in Cardiff in 1915. The role was revised in January 1918 and ostensibly split in two, with Minnie Pallister taking on the work of 'women's organiser' – but the regional council failed to appoint a men's organiser and Pallister was left to undertake the work of organising both men and women on her own.[90] As Pallister's star waxed during the war, she became an in-demand speaker, frequently using platforms to tell women that 'the socialist movement was theirs as much as man's' and encouraging them to 'come in and take part in the work'.[91]

Minnie Pallister was a considerable asset, especially as the ILP sought to engage more women in socialist politics; indeed, in politics in general. Two rallies in the autumn of 1918 stand out as an indication of her abilities: one held in Merthyr Tydfil, the other in Aberaman in the Cynon Valley. In September, Minnie Pallister spoke in the Aberaman workmen's hall at an ILP social organised specially to enrol new women members. More than sixty joined the party on the spot.[92] In Merthyr a month later, she achieved an additional forty members. 'Women', Minnie Pallister told activists in the town, 'had been left out of politics far too long and that was the reason why we had made such a horrible mess of our political life'. She added, 'Women would break down war. Because of her great universal motherhood, she would tear down the narrow nationalism of man, and put in its place the grand and lofty idealism of internationalism.'[93]

Soon Minnie Pallister was being described as 'Wales's Great Woman Orator', and there was talk in Llanelli that she be asked to run as the local parliamentary candidate.[94] In the event, she never stood for parliament in a Welsh constituency. In the early 1920s, Minnie Pallister became close to the Labour leader, Ramsay MacDonald, and worked with him as party organiser in Aberavon in 1922. Appointed as a national propagandist for the ILP the following year, in which role she penned pamphlets and books such as *Socialism for Women* (1923) and *The Orange Box* (1925) and was a frequent contributor to the *New Leader* newspaper, Minnie Pallister moved from the regional stage and stood as Labour's candidate for parliament in Bournemouth in 1923 and 1924. She was defeated on both occasions. Later in the decade she retired from frontline Labour politics, largely due to ill health, and found a successful career as a writer and radio broadcaster.

*

Given the developments in women's involvement in Labour politics before 1914, the impact of the First World War deserves a degree of scrutiny: to what extent did wartime conditions alter the premise of the suffrage campaign (as socialists and social

democrats saw it) and the role of the WLL and the women's sec-
ions of the ILP? Relatively early on in the war, Mary Keating-Hill
oke at an open-air rally in the Cardiff suburb of Llanishen and
told those present that it was necessary to 'keep the flag flying' on
the question of women's suffrage, and that with work opening
up for women 'the vote [was] a necessity to secure better conditions for them in the labour market'.[95] These material concerns,
which were by no means new to Labour Party activists, nevertheless gained momentum as women took on new roles across
the economy replacing men who had joined the armed forces.
Lecturers, too, responded with topics such as the 'economic position of women', the need for equal pay for equal work, rising
food prices and the cost of living, and the role of the Women's
Freedom League's National Aid Corps, which supported those
in financial difficulties, and its National Service Organisation,
which found jobs for women.[96] That was a wartime development
distinct from peacetime.

The work of expanding the Women's Labour League continued much as it had done before the war, of course. In 1916,
Grace Scholefield joined with James Winstone to establish a
new branch at Pontypool – some twenty members signed up
immediately, and delegates were appointed to attend a local peace
conference and the town's trades and labour council.[97] Much
of the WLL network in Wales already established before 1914
remained in place through the war years. By 1918, at least a dozen
branches covering most parts of Glamorgan and Monmouthshire
from Swansea to Newport, Barry to Aberdare, were still in existence.[98] The Abertillery branch, which had been in existence off
and on since 1910, had a membership of ninety and was report-
edly the 'largest women's organisation in the locality' by the time
it was remodelled as a women's section of the Labour Party in

the spring of 1919.[99] Alongside the branches were a small number of personalities, some local, some regional. There was the indefatigable Hetty Jones, the Bargoed branch president, who was to draw on her experience in the Women's Labour League to launch her campaign to become a member of Gelligaer Urban District Council. She was successfully elected in the early 1920s.

There was Minnie Pallister, then in her early thirties, and there were the emerging figures of Elizabeth Andrews in the Rhondda and Rose Davies in Aberdare. The latter was already a long-standing co-opted member of the local education committee, which she chaired in 1915, and during wartime joined the military service tribunal and the food control committee. 'In fact', remarked the *Daily Herald* in 1918, in an article recording her election as chair of the Aberdare Trades and Labour Council, 'she plays a leading part in every piece of good work for the town [and] has demonstrated that, given the chance, women are capable and efficient organisers of municipal and trade union work'.[100] The following year, she was approved as a prospective parliamentary candidate for Labour, and was elected to Aberdare Urban District Council in 1920.[101] Grace Scholefield, who was in her mid-fifties, had been at the forefront of ILP activism for more than twenty-five years in both west Yorkshire and south Wales. In retrospect, it is surely a matter of curiosity that she did not seek to become a councillor herself, or to hold the post of women's regional organiser for Wales when it was established shortly after the armistice. That role went instead to Elizabeth Andrews, who was to shape the women's sections of the Labour Party – and subsequent historical memory – in her own image in the interwar years.

Yet, in 1920, as a sign of the esteem in which Grace Scholefield was held, she was one of almost fifty women, including Rose

Davies, the first in Wales after the Sex Disqualification (Removal) Act was passed just before Christmas 1919, to become a justice of the peace.[102] Four years later, Elizabeth Andrews was awarded the same accolade. Although Grace Scholefield appeared in the 1921 edition of *Who's Who in Wales*, her status had already diminished. The entry read, simply: 'Prominent in Labour circles; during the war was associated with the Soldiers' and Sailors' Association, besides being on the Glamorgan War Agriculture and Education Committees'.[103] If the First World War had a dramatic impact on the organisation of women's Labour politics, then, it was the ushering in of a new generation who carried on the work begun at the start of the twentieth century, but with the new opportunities afforded by the 1918 Labour Party constitution and the creation of individual membership of the party. The old structures created through the auspices of the Women's Labour League and the ILP women's sections were fundamental to the Labour Party's subsequent ability to capture what remained of working-class membership of the Liberal Party and to associate newly enfranchised women voters with social democratic, rather than liberal, ideals.

If, as Ursula Masson noted of liberalism in Aberdare, and the assessment stands as a universal one, the Women's Liberal Associations in Wales 'failed to create a form of politics which would attract young working-class women', then it was not only because of a 'Liberal government apparently indifferent to their claim for citizenship', but also because of years of hard work by women activists within the labour movement and within the fledgling Labour Party itself.[104] Yes, these activists had supported an infrastructure which was overwhelmingly focused on winning improvements for male trade unionists and getting male representatives of labour elected to parliament, but they had also succeeded in getting elected to public bodies, proved the merit of independent organisation of women, and expanded the meaning of social democratic policy. They ensured in the decade between winning the vote for some adult women, in 1918, and all adult women over the age of 21, in 1928, that the Labour Party met the challenge of producing a politics and a platform which spoke for women as well as for men. That, in the formal construction of a social democratic Glamorgan and Monmouthshire in the interwar years, nursery schools and birth control clinics, public parks and swimming pools and pithead baths, were all part of an effective programme of government.[105]

Notes

1. David James, *Class and Politics in a Northern Industrial Town: Keighley, 1880–1914* (Keele, 1995); David James, 'The Emergence of the Keighley Independent Labour Party' (unpublished MA thesis, Huddersfield Polytechnic, 1980).
2. *LL*, 19 December 1896. The site was later the location of the *Merthyr Pioneer* office.
3. *Merthyr Times*, 23 July 1897.
4. *LL*, 3 October 1896. F. W. Smithson was Scholefield's business partner at the Gwaunfarren Baths. *Merthyr Times*, 21 May 1897.
5. *LL*, 21 December 1901. Nathan Scholefield subsequently represented south Wales on the ILP National Administrative Council.
6. *Merthyr Times*, 1 October 1896.
7. *LL*, 27 April 1906.
8. RBA, SWCC, MNA/PP/69/1: Dowlais ILP Minute Book.
9. *LL*, 23 November 1906, 26 February 1909.
10. *LL*, 13 September 1907.
11. *The Vote: Organ of the Women's Freedom League*, 6 July 1912.
12. *LL*, 19 July 1907, 9 August 1907, 1 November 1907, 21 August 1908, 25 June 1909, 23 July 1909, 24 May 1912.
13. *Votes for Women*, 16 April 1915.
14. *The Vote*, 9 December 1909, 5 March 1910.
15. *The Vote*, 12 November 1910.

16. Ryland Wallace, *The Women's Suffrage Movement in Wales, 1866–1928* (Cardiff, 2009).

17. Pat Thane, 'Women in the Labour Party and Women's Suffrage', in Myriam Boussahba-Bravard (ed.), *Suffrage Outside Suffragism: Women's Vote in Britain, 1880–1914* (Basingstoke, 2007), pp. 35–51.

18. *LL*, 24 April 1913.

19. *MEx*, 16 March 1907, 18 April 1908; *PO*, 25 February 1911.

20. *Common Cause*, 14 February 1913.

21. Masson, *For Women*, pp. 167–8.

22. June Hannam, '"I Had Not Been To London": Women's Suffrage – A View From The Regions', in June Purvis and Sandra Stanley Holton (eds), *Votes For Women* (London, 2000), p. 235.

23. 'Lists of Liberal and Labour MPs', in Catherine Marshall Papers, Cumbria Record Office: D/MAR/3/19. Cited in Ursula Masson, 'Divided Loyalties: Women's Suffrage and Party Politics in South Wales, 1912–1915', *Llafur*, 7/3–4 (1999), 116. The other coalfield Labour MP in the region, Thomas Richards, was not mentioned.

24. *The Vote*, 10 February 1912.

25. NLW, Samuel T. Evans Papers: 'Letter from Vernon Hartshorn to Samuel T. Evans, 11 November 1906'. Cited in Masson, 'Divided Loyalties', 116.

26. *LL*, 14 May 1914.

27. *LL*, 8 August, 15 August 1912.

28. *GG*, 10 April 1914.

29. *LL*, 25 July 1912.

30. Christine Collette, *For Labour and for Women: The Labour Women's League, 1906–18* (Manchester, 1989).

31. SCOLAR, Women's Labour League Records, WLL/5: Letter from John A. Kelly, 20 November 1906 (microfilm).

32. *BH*, 17 September 1909. For the advertisements, see, for example: *BDN*, 9 October 1908.

33. *BDN*, 17 September 1909.

34. *SWDN*, 23 October 1908; *AL*, 31 October 1908.

35. WWP, PY4/5, Aberdare Socialist Society [i.e. ILP] Minute Book, 27 January 1906; GLA, DXHJ/2, Aberdare Socialist Society List of Officers; *LL*, 6 March 1908, 24 April 1908.

36. GLA, Stan Awberry Papers, DAW/H/14/4, 'Swansea Socialist Party and Labour Party', by Griff Jones; Collette, *For Labour and for Women*, p. 64; *LL*, 26 November 1909.

37. *AL*, 2 February 1906.

38. This is not necessarily to imply that there was a rivalry between the two – as in the example of Grace Scholefield, there was relatively fluid movement between the ILP women's movement and the Women's Labour League, to say nothing of the absolute ease of movement between the ILP itself and the women's movement. This wider synergy is usefully discussed in June Hannam and Karen Hunt, *Socialist Women: Britain, 1880s–1920s* (London, 2001).

39. Wright, *Wales and Socialism*, p. 125; *The Vote*, 4 July 1913; *WM*, 28 June 1913.

40. *AL*, 25 April 1908.

41. Wright, *Wales and Socialism*, p. 125.

42. *LL*, 23 March 1906.

43. *EEx*, 8 February 1910. The Newport ILP, which had its own women's section, had a complex relationship with the local branch of the Women's Labour League. The two organisations variously existed as a separate force and as a merged one, taking on the identity of the ILP. *LL*, 19 February 1914.

44. *EEx*, 29 January 1910. The Merthyr branch had been formed the previous September: *MEx*, 25 September 1909.

45. *LL*, 14 October 1910.

46. *LL*, 4 August 1911.

47. *LL*, 4 August 1911.

48. *WM*, 12 August 1911.

49. *LL*, 11 August 1911.

50. *LL*, 24 March 1911.

51. *CT*, 12 February 1910.

52. *LL*, 15 March 1912, 10 May 1912.

53. The minutes of the Newport Insurance Committee, which record Mrs Morrish's work, are held at the Gwent Archives: D528.

54. *LL*, 24 July 1913.

55. Mary Morrish died suddenly in Ammanford in 1918, during a visit to her sister. By this time, the family had relocated to Banbury in Oxfordshire. *Amman Valley Chronicle*, 28 February 1918.

56. Beatrice Lewis became president of the branch in the autumn of 1910, following Elizabeth Henson's election to the Board of Guardians. *BDN*, 16 September 1910.

57. *BDN*, 17 January 1913.

58. *BDN*, 2 November 1906.

59. *BDN*, 13 March 1914.

60. *BDN*, 21 March, 4 April, 11 April 1919.

61. *BDN*, 21 July, 17 November 1916.

62. *BDN*, 22 April 1910, 24 October 1913.

63. *BDN*, 10 June 1910.

64. *BDN*, 30 September 1910; SCOLAR, WLL/164: Women's Labour League Branch History.

65. *BH*, 30 September 1910; *LL*, 14 October 1910. Motions on lodging houses were debated, for instance, in Jarrow and in Coventry, and in Bristol (with some of the Welsh branches in attendance). *LL*, 3 March 1911, 28 April 1911, 14 July 1911, 22 March 1912. On the engagement of the women's suffrage movement see *The Vote*, 26 August 1911, 17 February 1912, 24 February 1912; *Votes For Women*, 30 June 1911.

66. The *RS* had launched four months earlier in August 1911.

67. 'Matron', 'Our Women's Column', *RS*, 5 (December 1911).

68. Masson, in Masson and Aaron, *Salt*, p. 168.

69. *Rhondda Socialist*, 4 (November 1911).

70. 'Matron', 'Our Women's Column', *RS*, 8 June 1912.

71. 'Matron', 'Our Women's Column', *RS*, 21 December 1912.

72. *South Wales Worker*, 66 (30 May 1914).

73. Ruth Chalk, 'Our Women's Column', *Swansea and District Workers' Journal*, April 1912.

74. *League Leaflet*, February 1913; April 1913; those in Bargoed, Barry and Swansea were elected. *LW*, 1/1 (May 1913).

75. *Cambria Daily Leader*, 7 April 1913, 8 April 1913.

76. *LW*, 1/10 (February 1914).

77. *LL*, 29 May 1913.

78. *LL*, 19 June 1913; 31 July 1913.

79. *LL*, 4 September 1913.

80. *Llais Llafur*, 3 January 1914.

81. *Herald of Wales*, 28 February 1914; *Llais Llafur*, 28 February 1914.

82. *Llais Llafur*, 14 February, 7 March, 16 May, 23 May, 25 July 1914; *Herald of Wales*, 25 July 1914.

83. *Llais Llafur*, 9 January 1915.

84. *LW*, April 1915; October 1915; November 1915; December 1915; *Llais Llafur*, 4 April, 5 September 1914; *MPn*, 15 December 1917.

85. *LL*, 29 June 1916; *MPn*, 6 January 1917; 1 June 1918.

86. *LW*, December 1916.

87. *LW*, July 1916.

88. *LL*, 19 September 1912.

89. *Abergavenny Chronicle*, 12 June 1914; *Llais Llafur*, 1 August 1914; *GG*, 6 September 1916.

90. *MPn*, 8 June 1918.

91. *MPn*, 10 November 1917.

92. *AL*, 28 September 1918.

93. *MPn*, 19 October 1918.

94. *LL*, 3 April 1919.

95. *The Vote*, 25 June 1915.

96. *The Vote*, 12 February 1915, 5 March 1915, 6 August 1915.

97. *LL*, 29 June 1916.

98. *GG*, 28 November 1919; 5 December 1919; *Monmouth Guardian*, 16 May 1919; *BDN*, 4 April 1919.

99. *SWG*, 25 April 1919.

100. *DH*, 16 March 1918.

101. *Westminster Gazette*, 11 August 1919.

102. *The Vote*, 23 July 1920; G. Evelyn Gates (ed.), *The Woman's Year Book, 1923–1924* (London, 1924), pp. 649–55.

103. Arthur Mee (ed.), *Who's Who in Wales* (Cardiff, 1921), p. 431.

104. Masson, *For Women*, p. 123.

105. Leeworthy, *Labour Country*, pp. 161–310, *passim*. Contemporaries would have understood this as a capitalised 'South Wales', although I have employed Glamorgan and Monmouthshire here to avoid the anachronistic construction 'south Wales'.

3

Between the Acts

Elizabeth Andrews began her work as the Labour Party's women's organiser for Wales in March 1919. She was 36 years old. Her task, to which she was devoted for the next thirty years, she later explained to a younger generation, was to bring 'the new woman voter into the Labour Party'. She embarked with what she called a 'deep conviction and missionary zeal' and travelled across Wales to address party meetings, to establish new women's sections, and to demonstrate the commitment of the Labour Party to bring about universal female suffrage rather than rest on the partial achievements of the recent Representation of the People Act (or Fourth Reform Act).[1] It was a task to which she was unusually well suited. Already active in the labour movement in the Rhondda, where she had been secretary of Ton Pentre Women's Co-operative Guild for almost five years, she gained considerable administrative experience during the First World War as a member both of the county pensions committee for Glamorgan and of the maternity and child welfare committee of Rhondda Urban District.[2] She used the skills acquired in the public arena to great effect when called as part of a delegation of three miners' wives to give evidence before the Royal Commission on the Coal

Mining Industry – better known as the Sankey Commission after its chair, Sir John Sankey – in May 1919.[3]

Women in mining areas, she told the Royal Commissioners, a group which included Sidney Webb and R. H. Tawney, suffered from all sorts of hardships and iniquities – including being 'confined' to houses sodden with mildew and damp. The coal-owners, she added, had dog kennels with electric lights, but most mining families had no such luxury. 'I don't want the dogs to get a worse time', she said, 'but I [do] want the human beings to get as good conditions'.[4] One idea put to Elizabeth Andrews by the Royal Commissioners was that 'miners' wives acquiesce in bad housing conditions because they like low rent' – an proposition which she refused. 'Miners' wives', she explained, 'have had to pay a big increase in rent during the last ten years for the same houses and conditions as before'. What was needed was a system of socialised housing provision, with need, not ability to pay, being the main driver of allocation. She added that it was not just housing but facilities in the community which needed improving, too, including pithead baths and playgrounds for children.[5] When the government responded to the Sankey Commission report with the introduction of the Mining Industry Act (1920), it established the miners' welfare fund, which established a sum of money for precisely that purpose.

That Elizabeth Andrews was identified to the Royal Commissioners not as the Labour Party's women's organiser for Wales, but as a miner's wife, was a tactical decision. She was there not as a Labour Party representative, at least not directly, but at the request of the South Wales Miners' Federation. It was a subtle distinction, for in practice there was not a great deal of difference. The suggestion that miners' wives would present gendered evidence on housing and community infrastructure had itself come from Marion Phillips, the head of the newly created Labour Party Women's Department, who realised the potential impact of such testimony in the hearings themselves and, more importantly, in the wider press coverage. The three women famously stood in the King's Robing Room in the House of Lords, where the Commission hearings were being held, with press and Royal Commissioners alike recognising their fortitude. As Elizabeth Andrews observed, those present 'expressed surprise at our calmness when giving evidence'. But these were by no means typical miners' wives, they were well used to being in the public arena and were political activists in their own right: Mrs Hart, the Lancastrian member of the delegation, went on to be elected to Wigan County Borough Council early in 1927.[6]

Given Elizabeth Andrews's many achievements during her nearly thirty-year career as Labour Party women's organiser in Wales, it has long been assumed that she was singularly responsible for the growth of the women's sections.[7] Certainly, she made the most of the opportunity she was given in 1919 and faithfully recorded new developments in the pages of the *Labour Woman*. Thus, in May 1920, she noted the existence of a 'very active' women's section in Pontypridd, the name of the secretary of the Ynysybwl women's section, and the recent formation of the Tredegar women's section with a membership roll of fifty.[8] The following month, the *Labour Woman* published a list of no fewer than a dozen women's sections in existence in Monmouthshire, including Abertillery, Rhymney and Tredegar.[9] As captured in this way, the progress of Labour's women's infrastructure seemed rapid and a clear testament to the regional organiser's efforts. But Elizabeth Andrews began her work with already tilled soil. Several initiatives (including branch formation) were under way as she was coming into office, and the Labour Party and the ILP, in Glamorgan and Monmouthshire especially, were well used to women organisers and women's sections. Nor was she alone: Minnie Pallister continued her work on behalf of the ILP until 1922.

Elizabeth Andrews's journalism, which began in earnest in the early 1920s with regular columns for the *Labour Woman* and the *Colliery Workers' Magazine*, the monthly newsletter of the South Wales Miners' Federation, likewise followed on from previous efforts by Gwen Ray and Ruth Chalk, and joined Minnie Pallister's contemporaneous writing for ILP publications. It was official status, hard work and the rising power of the Labour Party, which formed a government for the first time in January 1924 and had eclipsed the Liberal Party as the natural opposition to the Conservatives by the end of the decade, which enabled Elizabeth Andrews to acquire a prominence and a range of titles and positions largely out of reach to an earlier generation of women activists. Reporting on her appointment as a magistrate in February 1924, the Women's Freedom League newspaper, *The Vote*, encapsulated the distance travelled.

> Mrs Elizabeth Andrews, the national organiser of the women's section of the Labour Party in Wales, has been appointed by Lord Haldane to the magisterial bench. Mrs Andrews has acted as member of the Consultative Committee to the Ministry of Health, and member of the Welsh Committee of the Commission of Public Morals, War Pensions, etc. She gave evidence before the Sankey Commission and the Regional Service Committee at Cardiff, and sat on the Committee that drafted the scheme for probational work in the Rhondda police courts.[10]

The National Council of Public Morals, to which *The Vote* referred, was at the forefront of the debate around Britain's declining birth rate in the early twentieth century and had issued a report in 1916 offering ideas for what it called 'the promotion of race regeneration – spiritual, moral and physical'.[11] In subsequent years, the Council issued a series of reports on parenthood under the guide of the 'National Birth-Rate Commission', and on other matters, including the cinema, which appeared to threaten the moral rectitude of the British population.[12] The Welsh Committee was established in late 1919.[13] Membership of such a body almost certainly explains Elizabeth Andrews's reticence when it came to birth control – a reticence which Ursula Masson noted with some surprise, given the efforts made by Labour-run councils in Glamorgan and Monmouthshire, such as at Abertillery and Pontypridd, to establish birth control clinics.[14] As the latter wrote, 'Andrews never addressed the topic in her monthly columns', and neither did she make mention of 'the campaigns by women in the party for dissemination of birth-control information' in her memoir. There was, in other words, a spectrum of opinion and organisational activity within the Labour Party: Elizabeth Andrews's social values, particularly those derived from her religious faith, were not fully representative, and the women's sections would continue to be a forum for diverse ideas about the labour movement, its purpose and its feminist potential.

Although, as Matthew Worley has noted, 'there was no attempt to give women equal representation on the [Labour] party's decision-making bodies', even in the aftermath of franchise reform in 1918, the creation of the Women's Department, the employment of regional organisers, and the provision of some representation on the National Executive Committee ensured that Labour was in a strong position to attract women as members, activists, and as newly enfranchised voters.[15] Indeed, as part of its direct appeal to women, Labour had promised during the First World War to create 'special facilities to the prospective women electors to join our ranks' and, in peacetime, worked to make good on that offer. In 1918, there was a wave of party publications including guidance notes on how to organise and operate women's sections covering all levels of the party, from the ward branch to the parliamentary division (or constituency). The most notable, Marion Phillips's *Women and the Labour Party*, was a clear-headed assertion of the party's belief that it was the natural platform for women. The organisational structure moved up from grassroots women's sections in local wards to constituency women's sections to advisory councils at the regional level to the national committees and annual conferences. Altogether, thousands of women were brought under the party umbrella.

In Wales, the regional advisory councils were often more radical in their outlook than was the regional organiser, and gave 'scope to venture out on new methods of educating the women in politics'.[16] Within a few days of each other, in February 1920, advisory councils were established in 'West Wales' (effectively Carmarthenshire, Swansea and the western districts of Glamorgan), Monmouthshire and East Glamorgan.[17] These replaced the older Women's Labour League, with existing conferences, committees, officers and members all absorbed. In northern counties, where the WLL had been weaker or non-existent, construction of regional infrastructure took longer. In the north-east, several women's sections were evident by 1924, including in Wrexham, Ruabon and Rhosllanerchrugog, with some effort at regional organisation taking place. An outing to Llandudno in the summer of 1924 provided, in the words of one newspaper, 'striking proof of the activities of the Labour women of North Wales'.[18] The Flintshire constituency party had its own women's conferences by 1930.[19] In the north-west, a women's advisory council for Caernarfonshire and Anglesey was formed in the second half of 1925.[20] That region's first Labour women's conference was held at Bangor in October, with Ellen Wilkinson as the guest of honour.[21] Margaret Bondfield spoke the following year.[22]

The Monmouthshire Labour Women's Advisory Council was the first to make a name for itself when, at its inaugural conference at the Ebenezer Lecture Hall in Abertillery in May 1920, delegates debated whether women were 'slaves of men and children' and whether the present generation of women were 'wise'. The council's inaugural president, Mrs Adams of Abertillery, declared that those men who had opposed suffragettes most bitterly were on the losing side.[23] Members concluded that 'women of the past died premature deaths because they [had] made themselves slaves of their husbands' and that the 'young women of to-day were agreed they were not going to be soft. God never intended women to become slaves of their children or their husbands, and in future they did not intend to be'.[24] News of the Monmouthshire conference soon spread, prompting some controversy, particularly amongst moderate and right-wing commentators. The conservative *Hull Daily Mail*, for example, wondered whether men were 'being gradually put in [their] proper sphere' and warned that 'there are to be no more motherly women, at any rate if the members of the Monmouthshire Labour Women's Advisory Council have their way'. Beware, they said, of the 'new feminine race'.[25]

Language of the kind employed by members of the Monmouthshire Labour Women's Advisory Council is suggestive. Historians have tended to argue that 'Labour's approach to its female members and potential elections was infused with the gender preconceptions of the time', or that the party's authorised identity – that of the 'Labour Woman' – typically involved 'much more emphasis on "Labour" than on "Woman"', with feminist concerns marginalised in favour of those which fitted most comfortably with the aims of the party.[26] Certainly, leading figures on the national stage, such as Margaret Bondfield and Marion Phillips, insisted on the universality of Labour's perspective and on the indivisible nature of men's and women's interests. 'I always said it was a mistake on the part of some of the ultrafeminist suffragists', Bondfield told her parliamentary colleagues during a debate on the Fifth Reform Act in 1928, 'to argue the specific woman point of view in connection with political questions'.[27] Bondfield's perspective was not wholly shared by those on the left, such as Ellen Wilkinson or Jennie Lee, who were marked more by access to higher education and the possibilities of social mobility. Their political radicalism and feminism reflected that intellectual conditioning.[28] And such a spectrum of opinion was apparent at all levels of the Labour Party.

One of those involved in the Monmouthshire Labour Women's Advisory Council in the 1920s, including as president in 1927 – the final year of her life – was Beatrice Green (née Dykes), a former schoolteacher. Her public sentiments illustrate that 'Labour' and 'woman' were at least equal in grassroots thinking. The earliest mention of her as an activist was in January 1921, when she gave a lecture to the Abertillery Labour Party's women's section on women and the state, a subject 'so big that she could only touch [on] the fringe of it'. She told delegates that

> for too long the idea [has] been allowed to circulate that woman's place [is] in the home, and man's in the world. With the

inadequate measure of franchise, woman [is] realising that politics [have] a direct bearing upon her home, and that she [has] to get out in order to put things right.

It was a clarion call for women to become active campaigners, as well as an assertion of the need for equal pay and equal representation. Failure to secure the rights of women in the workplace had resulted, she argued, 'in the social evil of our time'.[29] Sue Bruley has argued that Beatrice Green's ascent was indicative of stand-out qualities rather than typicality as a Labour woman.[30] Whilst this may well be true, to a certain extent, the existence of equivalent figures in most towns across the coalfield suggests that the women's sections succeeded in providing a platform for eminently capable political activists. Their rise was not by their talents alone.

Indeed, in Abertillery itself, Beatrice Green was part of the second generation of Labour women activists, and her work built on the foundations laid by Ethel Barker, Edith Haskins and others who had been involved locally in the Women's Labour League. It was because of the continuity between the WLL and the subsequent women's section, and the relative stability of political organisation which such longevity provided, that Beatrice Green was able to move on to the regional and then, as a member of the Women's Committee for the Relief of Miners' Wives and Children in 1926, on to the national stage.[31] That aspect of her experience was more unusual, but the rest was not. Her husband, Ron, was a member of the Abertillery Trades and Labour Council, and the Greens were known as a political family.[32] In this respect, Beatrice Green was like her contemporary Sarah Ann Moon, the secretary of Tredegar Labour Party's women's section, who worked alongside her in the 1920s as treasurer of the Monmouthshire Labour Women's Advisory Council. Moon's husband, Ted, had been president of Tredegar Trades and Labour Council in 1912 and served as a district councillor from 1928 until his death in 1932. Another political family.

A more distinct campaigner, who was by vocation a schoolteacher, and who never married, was Myra O'Brien. Born to Irish parents in Cape Town in 1869, Myra O'Brien spent much of her childhood in Kilrush in Ireland. She moved to Pontypridd in 1899, after a brief period during which she taught in Holywell, Flintshire, and began teaching at St Michael's Roman Catholic School, where she remained until her retirement in 1934.[33] She was elected to Glamorgan County Council that same year. Myra O'Brien's position as headteacher at St Michael's placed her at the heart of Catholic life in the town. For at least a decade, alongside her duties at the school, she was the organist at St Dyfrig's Church.[34] Her faith and heritage led her towards involvement in the Irish home rule campaign, the United Irish League and, eventually, the Irish Self-Determination League, which had a substantial local presence. Together with the town's miners' agent and, from 1931 until his death in 1937, the member of parliament, David Lewis Davies, she was an important bridge between the Labour Party and Pontypridd's Irish Catholics.[35] Religious faith was mirrored in a lifelong commitment to trade unionism, the Labour Party and the wider women's movement. As her obituary, published in November 1935, observed, O'Brien's

> connection with the Labour Party was a long one and she had been president of the Pontypridd Labour Women's Section since its inception. For three successive years she was chairman of the Pontypridd Trades and Labour Council and was a member of the Executive Committee and a past

President of the Pontypridd Divisional Labour Party ... Her popularity among the members of the teaching profession was evidenced by her election to the Presidency of the local Branch of the N.U.T., and to that of the local Branch of the National Association of Head Teachers. For many years she was a member of the Executive Committee of the former.[36]

Her path through the women's infrastructure of the party was typical: she served twice as president of the East Glamorgan Labour Women's Advisory Council, including in 1929–30, and was the most prominent member of the women's section in Pontypridd.[37] She was a key figure in the Pontypridd Women's Co-operative Guild and served as president of the Ynysybwl Co-operative Society's education committee in the mid-1930s. But it was her position as chair of Pontypridd Trades and Labour Council between 1922 and 1925, and her subsequent election as chair of the constituency party, which put her in a relatively unusual position as a figurehead at that time. Albeit, by no means uniquely so.[38] Margaret Ann Williams, who lived at Aberbeeg near Abertillery, but who was originally from the Rhondda, served as president of the Llanhilleth Trades Council and Labour Party in the 1920s. She was, recorded the *South Wales Gazette* following her death in 1929, 'a very prominent figure in the public life of the district'.[39] Mary McPhail, the first woman to chair Merthyr Tydfil Trades Council and Labour Party, a post to which she was elected in early 1940, rose to that position through her work for the Dowlais branch of the Women's Co-operative Guild.[40]

*

The question which ought to occupy our examination of the women's movement in the 1920s, then, is not so much whether a figure such as Beatrice Green was unusual or not – as shown, she was, and she was not – but whether women were successful in changing the Labour Party's stance on decision making, materialism and the moral economy of the community. That women struggled to effect change at the national level is not in doubt. For all its progressive commitments to equality, which were sincere, Labour remained wedded to the idea of the 'common interest' and to a vision of politics which appealed 'to citizens irrespective of sex'.[41] Likewise, women were unable to overturn the grip of the South Wales Miners' Federation on the selection of parliamentary candidates in the safest Welsh seats. Those men elected to parliament tended to serve for long periods. In Aberdare, for example, the seat changed hands only once between 1918 and 1945, when George Henry Hall defeated Charles Stanton in 1922; in Ebbw Vale, the situation was even more dramatic – a single change in representative between 1920, when the seat was won by Evan Davies, and Aneurin Bevan's death in 1960. Bevan himself was first elected in 1929.

Outside the southern coalfield, in rural areas to the west and in the north, Labour did not always field candidates, further reducing opportunities for women to stand for parliament. For each of the parties, Wales's northern constituencies proved more fertile ground for women candidates: the aristocratic Lesley Brodrick, who stood in Denbigh in 1922 and 1924, came closest to winning a seat for the Conservatives, and Megan Lloyd George won Anglesey for the Liberal Party in 1929. She held the seat until her defeat in the 1951 general election. Labour's Frances Edwards (perhaps better known by her married name, Frances Kerby), achieved more than 16,000 votes when she stood in Flintshire in 1931. That was the highest number of votes cast for any woman candidate in Wales between the wars. Given her obvious appeal to voters in Flintshire, Frances Edwards's campaign merits closer examination. Her election agent, Huw T. Edwards, at the time secretary of the North Wales Labour Federation, later described his namesake as 'a young girl of twenty-four who was a teacher in Manchester. Her father came from Conwy but her mother was an Irish woman, with the result that she herself was a bundle of Celtic fervour'.[42]

Born in Salford, Frances Edwards was indeed a school-teacher – she worked at West Liverpool Street Girls School in Salford. Having joined the Labour Party at the age of 15, she became a well-known activist in and around Manchester, and in 1944, in recognition of her many years of work for the party, she was appointed women's regional organiser for the north-west of England.[43] In her election campaign, and in the years before and after, Frances Edwards stressed a feminist point of view, even as she was clearly encouraging support for the Labour Party. In 1930, describing the conflict which might arise between men and women in domestic affairs, she argued that women should 'fight if necessary in opposition to the men who are seldom the Chancellor of the Exchequer in their homes and so do not understand'.[44] In 1934, she returned to the theme, appealing to women to rid themselves 'of their apathy towards municipal and national elections' because, in her view, 'women are the mothers of the citizens, and your duty is to prepare for the heralding in of a new social order'.[45] And in 1931, she told a rally in Chester, where she was supporting the local Labour candidate, Joseph Lewis, that 'Labour believed in women and children first'.[46]

Frances Edwards's achievement in Flintshire in 1931 offers a tantalising counterfactual. Had the parliamentary selection process been open to women in winnable constituencies, Labour would probably have succeeded in breaking the glass ceiling

long before it did so in 1950. There is no doubt that Frances
Edwards's vote tally reflected her efficacy as a political fighter
and campaigner and that her efforts helped to lay the ground-
work for Eirene White's eventual success in Flintshire East
– the successor constituency – nearly two decades later. Indeed,
Frances Edwards proved that even in unwinnable Welsh seats,
even with a degree of unease registered by male organisers,
would-be Labour voters were not put off by women candidates. Quite the opposite. In its reporting of the 1931 election,
the *Flintshire County Herald* frequently noted the large crowds
which attended Frances Edwards's campaign meetings, and that
at Holywell it was the largest gathering in many years.[47] Such
was the Flintshire Labour Party's confidence in her that she
was unanimously reselected as their parliamentary candidate
early in 1932, although she eventually stood in 1935 in Darwen
in Lancashire.[48] In the nadir of Labour's political and electoral
fortunes, then, women proved themselves able to break through
in areas where men could not.

But national and parliamentary politics were not local politics, and a distinction must be made between what Labour
failed to do at one level, and what it might have achieved had
circumstances been different, and what it succeeded in doing at
another. At the level of local and regional government and in the
construction of municipal social democracy there were ample
opportunities for women to get involved, to provide leadership
and to bring to bear their collective point of view. This theme has
been the subject of considerable debate amongst historians. In
his influential study of gender and municipal Labour politics,
Duncan Tanner argued that it was individual women, such as
Elizabeth Andrews or Rose Davies, working alongside men in
elected positions, but crucially from within the Labour machine,

who introduced reforms and brought about change at the local level.[49] Pat Thane, by contrast, has asserted the collective import-ance of the women's sections, albeit she was not writing, per se, about the Welsh context.[50] My reading of the evidence, gathered from mass newspaper digitisation, which was not available when Tanner was conducting his research in the early 2000s, qualifies his assessment. Rose Davies, Myra O'Brien, Margaret Williams and many others recognised that their position was as much that of a delegate who acted on behalf of the women's sections, as it was an individual one of their own.

Thus, in December 1926, to offer a concrete example of the process, Llanhilleth Labour Party's women's section success-fully demanded representation on the local housing committee and proposed that Margaret Williams should be the representa-tive.[51] Although she gained a reputation as an 'ardent worker' on the committee, the relationship between her position and the perspective of the women's section was clear.[52] Indeed, her equivalent from Abertillery was directly elected by section mem-bers.[53] This was a widely implemented procedure. Pontypridd's maternity and child welfare committee, established in 1919, had two positions reserved for women nominated by the trades and labour council.[54] Although ratified by annual election at a meeting of the trades and labour council, responsibility for nominating individuals to fill the roles was itself delegated to the women's sections and to the women's co-operative guild.[55] Additional co-opted members would be put forward by other women's organisations, such as the mother's union. At Aberdare, ratification of women nominated to serve as co-opted members of the education and child welfare committees was similarly the responsibility of the trades council.[56] And at Colwyn Bay, by no means traditional Labour territory, nominations came directly from the Women's Co-operative Guild, and those co-opted were recognised representatives of the Guild itself.[57]

Individual activists and campaigners undoubtedly followed their interests or professional skillset, of course. Myra O'Brien was heavily involved in the Pontypridd and District Institution for the Blind, which she helped to establish in 1919 and served as secretary until her death in 1935.[58] Additionally, she joined the College of Teachers of the Blind in 1931 and was elected vice president of the South Wales and Monmouthshire Association for the Blind in 1934.[59] From such a background she was able to exert influence over municipal policies in relation to the disabled. During the 1920s, she served as a co-opted member of the maternity and child welfare committee, the education committee (in which capacity she helped to steer the lowering of the school entry age from 5 to 3[60]) and was the chair of the town's parks representative committee. The latter committee had been established to raise funds for the purchase of Ynysangharad Fields as a permanent war memorial. As chair, she was selected to serve as a co-opted member of the council's own parks committee, which came into existence after the park opened in 1923, and so was able to influence its growth and development. But for her comparatively early death, Myra O'Brien would have been the first woman council chair in Pontypridd, thereby fulfilling 'a wider vocation to improve the living conditions for the working class as a whole' – the hallmark of the interwar Labour woman.[61]

Thus far, it has been apparent that women emerged into executive and leadership roles within the Labour Party at a local level, but what sort of impact did this have on the provision of facilities? Although the powers of local authorities differed across Wales, depending on whether it was an urban district, rural district, borough, county borough or county council, there was a degree of consistency as to which council committees had women members. These typically included education, maternity and child welfare, hospitals, housing, leisure facilities, and old age pensions. This accorded with Labour's belief that 'women are specially concerned with the development of the social services'.[62] It also meant that, particularly on councils where Labour were in control, Labour women had a clear voice in the management of municipal affairs across almost the entire spectrum of infrastructure.[63] In both the presence and absence of co-option to or representation on council committees, the Labour women's sections and branches of the Women's Co-operative Guild applied direct pressure to council committees to bring about change. Such pressure could result in the provision of public lavatories for women in Tredegar, for example, or a commitment to build more council houses in Cardiff.[64]

One area where women's involvement in municipal politics was most obviously felt was in the development of nursery education.[65] Labour's initial debate on the subject, prompted by delegates from Bradford, had taken place at the party's annual conference in Manchester in 1917. Five years later, ahead of the 1922 general election, Labour issued a pamphlet entitled *Motherhood and Child Endowment* wherein it set out the case for what it called an educational revolution. Education, the party argued, 'should be free from nursery school, at which the child can be admitted at two years of age, through the primary and secondary schools and the Universities, maintenance allowances being available when needed'.[66] Nor did Labour stand still. In 1927, the party produced a landmark report in conjunction with the Trades Union Congress which shaped its message on education for the rest of the interwar period. *From Nursery School to University*, which carried a forward by Ramsay MacDonald, set out in clear terms the party's position. On nursery education, it argued that 'it should be the duty of the [local] authority to provide nursery schools for children over two and under five, where formal notice had been given by the parents that a certain number of children were prepared to attend'.[67]

Although it was national party policy, and was generally encouraged by women's sections across Wales, as well as by Elizabeth Andrews, support for nursery schools was by no means universal. The women's section of Caerphilly Labour Party, for example, resisted provision of nurseries in that part of the coalfield on the basis that 'the women comrades thought it would tend to give mothers more time to gossip', and in Abertillery, despite the issue being raised in the mid-1920s by the district medical officer, Monmouthshire Labour Women's Advisory Council and women's section activists, such as Beatrice Green, they were to some extent resisted, because 'the industry is mostly coal mining, and little or no female labour is employed' there was 'no demand for an institution of this kind'.[68] Nevertheless, contrary to this assertion, several nursery classes would be established and were to be warmly welcomed by parents, because they 'specially prepare the children for continuation in the junior schools'.[69] Monmouthshire County Council were similarly supportive.[70] In 1939, perhaps to iron out these inconsistencies, the South Wales Regional Council of Labour issued a set of policies which included a proposal to establish nursery schools in every part of Glamorgan and Monmouthshire.[71]

In her memoir, Elizabeth Andrews recorded that the first Welsh nursery school was situated 'on the hill side at Ynyscynon, Llwynypia, Rhondda'.[72] Although it opened relatively early, in September 1935, and there had been discussion about municipal provision of nursery schools in the Rhondda since the mid-1920s, it was not, in fact, the first.[73] That honour fell to the Emergency Open-Air Nursery School opened in Dowlais in October 1933. A few months later, in May 1934, a second opened at Brynmawr. They were supported financially by the Save the Children Fund and underwritten largely by Nancy Astor, who officially opened both. A fourth nursery school, which was run by a local council and was frequently visited by women's sections keen to learn about such facilities, opened in Swansea in May 1936.[74] Katherine Bruce Glasier cut the ribbon.[75] It had been conceived of five years earlier but was significantly delayed because of the austerity of the early 1930s. The Alaw nursery school in Trealaw followed in December 1939, and the much delayed Severn Road nursery school in Cardiff, which had been conceived of in 1936, but campaigned for by Labour women since the mid-1920s, opened in March 1940.[76] Merthyr Tydfil County Borough Council adopted the Dowlais nursery, amidst wild complaints of financial profligacy, in 1939.[77]

Establishing this chronology is important because nursery schools emerged in parallel through voluntary and municipal action. Elizabeth Andrews's narrative evacuated voluntary provision of nursery schools and, in so doing, nuanced discussion about how public services could and should be provided – an echo of the wider debate about public health.[78] There is no doubt that there was a strong degree of scepticism about charitable intervention into the coalfield, especially amongst Labour Party members. As early as 1920, the Ton Pentre branch of the Women's Co-operative Guild, with Elizabeth Andrews as its secretary, passed a resolution protesting against middle-class women from London 'who know very little, if anything about the lives of the miners coming into the valley and endeavouring to influence miners' wives'.[79] Elizabeth Andrews was to make a similar point in a column for the *Labour Woman* in 1937. 'We have become', she wrote, 'not only centres of poverty but centres for every charitable experiment'.[80] Employment was at stake. The laying out of leisure facilities by miners' welfare committees who had chosen to volunteer their labour was one thing, but charitable trusts imposing 'voluntary labour' on destitute communities was quite another, particularly where that imposition came with a string of values inimical to socialism.[81]

Unsurprisingly, Elizabeth Andrews, together with her allies in the South Wales Miners' Federation, was dismissive of Nancy Astor as an unknowing philanthropist and propagator of voluntaryism, and the sort to take credit for work which was not really theirs to claim. 'The Labour women', Andrews wrote in response to the opening of the nursery schools in the Rhondda and Swansea, 'are glad that their propaganda is bearing fruit at last, though at this stage there will probably be others who will try to claim some of the credit'.[82] Indeed, there were plans for a municipally run nursery in the Rhondda, which had first been drawn up in 1920. And yet the nurseries built and operated by volunteers were as valued as those run municipally, which suggests a certain flexibility in the moral economy of the community: that having a facility was more important.[83] One mother wrote to Nancy Astor in 1938 to

> appreciate you for what you have done, as a mother for our children, which attend the New Road Nursery School Dowlais ... It is nice, that there are such places for our children to go to, as the food, and the care, they get is wonderfull [*sic*].[84]

If the overall aim of Labour women was to 'fit the world for the child', as Elizabeth Andrews put it, then the advent of early years education at the municipal level, and its take-up by families, was surely a testament to their success and to their influence.[85]

*

Most of those involved in the Labour Party's women's sections did not stand as councillors or as parliamentary candidates, nor did they put themselves forward as branch officers, delegates or co-opted members of council committees. Despite dutifully attending branch meetings, taking part in campaigns, and debating the same ideas as their more easily identifiable counterparts, they have remained anonymous. There is good reason: the records of women's sections have survived much less frequently than those of the main executive committees, and the latter tend only to mention officers or delegates. Occasional roll calls of branches contained in summaries of events published in newspapers do provide glimpses of who was who, but these cannot replace the sustained record of discussions contained in minute books and other section-level material. Of the scores of women's sections formed in Wales in the 1920s and 1930s, just a handful of minute books survive, covering parts of the Caerphilly, Gower, Newport, Rhondda West and Swansea East constituencies. The records of the women's advisory councils are similarly thin, with coverage best for East Glamorgan and more limited for West Wales. Unfortunately, the records of the Monmouthshire Labour Women's Advisory Council are not extant. As such it is difficult to be precise about who was involved, when and why.

This is as true of a small ward-based section, such as Tynewydd in the upper Rhondda Fawr, or Penderry in Swansea, or the substantial Newport women's section, which mushroomed from an initial membership of just over fifty on its formation shortly after the First World War to more than 1,000 by 1924.[86]

The combined membership of the nearly forty women's sections in East Glamorgan was itself more than 1,100 by 1925.[87] Only a small proportion of these women will ever be identified. Nevertheless, section records, such as those of Tynewydd, which are now held at Rhondda Heritage Park, are instructive and provide a rare degree of micro-level detail.[88] The records begin on 28 August 1920 and note that Elizabeth Andrews travelled to Treherbert to speak with a group of fourteen women active in the Labour Party, with a view to establishing a women's section. It was duly formed as the Treherbert Labour Women's Section. For several months thereafter, the group met at Bethany Baptist Church. They discussed politics, arranged the sale of the *Labour Woman* and W. H. Mainwaring's radical newsletter, *The Worker's Bomb to Destroy Ignorance and Prejudice*, and took steps to affiliate to the district trades and labour council. During the 1921 miners' lockout, members took an active role in the community, establishing a feeding programme and organising parents and children in a threatened school strike. It would go ahead, they warned the authorities, 'if the Guardians do not provide sufficient money to maintain [the children]'.

The minutes ascribed to the Treherbert Women's Section between 1920 and 1921 stop amid the industrial turmoil of the miners' lockout, and the remaining pages were then used to record the activities of the Tynewydd women's section, which was formed in October 1924. This recycling suggests a degree of continuity between the two branches, but it also prompts the question of the relationship between the 1920 Treherbert formation and that founded in 1918 with the support of Mary Mainwaring (wife of W. H. Mainwaring) and T. I. Mardy Jones.[89] No reference was made to the earlier branch in the 1920–1 minutes. Was it the case that women's activism in the Rhondda in the immediate post-war period was in a state of flux and more volatile than the movement elsewhere? This seems unlikely; in fact, the women's movement grew rapidly in the two Rhondda constituencies between 1918 and 1920, with sections formed in Maerdy, Ferndale, Tylorstown and Porth in Rhondda East, and Tonypandy, Ystrad, Ton Pentre and Cwmparc in Rhondda West.[90] The true explanation for the apparent stop–start development of the women's section in Treherbert and Tynewydd is unlikely ever to be known. Once reconstituted in 1924, however, the section survived for the rest of the interwar years.

The records kept for the Tynewydd section run from 1924 until 1934, although an account book covers the period through to 1937. Together they demonstrate the expansion and contraction of the section in that period and the response of members to major events. Until 1926, much of the work of the section was as it was in 1920 (and as it was in other women's sections): organising talks, selling literature, collective singing and entertainment, and various public activities. Elizabeth Andrews spoke to members about food supplies, nursery schools, and the need for good quality milk. W. H. Mainwaring, then the district miners' agent, spoke about the effects of unemployment legislation. Martha Ann Herman (née Rees, 1892–1976) spoke about birth control. Relatively little is known about Mrs Herman: she was from a mining family, as was her husband, and for a period before the latter's death they lived in Buckinghamshire, where William Herman (1894–1945) was steward of the trades and labour club in Chepping Wycombe. Martha Herman herself was one of the most prominent women activists in the Rhondda in the 1920s. In July 1926, for instance, she spoke at a major women's rally in London alongside Margaret Bondfield, she was active with Beatrice Green on the Women's Committee for the Relief of

Miners' Wives and Children, she was involved with the touring
miners' choirs, she wrote articles for the *Labour Woman* pointing
to destitution in her community, and she visited Russia as part
of a worker's delegation in the autumn of 1927.[91]

On her return to Britain, Martha Herman was invited by several Labour women's sections in the Rhondda to speak about her
experiences in the Soviet Union. She addressed the Tynewydd
women in December 1927 and 'gave a vivid outline', pointing to
the 'conditions prevailing there at the present moment'. The section secretary recorded in the minutes that Mrs Herman had told
them that 'real peace and progress for the workers in this country
can only be achieved by international working class solidarity'.[92]
From reports of her public speaking, which are by no means
numerous, Mrs Herman was clearly a very effective orator, able
to paint vivid, emotionally affective pictures of situations at home
and abroad. At the rally in London in 1926, she impressed upon
her audience, amidst cries for shame, how she had seen pit boys
fainting 'in the queues waiting for their one meal'.[93] Appealing
to the maternal instincts of the women in the crowd, Martha
Herman performed her duties as a Labour woman perfectly, but
it is too easy to interpret women's activism or deployment in
certain situations as 'soppy' or cynical. The material analysis
presented by Martha Herman, Beatrice Green and others was
much too sharp – and heartfelt – to be anything other than a
realistic expression of personal understanding.

Moreover, the high level of political debate and intellectual
engagement within the Labour women's sections in Wales has
been relatively little appreciated. In April 1921, the women's
section of Cardiff East Labour Party hosted the poet Anna G.
Lang, who spoke to them on the need for international fellowship between British women and their Irish sisters.[94] The Irish

war of independence, which had raged since January 1919, and cost the lives of nearly 2,000 people, was then nearing its conclusion. In 1924, the women's section of Cardiff's south ward was inspired after a talk to write to Ramsay MacDonald's Labour government to urge legislative action on rent control.[95] The same year, Tredegar Labour Party invited Stella Browne to tour the Monmouthshire valleys and speak to members about birth control.[96] Newport followed it up in 1933 with a speaker from the National Birth Control Association.[97] Pithead baths were a particular demand of the women's sections in the Rhondda, and in early 1919 they pressed the executive of the South Wales Miners' Federation to act to ensure baths were erected across the coalfield.[98] And land value taxation schemes were widely discussed, particularly in the Pontypridd area and in Cardiff, where the women's co-operative guild branches, Labour women's sections and trade union officials were supportive.[99]

Even in small sections, such as Tynewydd, activists absorbed themselves in the full range of contemporary ideas and concepts appropriate for a social democratic movement. During the general strike and miners' lockout, as in the 1921 lockout, there was considerable discussion and organisation around maintaining food supplies for mining families, but debate in 1926 went much further. In July, the Quaker Emma Noble, who was then a Labour councillor in Swindon, arrived to deliver what the minutes recorded as a 'plain talk' about the current situation and her experience of visiting the Rhondda. Noble was to move to the area with her husband, William, the following year to establish the Maes-yr-Haf settlement. During the year, the branch organised a series of evening classes and question time sessions, which were held at the spiritualist church. Members debated A. J. Cook's performance as a miners' leader, pension policies, party manifestos, and ideas such as 'How long are we going to be without joy?', 'Is it worth the sacrifice to be a true Labour woman?' and 'How long must one live in England before one can be naturalised?' Debate was steadily feminised, too. Speakers before 1926 had tended to be councillors or other key figures in the Rhondda Borough Labour Party and were typically men. As the events of 1926 wore on, the choice of branch visitors and guest lecturers became resolutely female.

Understandably, the politicised context of 1926 had a direct impact, not only on the terms of party debates, but also on the number of people attending branch meetings, as is illustrated in figure 1. In 1925, the Tynewydd section had an average attendance of around fifteen people during the six months from June to December. The equivalent period for 1926 saw attendance rise threefold and peak in mid-November at nearly sixty members. Although this level of politicisation and activation was not entirely sustained for the rest of the decade, branch attendances and membership between 1927 and 1929, were higher than they had been in 1924 and 1925. This was to have consequences for the labour movement in the 1930s, with Labour women presenting an especially strong barrier to the formation of a 'united front' in the Rhondda between the Labour Party and the Communist Party. 'Most of the women', characterised the novelist Rhys Davies in 1937, 'were against [communism], at the same time being more revolutionary in their home talk than the reddest local man; the women, raging in efforts to feed and clothe, wanted those responsible hanged, drawn and quartered'.[100] The women's sections became the strongest allies of W. H. Mainwaring in his, at times bitter, struggles against the communist insurgency in his Rhondda East constituency.

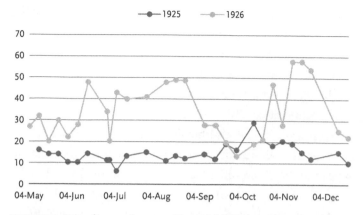

FIGURE 1: Branch attendance at Tynewydd Women's Section, 1925 compared with 1926

Source: Tynewydd Women's Section, Minute Books, Rhondda Heritage Park

The origins of the anti-communist stance taken by Rhondda's Labour women lay in the aftermath of the 1926 miners' lock-out, when the radicalisation of various sections of the Rhondda Labour Party – particularly in the Rhondda Fach – and the South Wales Miners' Federation lodges led to the disaffiliation crisis of 1927 and to the expulsion of Mardy Lodge in 1929.[101] The crisis led to an overt split across the labour movement between the left-wing minority, which was oriented towards the Communist Party, then at its interwar peak, and the moderate majority. During the early months of 1927, each side took every opportunity to set out its case. In May, Mrs Evans, one of the section members in Tynewydd, spoke about the growing divergence between the 'left and right wing in the labour movement' and urged the women present to support the former. She was followed a couple of months later by Glyn Jones, a communist from Treherbert, who spoke about 'trade unionists and Labour politics'. He returned in the spring of 1928. The minutes record that 'many questions were asked in regard of [the] right and left wing'. To dampen division, one senior member of the women's section insisted that 'we remain as we are', letting any decision of which side to support lie on the table indefinitely. The plea failed.

In July 1928, the Tynewydd women's section secretary reported on a meeting of the 'Women's Front Committee' in Tylorstown. This was probably the All-Rhondda Left Women's Movement, a communist front which aimed at uniting left-wing activists in support of the Communist Party.[102] Others were involved in the National Minority Movement and attended events locally and in London, or joined the Friends of Soviet Russia or the National Unemployed Workers' Movement. George Thomas, the communist organiser from Treherbert, whom the police regarded as a 'very able leader', appeared at the Tynewydd section in September 1928 to put the case for the left once more. Members listened to Thomas, although in a sign that the moderates were gaining the upper hand a letter inviting the section to support the National Minority Movement was set aside and ignored. Eventually, in April 1929, shortly before the general elections, efforts to maintain the integrity of the section, despite the pressure of a growing civil war between the left and more moderate members, broke down. The Rhondda Labour Party was itself cleaved in two by the same tensions. On 23 April, the matter in Tynewydd came to a head at a whist-drive fundraiser. Moderates packed the event and succeeded in passing a resolution to affiliate to the National Labour Party. The communist-aligned minority walked out in disgust.

Labour emerged as the largest party at the general election the following month. They promised 'to pursue and apply the principle of equal treatment for men and women', and Ramsay MacDonald introduced Britain's first woman cabinet minister, Margaret Bondfield, as Minister of Labour. She quickly drew

the ire of the left, part of the souring of relations between the
Communist Party and the Labour Party. Already during the
general election campaign, in language consistent with the
'class against class' tactics employed by the Communist Party
at that time, Margaret Bondfield had been labelled a 'social fascist' by her communist opponent, Wal Hannington, the leader
of the National Unemployed Workers' Movement. Although
MacDonald's government initially improved access to social
security and increased rates of payment, the economic shocks
caused by the Wall Street Crash in October 1929 saw unemployment rise sharply and the costs of welfare increase from
£12 million in 1928 to almost £125 million by 1931. Margaret
Bondfield's department, and the minister herself, came under
ever closer scrutiny as they sought to tackle the crisis with greater
investment in government training centres for the unemployed
and then making attendance compulsory.[103]

The relative absence of contemporary debate about Margaret
Bondfield's policy amongst the Labour Party women's sections in
Wales would suggest that compulsory training for unemployed
men and women was not as controversial an approach as might
seem, either in retrospect or with the communist position in
mind. Certainly, some women's sections heard from members
of parliament and were given opportunities to pose questions
about the schemes developed by the Ministry of Labour.[104] But as
the governing party municipally and nationally by 1929, Labour
found itself in a nuanced position – its representatives, including members of the women's sections, such as Jessie Boyes of
Ogmore Vale, sat on public assistance committees (the local
bodies responsible for administering social security) and had
to make decisions in the face of declining revenues as well as
increased public scrutiny. The compromise lay in establishing

information committees, such as that which operated at Taibach from November 1931, which were staffed by members of the local Labour Party and the women's sections and aimed at providing advice about unemployment schemes and how to apply for benefits.[105] They were to be a modest counterpoint to the communist-aligned National Unemployed Workers' Movement and local unemployed associations, which were themselves often subject to communist influence or leadership.

For their part, as we explore in the next chapter, communist women developed their own approach to organisation and debate as the two parties sharply diverged in the early 1930s. These women used their experiences of unemployment and poverty to craft grassroots, street-level politics which stood against austerity, fascism and war; which looked to the Soviet Union as a model of what life *could* be like for working-class women if workers were in control; and which used annual events such as International Women's Day to establish a radical left wing of the interwar women's movement. Often communist women struggled against hunger and starvation, against police surveillance and harassment, and against the constant threat of arrest and imprisonment. In their view, the fight was not only against a state which harangued them but also against a Labour Party which had turned coat and sided with the capitalists. After all, on the magistrates' benches when communists were fined or sent to prison or admonished for their riotous behaviour were those Labour women who had risen through the ranks: Rose Davies and Elizabeth Andrews. Lauded by their own supporters, amongst communists these women seemed to symbolise what had gone wrong in the labour movement during the 1920s as it became the electoral hegemon. It was quite the opposite of their own sense of purpose and historical image.

Notes

1. Elizabeth Andrews, *A Woman's Work is Never Done* (Cardiff, 1956), pp. 21–3.

2. J. D. Jenkins, *Medical Officer of Health Report for 1918* (Tonypandy, 1918), pp. 22–3; J. D. Jenkins, *Medical Officer of Health Report for 1919* (Tonypandy, 1919), pp. 23–5.

3. The other women were Mrs Hart from Wigan in Lancashire and Mrs Brown from Lanarkshire in Scotland. *DH*, 31 May 1919.

4. *DH*, 25 June 1919.

5. *Workers' Dreadnought*, 7 June 1919.

6. *The Vote*, 21 January 1927.

7. Evans and Jones, 'Women in the Labour Party', p. 220; Newman, '"Providing an opportunity to exercise their energies"'.

8. *LW*, May 1920.

9. *LW*, June 1920. The sections noted were Aberbargoed, Abertillery, Bedwas, Cwmfelinfach, Machen, Maesycymmer, Nantyglo, Oakdale, Pengam, Rhymney, Tredegar and Trethomas.

10. *The Vote*, 29 February 1924; *WM*, 19 February 1924.

11. National Council of Public Morals, *The Declining Birth Rate: Its Causes and Effects* (London, 1916).

12. National Council of Public Morals, *Problems of Population and Parenthood* (London, 1920); National Council of Public Morals, *Youth and the Race* (London, 1923); National Council of Public Morals, Cinema Commission, *The Cinema* (London, 1917); National Council of Public Morals, Cinema Commission, *The Cinema in Education* (London, 1925).

13. *WM*, 19 September 1919, 19 November 1919.

14. Ursula Masson, 'Introduction', in Elizabeth Andrews, *A Woman's Work Is Never Done* (Dinas Powys, 2006 edn); Kate Fisher, 'Teach the Miners Birth Control: The Delivery of Contraceptive Advice in South Wales, 1918–1950', in Pamela F. Michael and Charles Webster (eds), *Health and Society in Twentieth Century South Wales* (Cardiff, 2006).

15. Matthew Worley, *Labour Inside the Gate* (London, 2005), p. 40.

16. Andrews, *Woman's Work*, p. 23.

17. *WM*, 6 February 1920; 7 February 1920; 9 February 1920.

18. *Rhos Herald*, 23 August 1924.

19. *FCH*, 4 November 1932. This is recorded as the 'third annual conference', which supposes establishment in 1930, although it was not reported at that time. *FCH*, 10 October 1930.

20. *LW*, December 1925.

21. *NWWN*, 29 October 1925.

22. *DH*, 4 October 1926.

23. *SWG*, 21 May 1920. The founding secretary was Margaret C. Thomas of Caldicot. She became president of the council in 1934. *WM*, 5 February 1934.

24. *Warwick and Warwickshire Advertiser*, 22 May 1920.

25. *Hull Daily Mail*, 19 May 1920.

26. Worley, *Labour Inside*, p. 41; David Howell, *MacDonald's Party: Labour Identities and Crisis, 1922–1931* (Oxford, 2002).

27. HC Deb, 29 March 1928, c1415.

28. Laura Beers, *Red Ellen: The Life of Ellen Wilkinson, Socialist, Feminist, Internationalist* (Cambridge, MA, 2016); Matt Perry, '*Red Ellen' Wilkinson: Her Ideas, Movements and World* (Manchester, 2014); Patricia Hollis, *Jennie Lee: A Life* (Oxford, 1997).

29. *SWG*, 7 January 1921.

30. Bruley, *1926*, 101; *WM*, 9 February 1927.

31. *DH*, 2 December 1927.

32. *SWG*, 15 October 1920.

33. *PO*, 10 November 1934.

34. *St Dyfrig's Church: Centenary Souvenir* (Pontypridd, 1963). In the early part of the twentieth century the church was known by its Latin name, St Dubricius.

35. Paul O'Leary, *Immigration and Integration: The Irish in Wales, 1798–1922* (Cardiff, 1998), p. 285.

36. *PO*, 23 November 1935.

37. *PO*, 25 February 1928, 1 March 1930.

38. Contemporary national examples included Southampton (*DH*, 7 February 1922) and Northampton (*Northampton Chronicle and Echo*, 16 February 1922). Leeds followed in 1923. *DH*, 2 March 1933.

39. *SWG*, 1 November 1929; *WM*, 28 October 1929.

40. *MEx*, 10 February 1940. Mary McPhail had also served as the national chair of the Women's Co-operative Guild and was a member of the national council of the Co-operative Party.

41. Labour Party, *Labour and the Nation* (London, 1928), pp. 32–3.

42. Huw T. Edwards, *Hewn From The Rock* (Cardiff, 1967), p. 86; Paul Ward, *Huw T. Edwards: British Labour and Welsh Socialism* (Cardiff, 2011), p. 69.

43. *FCH*, 16 October 1931.

44. *LW*, September 1930, 137.

45. Sam Davies and Bob Morley, *County Borough Elections in England and Wales, 1918–1939: A Comparative Analysis, Volume II* (Aldershot, 1999), p. 439.

46. *FCH*, 23 October 1931.

47. *FCH*, 23 October 1931, 30 October 1931.

48. *FCH*, 12 February 1932.

49. Tanner, "Gender, Civic Culture and Politics in South Wales'.

50. Pat Thane, 'Women in the British Labour Party and the Construction of State Welfare, 1906–1939', in Seth Koven and Sonya Michel (eds), *Mothers of a New World: Maternalist Politics and the Origins of Welfare States* (London, 1993).

51. *SWG*, 31 December 1926.

52. *WM*, 28 October 1929.

53. *SWG*, 23 April 1926.

54. *PO*, 6 September 1919.

55. *PO*, 28 April 1923, 24 May 1924.

56. *MEx*, 23 February 1935.

57. *NWWN*, 23 June 1921.

58. *The New Beacon*, 15 April, 15 November 1936; Henry J. Wagg and Mary G. Thomas, *A Chronological Survey of Work for the Blind* (London, 1932), pp. 139, 167, 170.

59. *The Teacher of the Blind*, 20/1 (October 1931), 30; *The New Beacon*, 15 September 1934.

60. The policy was adopted at the end of the 1920s. See the detail recorded in Pontypridd Urban District Council, *Annual Report of the Medical Officer of Health, 1933* (Pontypridd, 1933), p. 123. Officials boasted that this reduced the 'problem of the toddler'. Pontypridd Urban District Council, *Annual Report of the Medical Officer of Health, 1929* (Pontypridd, 1929), pp. 49–50.

61. Graves, *Labour Women*, p. 170.

62. Labour Party, *Labour and the Nation*, p. 32.

63. This could attract the ire of those who were from other party political backgrounds and who felt their voices were being attenuated. 'The practice of allocated [co-opted] positions to one party only is being bitterly criticised in the urban area', complained one resident of Blaina in Monmouthshire in 1931. *South Wales Gazette*, 11 December 1931.

64. *MEx*, 29 August 1925; *WM*, 18 September 1935.

65. This section partly draws on Rebecca Gill and Daryl Leeworthy, 'Moral Minefields: Save the Children Fund and the Moral Economies of Nursery

Schooling the South Wales Coalfield in the 1930s', *Journal of Global Ethics*, 11/2 (2015), 218–32.

66. Labour Party, *Motherhood and Child Endowment* (London, 1922), p. 7.

67. Labour Party, *From Nursery School to University* (London, 1927), p. 5.

68. Abertillery Urban District Council, *Report of the Medical Officer of Health for 1925* (Abertillery, 1925), p. 81; Abertillery Urban District Council, *Report of the Medical Officer of Health for 1938* (Abertillery, 1938), p. 50; *South Wales Gazette*, 27 February 1925.

69. Abertillery Urban District Council, *Report of the Medical Officer of Health for 1938* (Abertillery, 1937), p. 97. The classes were held at Blaentillery Infants, Blaenau Gwent Infants and Queen Street Infants.

70. Monmouthshire County Council, *Report of the Medical Officer of Health for 1936* (Newport, 1936), p. 26.

71. *WM*, 10 July 1939.

72. Andrews, *Woman's Work*, p. 46.

73. Rhondda Urban District Council, *Report of the School Medical Officer for 1925* (Treherbert, 1925), pp. ix–x.

74. For instance, the visit of Neath Labour Party's women's section in July 1936. *Neath Guardian*, 17 July 1936.

75. Liverpool University, Special Collections, Katherine Bruce Glasier Papers. Swansea Education Committee, *Programme of the Opening and Particulars of the Nursery School Opened by Mrs Bruce Glasier, 7 May 1936*; Swansea County Borough Council, *Minutes*, 18 February 1931.

76. A programme marking the opening of the Alaw Nursery is held at the Glamorgan Archives, BMT/E/8/14. For the opening of Severn Road Nursery, see Cardiff County Borough Council, *Report of the Medical Officer of Health for 1940* (Cardiff, 1940), p. 86. On the earlier campaign, *WM*, 19 December 1925.

77. *WM*, 25 April 1939, 19 July 1939.

78. Barry M. Doyle, *The Politics of Hospital Provision in Early Twentieth-Century Britain* (London, 2014); George Campbell Gosling, *Payment and Philanthropy in British Health Care, 1918–48* (Manchester, 2017); Steven Thompson, *Unemployment, Poverty and Health in Interwar South Wales* (Cardiff, 2006).

79. *DH*, 18 September 1920.

80. *LW*, November 1937.

81. Alun Burge '"A Subtle Danger?": The Voluntary Sector and Coalfield Society in South Wales, 1926–1939', *Llafur*, 7/3–4 (1999), 127–42.

82. *LW*, January 1936.

83. *WM*, 4 January 1938.

84. Astor Papers, Special Collections, University of Reading Archives, MS1416/1/1/1857: 'Letter, dated 6 November 1938, from Mrs Williams, 101 High Street, Penydarren'.

85. Andrews, *Woman's Work*, p. 20.

86. Worley, *Labour Inside the Gate*, p. 63.

87. Bruley, *1926*, p. 92.

88. Rhondda Heritage Park, Trehafod, RHO 2017.288–92.

89. Williams, *Democratic Rhondda*, p. 107.

90. Bruley, *1926*, p. 91.

91. *DH*, 28 June 1926, 28 August 1926, 11 November 1926, 5 December 1927.

92. Tynewydd Women's Section Minutes, 14 December 1927. The delegation had been invited as part of the tenth anniversary celebration of the Bolshevik Revolution. *Soviet Russia To-Day: Report of the British Workers' Delegation, 1927* (London, 1928).

93. *DH*, 29 June 1926.

94. *DH*, 5 April 1921.

95. *DH*, 1 March 1924.

96. *New Generation*, January 1924, 8–9. Browne had previously visited the Rhondda at the behest of the Communist Party. *New Generation*, September 1923, 107; October 1923, 116–17; December 1923, 144.

97. Worley, *Labour Inside the Gate*, p. 63.

98. *WM*, 10 February 1919.

99. *Land & Liberty*, 287, April 1918, 83; no. 313, June 1920, 429.

100. Rhys Davies, *Jubilee Blues* (London, 1937).

101. The wider crisis is discussed in Williams, *Democratic Rhondda*, pp. 155–6.

102. 'Weekly Intelligence Summary', 11 April, 3 July 1926, 18 November 1927.

103. John Field, *Working Men's Bodies: Work Camps in Britain, 1880–1940* (Manchester, 2013).

104. *WM*, 16 January 1930.

105. *NG*, 27 November 1931.

4

Against Fascism, Austerity and War

By the middle of the 1930s, Ceridwen Brown was a desperately thin, sallow-faced woman suffering from the grief of having buried her eldest child. She was not yet 40. With her family out of work and with little money coming in, she was also starving. Family meals were limited, her own even more so, as food was redirected to her children – they grew used to the idea that an evening repast was indulgent or unnecessary. Yet, on the morning of 4 February 1935, having walked to Merthyr Tydfil over the mountain from Aberdare, it was to her that a crowd of nearly 3,000 men and women looked for leadership and guidance. After more than six years of austerity and almost a decade and a half of poverty, the crowd had gathered outside Iscoed House, the offices of the Unemployment Assistance Board, to exact revenge on the system which oppressed them. 'This was to be a women's demonstration', recalled Griff Jones, an unemployed miner and later International Brigade volunteer, who was present. 'The place was packed', he said, 'they were all crowded in ... [then] the actual gate of Iscoed House gave in and they started moving'. The crowd went inside the building. Windows were smashed. The stairs were ripped up. Fixtures, fittings, telephones, everything that could be destroyed, was destroyed. As much of the paperwork as possible was set alight.[1] The police tried to intervene, but the crowd refused to listen to the authorities. They recognised only the leadership of Ceridwen Brown and one other: Jack Williams of Dowlais, who was to fight in Spain.[2]

The previous day, the coalfield had been shaken by hundreds of thousands of people marching against the new means test regulations. Tens of thousands more attended similar rallies in central Scotland and the industrial north of England. Ceridwen Brown had herself been part of the 50,000 strong who marched through the Cynon Valley. 'When one remembers that thousands of these people', the *Aberdare Leader* put it a week later, 'had walked to Mountain Ash from Hirwaun, Llwydcoed, Cwmdare, Trecynon, and had to walk back again – many of them tramping in the wind and rain one is impressed by the determination of the people in making this great protest. The Government *must* listen'.[3] For once, they did. Just weeks after the new regulations had come into effect, they were abandoned. But the damage to reputations had been done. With the government having claimed that welfare payments would rise, and that the means test would provide greater equity across the country, rather than a mixed system of higher or lower payments according to a 'postcode lottery', the opposite proved to be the case. Hundreds of thousands of claimants – already poor – faced significant reductions in their standard of living. Starvation increased. Poverty deepened.

From the point of view of the authorities, Ceridwen Brown was a menace and a significant danger to public order. As an active communist, and someone who was known to have been to Moscow more than once, she was put under regular police surveillance. Her physical characteristics and photographs of her at demonstrations or on marches, captured using methods developed by Scotland Yard for spying on suffragettes before the First World War and by Special Branch in Ireland, were housed in special files stored at the Glamorgan Constabulary's headquarters in Cardiff.[4] The intelligence services in London maintained its own files on her, in which were contained intercepted correspondence, notes tracking her engagements with other activists, verbatim logs of speeches she had delivered, and the tittle-tattle given to the state by neighbourhood curtain twitchers and gossips. To MI5, Ceridwen Brown was simply PF43093 – her personal file number. She was born Ceridwen Thomas in Aberaman in the Cynon Valley on 10 October 1896. It was a mining family and staunchly Labour. Her father, Morgan, and brothers all worked underground. Her younger brother, John, even sat on the committee of the local miners' federation lodge. But left-wing politics were shared with religion: the Thomases were committed members of Gwawr Baptist Chapel, situated a few doors down from where they lived.

In the summer of 1914, Ceridwen Thomas married Edward Brown, a miner from Aberaman who was four years her senior. The couple's eldest daughter, Jennie, was born the same year – she died of tuberculosis, exacerbated by malnutrition and poverty, in 1931.[5] Edward joined the army in late March 1915 but was discharged six months later, on the grounds that he was 'not likely to become a good soldier'.[6] He returned to Aberaman and to his job underground. The following year, the day after Ceridwen Brown's twentieth birthday, the couple's only son, Ronald, who was later to serve in the International Brigades, was born.[7] A younger daughter, Doreen, followed in January 1919. According to her later testimony, Ceridwen Brown became 'more independent minded' after marriage and steadily lost the religious faith she had had as a child, although the impress of demonstrations and public speaking, which she gained through the chapel, remained with her.[8] She used those skills when addressing gatherings on street corners or waste ground, in election campaigns; or in the hunger and women's marches of the 1930s, when she was often to be seen wearing her trademark trench coat and red beret, a sartorial style picked up in Moscow.

Ceridwen Brown's transition from the Labour Party into the Communist Party – of which she was a founder member, although her husband was not – seems to have been a family affair.[9] Towards the end of the First World War, a group of miners in the Cynon Valley established a branch of the Unofficial Reform Movement, which itself had been founded in the Rhondda in the aftermath of the 1910–11 Cambrian Combine Dispute and was responsible for the syndicalist manifesto the *Miners' Next Step*, published in 1912.[10] Unofficial Reformers debated and discussed the likely future of the coalfield, and continued to stress the necessity of industrial democracy – collective ownership of the mines by the miners – over the aspirations of political democrats, who pointed to winning seats in parliament and forming a Labour government as the best chance for reform. The Russian revolutions of 1917 added further complexities to the political and industrial question, with the most radical activists seeking to foment a revolution inspired either by the social democrats of February/March or the Bolsheviks of October/November 1917. It was in view of the latter, that a group came together to form a branch of the Socialist Labour Party (SLP) in Aberdare shortly after the end of the war.[11]

At a national level, the SLP was in negotiations with Britain's other Marxist political party of the time, the British Socialist Party, to form a new unified organisation modelled on the

Bolsheviks: the Communist Party of Great Britain (CPGB). The key sticking point of the unity talks was whether the new party should affiliate to the Labour Party, or whether it should be independent. The SLP executive was opposed to affiliation, whereas the BSP, which was the larger of the two and was itself already affiliated, was in favour. At the grassroots of the SLP, there were those who sided with the BSP's position on the Labour Party, and some activists and their branches broke away, forming the small (and short-lived) Communist Unity Group. The Aberdare SLP was one of those which split away and, under its new identity, the Aberdare Communist Unity Group, it was represented at the conferences held to establish the CPGB in the summer of 1920. The Aberdare delegate was J. E. Thomas from Aberaman – almost certainly Ceridwen Brown's brother, John. She was herself probably involved in the Communist Unity Group, although in the absence of any documentation it is difficult to be absolute in that conclusion, and it was through this route that she became a founder member of the CPGB.

The decision to join the Communist Party changed the trajectory of Ceridwen Brown's life. It meant that she was eventually excluded from the traditional elements of the labour movement open to women in the Cynon Valley, from the co-operative guilds to election as a delegate to the trades council to co-option to council committees, and so she had to join with friends and fellow activists to create new alternatives. Those alternatives provided part of the most meaningful grassroots opposition to the Labour Party in Glamorgan and Monmouthshire in the 1930s. And they provided Ceridwen Brown with a means of rising to a degree of local prominence, which all the other parties endeavoured to stifle: she was to be a leading communist activist in the interwar years, unusual both because she was a woman and because she was not a schoolteacher. Unlike Evans (as Gwen Ray was known following her marriage in 1920), Mavis Llewellyn or Annie Powell, the other local women who rose through to the top rank, Ceridwen Brown lacked a formal education beyond the elementary level, and her politics were perhaps more visceral than intellectual. But in the tense turbulence of the 1930s, when political decisions were a matter of life or death, starvation or survival, that emotional appeal proved effective on its own terms.

*

It took almost ten years for Ceridwen Brown to come to public notice, just at the point relations between the Labour Party and the Communist Party entered their bitterest and most discordant phase. Standing as a candidate for the district council elections in Aberdare in 1929, the *Western Mail* declared that Ceridwen Brown was 'an avowed communist' and the paper took great delight in reporting her defeat.[12] Two years later, Ceridwen Brown was nominated by the Communist Party to stand in the general election as the party's candidate in the Aberdare constituency. However, ill from starvation and grieving the loss of her daughter, Jennie, she withdrew, leaving the sitting Labour MP, George Hall, to be returned unopposed.[13] Had Ceridwen Brown stood in 1931, even in the face of certain defeat, she would have been both the first communist and the first woman to run for parliament in the constituency – a novelty difficult to overestimate. In fact, she would have been the first communist woman to run for parliament anywhere in Wales. It was not until the 1950s that Mavis Llewellyn and Annie Powell ran (respectively) in Ogmore and in Rhondda East. The first woman to stand in Aberdare, almost half a century later, in 1979, was the Communist Party's Mary Winter.[14]

The state, of course, knew rather a lot about Ceridwen Brown and her associates, a level of detail which reflected the anxiety about communist and left-wing activity in interwar Britain. Every week the chief constable of Glamorgan, Lionel Lindsay, issued a fresh surveillance memorandum, most copies of which were subsequently destroyed, which was akin to the Home Office's *Report on Revolutionary Organisations in the United Kingdom*, issued to members of the cabinet. Lindsay's memoranda detailed what the police knew about communist activity and provide a useful guide to Ceridwen Brown's emergence as one of the key members of the Communist Party in interwar Wales. The documents shed light on the multiple forms of activism in which Ceridwen Brown engaged and show the process of building up the far left of the women's movement, the attempts made to work within the traditional boundaries of the labour movement, and the subsequent divisions and stark separations, as well as some of the limitations of this type of campaigning. They also provide nuance to general understandings of who was, and was not, important within communist circles. Mary Lloyd, Ceridwen Brown's neighbour and fellow activist, does not appear in any of the police intelligence. This is despite later assertions that the Lloyds were 'in the Communist Party before the Paris Commune'.[15]

Ceridwen Brown first appeared in the police intelligence reports early in 1925, when she was recorded as the leader of a co-operative group in Aberaman. Although unnamed, this was probably a branch of the Women's Co-operative Guild attached to the local Cwmbach-Aberaman Co-operative Society. The date is significant because not long afterwards the national Women's Co-operative Guild appointed Eleanor Barton (1872–1960) as its general secretary, and she adopted the stance that those not in sympathy with the Labour Party and its objectives – including members of the Communist Party – should be ejected.[16] This mirrored Labour's own resolution passed at its annual conference that year when delegates agreed to the expulsion of communists from the party's membership. Whilst this was difficult to implement, particularly in the valleys of Glamorgan and Monmouthshire, the consequences were such that communist women began to develop their own sections independent of the traditional labour organisations.[17] By 1926, on the eve of the miners' lockout, Ceridwen Brown was thus recognised as the leader of the communist women's section in the Cynon Valley, as well as a founder member of the Aberdare branch of the party. She joined a small cohort of women, in communities such as Abertridwr, Ton Pentre and Maerdy, who developed communist women's sections before the mushrooming of party activity during the miners' lockout and its immediate aftermath.

In terms of interwar gender politics, the communist women's sections were as rooted in ideas about family and the domestic consequences of poverty and material inequality as were their Labour equivalents. This is hardly surprising, given they were responding to the same conditions and circumstances, had their roots in common organisational ancestors, and drew on the same broad understanding of what was wrong in contemporary society. They differed chiefly in what answers to provide. Thus, alongside her duties as the organiser of women, Ceridwen Brown found herself tasked with establishing a local branch of the Young Pioneers League, the communist children's movement founded nationally in 1925, and the Young Communist League – the party's youth wing. This commitment to nurturing the world-view of young people and women was characteristic of the familial world of interwar communism. Although the party's 'writ did not run to the child's early years in the home', it frequently attempted to exercise influence on party members who were parents, and on mothers especially.[18] Ceridwen Brown was herself an enthusiastic adoptee of 'communist maternalism' and successfully drew each of her children into the party's sphere of influence. Her husband, Edward, who was not then a party member, took a secondary role in the personal development of his children.

In attestation papers for the International Brigades, for example, Ronald Brown clearly pointed to the influence of his mother in shaping his own political beliefs – his father was not mentioned. The form enquired, amongst other things, as to a volunteer's party allegiances and who had supported their application to join the international communist movement (if they were involved at all). Ronald was a member of the Young Communist League, which he had joined in Aberaman two years before leaving for Spain in 1937, and in response to the second question, he replied simply '*madre*'. His mother. Ceridwen Brown had also supplied her son's political education and guided his reading knowledge of Marxism, although this was limited to perusing copies of the *Daily Worker* and elementary pamphlet literature, such as the *Communist Manifesto*. This dynamic was repeated with other young people who came into contact with Ceridwen Brown and helped to forge a close bond between the communist families in the Cynon Valley. Doreen Brown was the best friend of Olive Greening, whose brother Edwin fought in the Spanish Civil War alongside Will Lloyd. The latter was the son of Mary Lloyd, known affectionately to this group as 'Ma Lloyd', an indication of her status. Olive Greening subsequently married Alistair Wilson, who was elected as a communist councillor in Aberdare in 1938.

*

But just how many women joined the communist wing of the women's movement in the interwar years, and who were they? In her research, undertaken in the early 1970s, Sue Bruley was told by former activists that there were at least 200 women in the Communist Party in Glamorgan and Monmouthshire. They were spread across several branches. Names were, however, elusive. Fewer than a dozen women came to light in that research, mostly from the Rhondda.[19] This was a broadly accurate appraisal. Membership statistics held in the Comintern archives in Moscow confirm that there were approximately 200 communist women by April 1938, that figure compared with almost 800 men.[20] A year earlier, there had been around 125 women in the party, a figure which fell during the first half of the year.[21] At the end of October 1937, there were just over 100 women active in the Communist Party's South Wales District.[22] The number of men active remained relatively stable over the year. A comparative figure produced in April 1937 showed that in Scotland there were around 300 women compared with more than 2,000 men, and in the North Wales District there were six women and sixty men.[23]

The rising figures for the South Wales District can be misleading in retrospect; most branches had only one or two women on their membership roll, with three-quarters of women active in just five places: Blaengarw, Cardiff, Nantymoel, Newport and the Rhondda. They met in separate women's sections, of which there were thirteen by 1938, although this did not exclude women from assuming branch committee roles in some areas and collaborative working.[24] Organisation of the communist women's movement was relatively sophisticated. Sections and members were linked together by a District Women's Committee led by Mavis Llewellyn (1908–78) and Irene Paynter (née Francis,

1914–40), who were given seats on the South Wales District Committee, with Ceridwen Brown and Ethel Horner also involved. Activities included annual International Women's Day demonstrations and district conferences, as well as the application of pressure for policy changes at a national level.[25] The largest concentration of women members in Glamorgan and Monmouthshire was in the Rhondda, a cohort consisting of a quarter of the regional membership total at the end of the 1930s. The local structure consisted of women's sections attached to individual branches and an all-Rhondda women's district committee.

One of those involved in the Rhondda was Elizabeth Jessie Collingbourne (née Jones, 1889–1968) of Tylorstown. Before her marriage in 1915, she had worked as a schoolteacher. Her husband, James, was a miner turned general labourer, who joined the massed ranks of the unemployed in the aftermath of the 1926 miners' lockout. Unemployment had been the catalyst for their mutual radicalisation. Elizabeth Collingbourne joined the Tylorstown women's left movement, as the local women's section of the Communist Party was known, and was elected its president. She was also vice president of the all-Rhondda women's district committee and sat on the regional executive of the Young Communist League, alongside Ceridwen Brown. As an indication of Elizabeth Collingbourne's long commitment to the communist cause, she was one of a handful of Welsh party members interviewed for a special memorial edition of the *Daily Worker* published in July 1960 to mark the death of Harry Pollitt. Amongst the other Rhondda voices in the paper were Annie Powell and former district councillor and Young Communist League organiser James Morton. The *Daily Worker* reported that 'Mrs Collingbourne recalled one of the many meetings she chaired for [Pollitt] when he and John Strachey were speaking from the same platform ... [Pollitt] gave the working-class movement everything right up until the time he died'.[26]

The last of the Rhondda communists interviewed was Ellen Rachel Paddock (née Payne, 1895–1971), known as Nellie. Paying tribute to Pollitt, Nellie Paddock recalled that he 'gave hope to a lot of us women, there was no-one like Harry or his wife Marjorie for the womenfolk'. Married in 1917, Nellie Paddock lived in Trealaw with her husband Sam (1893–1961), an unemployed miner. Their communism was a family affair. Sam Paddock stood as the communist candidate for Trealaw in the 1932 district council elections, although he was easily defeated by senior Rhondda Labour Party figure Mark Harcombe.[27] Nellie Paddock's brother, Albert, was also a member of the Communist Party. Her own role in the Rhondda Communist Party was to organise the Mid Rhondda Young Communist League. In the 1930s, she took part in a considerable amount of street campaigning, but she has been forgotten, or side-lined, even when she was in the thick of the fighting. Or in the lead. In the summer of 1936, Nellie Paddock was one of almost forty men and women arrested following a showdown with Oswald Mosley's Blackshirts on the De Winton Field in Tonypandy. According to one eyewitness, who gave testimony at the county assizes that autumn, Nellie Paddock was in the front of the anti-fascist counter-demonstration, 'screaming like a fury'.[28]

When sentences were handed down by the judge in December, Harry Dobson famously received six months. He was to join the International Brigade shortly after his release.[29] Sam Paddock was gaoled for twelve months. Nellie Paddock, the only woman to receive a custodial sentence at the trial, a fact generally ignored by historians of these events, was sent down for three months.[30] Her imprisonment, which was controversial, prompted both of Rhondda's Labour members of parliament, Wil John and W. H. Mainwaring, neither of whom was especially well-disposed to communists, to petition the Home Secretary for early release.[31] Unfortunately for Nellie Paddock, the fracas on the De Winton Field was by no means her first brush with the authorities. She was a seasoned street-fighter, in all senses of the term. In March 1930, for instance, she was arrested for refusing to disperse when ordered by the police. In a show of defiance, she sang the *Red Flag*.[32] A few months later Nellie Paddock was in trouble again, this time for participating in a demonstration in the public galley inside the police court in Pontypridd. The communist schoolteacher Gwen Ray Evans and Betty Ford, a visiting activist from Bradford, were before magistrates for having made an unauthorised street collection. After magistrates concluded proceedings, issuing fines and bound-over orders, Nellie Paddock and a small group of friends sang *The Internationale* as loudly as possible. According to the press, a 'general melee followed', during which umbrellas were used by the communists in the gallery as batons. Eventually the group was ejected from court.[33]

A week later, it was Nellie Paddock's turn in the dock. She appeared before magistrates on two counts of assaulting a police officer. According to the officer involved, he had tried to break up a street rally with several communists, including Will Paynter, taking it in turns to speak from a soapbox in the centre of Porth. As each speaker was pulled down from the box by the police officer, another took their place. Eventually Nellie Paddock got on. When the police tried to remove her, she resisted. 'Police Constable Wales put her off', reported the *Western Mail*, and so 'she clenched her fist and struck Wales a violent blow behind the ear'. He ran off in search of help. Nellie Paddock shouted after him that he was the 'Mussolini of Porth'.[34] The group then moved on to the nearby village of Llwyncelyn, where they resumed their rally. Such confrontation, and other events which resulted in neither court action nor newspaper reports, except in the *Daily Worker*, gave Nellie Paddock a reputation amongst the police for always being 'wherever there was likely to be a disturbance'.[35] This stood against her during the trial at the county assizes in 1936, but it was a reputation which she clearly relished – it proved her commitment to fighting against injustice, fascism, capitalism and war, and to the struggle for the long-anticipated worker's revolution.

Amongst the other Rhondda women caught up in the anti-fascist violence in Tonypandy in 1936 were Will Paynter's partner, Irene Francis, who was arrested by police but avoided a prison sentence, and Betty Sweet (née Ford), by then a member of the Maerdy Council of Action and the agitprop officer for the Maerdy branch of the Communist Party. Betty Sweet's husband, Jesse, who studied at the International Lenin School in Moscow and was later to serve as one of the cohort of communists elected to Rhondda Urban District Council, was branch secretary in Maerdy – the pair had married in 1931. Like Nellie Paddock, Betty Sweet was a veteran of the struggle and regularly in trouble with the police. Early in 1932, she was tried for incitement to riot and unlawful assembly at the county assize for her part in anti-bailiff action the previous November.[36] She was found guilty for unlawful assembly, but not guilty for incitement to riot.[37] The following year, she was again charged with obstruction of the highway and using threatening language.[38] On each occasion, Betty Sweet appeared in court alongside her husband and her parents-in-law, Esther and Alfred, as well as alongside friends such as Helen Tudor, who was likewise found guilty for her part in the anti-bailiff action, and Sarah Evans.[39]

Esther Sweet was a communist matriarch, to whom many involved in the radical women's politics of the Rhondda, looked for guidance. According to testimony provided in court by eyewitnesses in 1932, she had shouted, at the top of her voice, 'stand by the Council of Action and to [hell] with the police'.[40] For their part, the police thought her a 'most impossible, aggressive and dangerous woman who never misses a demonstration or procession'.[41] Esther Sweet had first come to the attention of the authorities in 1928, when she took part in and helped to organise, with Helen Tudor and others, a demonstration against the celebration of Empire Day (24 May) by employees of Locket's Colliery in Maerdy.[42] The protestors felt that the celebration should have marked Labour Day (1 May) instead, particularly at a time when unemployment was high, and many people were starving. The communists' original aim had been to head up the march, blocking out the image of children waving the Union flag with more radical banners and slogans. A series of delays meant that they 'found their party of about fifty forestalled and they had to follow [the march] instead'.[43] To ensure the protest was not a complete failure, they handed out squares of red tissue paper to the children who were marching.

In the weeks leading up to Empire Day, communists in the upper Rhondda Fach had handed out leaflets to children and parents at school gates; the typewritten leaflets described imperialism and its horrors, and forced a confrontation with Britain's colonial practices overseas. The *Western Mail* thundered in response that, 'the children of Mardy, as well as their parents, have learned that the ruin of the coalfield was the result of Communist propaganda in the past'. In the end, the communists, many of whom were women, were arrested by the police and charged with obstruction. Most were found guilty by magistrates and fined five shillings. Arthur Horner's wife, Ethel, who was regarded as the instigator of the protest, received a heavier fine of twenty shillings. The women collectively refused to pay, they could not afford to do so, and were sent to Cardiff Gaol instead. Ethel Horner and Esther Sweet were put to work in the laundry, content at having made a stand and willing to serve their short custodial sentences. Behind the scenes, however, the Communist Party arranged for the fines to be paid through the International Class War Prisoners' Aid Society, the British branch of the Soviet International Red Aid funded by the Comintern in Moscow. The women were released on 5 July 1928.[44]

They were welcomed back to Maerdy as heroes. A celebratory demonstration was held in Maerdy Square that afternoon. It was a lively affair, which soon turned sour when the police intervened to disperse the crowd. Ethel Horner was again summoned to appeared before magistrates for obstruction, with Jesse Sweet and Dai Lloyd Davies, the latter a councillor and chair of Maerdy Miners' Lodge, summoned for obstruction and abusive language. For a repeat offence, Ethel Horner was bound over for twelve months, with three sureties totalling forty pounds to ensure that she did so. The alternative was a further stint of six weeks' imprisonment.[45] Sharp confrontations with the police and regular appearances in court, symptoms of apparent danger and disrepute, alienated communist women from their Labour Party and Women's Co-operative Guild counterparts. Both stressed respectability and closely adhered to internal regulations disbarring communists from membership, with the result that there was very little cross-over of personnel. The Pontypridd branch of the Women's Co-operative Guild regularly resisted attempts at rapprochement between the Labour Party and the Communist Party in the 1930s, ordering its delegates on the town's trades council to vote against favourable motions, refusing to participate in united front action, and opposing efforts to sell communist literature at Labour Party meetings.[46]

Within Rhondda Labour Party, too, the chief opposition to united front activity came from the women's sections.[47] Elizabeth Andrews, especially, led a concerted campaign against communists, whom she thought were hostile to the interests and advancement of the Labour Party. In a speech to delegates of the Monmouthshire Labour Women's Advisory Council ahead of the general election in 1929, she observed that

> communists are going to fight in Rhondda East, Ogmore, and Caerphilly divisions, not because they hope to win but because they hope to get a sufficient number of votes to upset the Labour people. Then they talked about a united front! The time has come when we must be definite on this question – we cannot serve two masters.[48]

Unsurprisingly, a confidential report produced by the Communist Party in 1937 noted that 'there is a strong feeling of hostility towards the party, especially on the part of the women'.[49] Just nine communist women had succeeded in joining a Labour Party women's section, none of them in the Rhondda – they were too well known to successfully infiltrate the Labour ranks.[50] It was, explained Idris Cox in a speech to the 1937 South Wales Communist Congress, 'a serious feature' of the party's stagnation in the district.[51]

Cox went on to blame the failure to integrate communist women into the Labour Party's women's sections and the

Women's Co-operative Guild on a lack of concerted effort at the local level. More problematically, he also blamed the existence of a separate communist women's movement and the working women's guilds, which, he said, had driven 'active Labour women further away'. In effect, he was turning over responsibility to the women themselves. Years later, speaking to Sue Bruley, Cox set out a different explanation for the limited growth of the communist women's movement, either within or without the Labour Party. Women, he said, seemed unable to participate in communist activity 'to the same extent as the men' because the party's 'main struggle was over wages and conditions of work, which they had no part in'.[52] This flatly contradicted the party's own material, including that produced by the South Wales District Committee in the 1930s, which stressed that 'women are much closer to most working-class issues', such as housing, rent and food prices, and that there should be 'women's groups' which could take into account the fact 'women have to face special problems'.[53] Women's conferences were also planned to debate the rising cost of living.[54]

It was hoped that a campaign on prices would provide common ground and overcome the hostility of Labour women to working with the Communist Party. But as with other areas of common interest, such as the means test regulations, support for the Republican government during the Spanish Civil War, and the peace movement, mutual antipathy ensured that the approaches taken were usually distinct. Delegates to the annual conference of East Glamorgan Labour Women's Advisory Council in September 1936, for example, heard Margaret Bondfield appeal for 'the importance of working for peace amongst European nations' – the Spanish Civil War had broken out a few months earlier and this stance was consistent with

Labour's then policy of non-intervention.[55] A policy opposed by the Communist Party, which favoured active engagement. The Women's Co-operative Guild in Pontypridd, by contrast, took the lead in gathering local responses to the 1934–5 peace ballot, which was organised by the League of Nations Union to judge British attitudes to foreign policy and the League of Nations itself.[56] Co-operative women across the country were also the main sellers of the white peace poppy, despite considerable hostility from the Royal British Legion, who insisted that the red poppy was the true national symbol of remembrance.[57]

Idris Cox's finger-wagging in 1937 came after almost a decade of concerted effort by women in the Communist Party, not least Gwen Ray Evans and Mavis Llewellyn, to establish their own movement. In 1925, Gwen Ray Evans was selected as one of two Rhondda delegates to attend the Communist Party's national conference for women; three years later, she agreed to be co-opted on to the party's South Wales District Committee to head up the fledgling women's department. She used her role to press for a more direct appeal to women, and wrote regular newspaper columns to that effect. One such column, published in the *Daily Worker* on 26 January 1935, began:

> Last Tuesday, I overhead a respectably dressed woman on Porth platform say: "If the men take this lying down they deserve to go to a hot place. The women have had to put up with it all along". Right! But what are the women doing?

She urged women in the coalfield to take inspiration from women workers of the Putilov factory in St Petersburg who had protested on International Women's Day, 1917, and called on the Tsarist government to provide food, better pay, better jobs, peace and democracy, or face a revolution. 'It was the women', she explained:

> marching in the streets of Leningrad [as St Petersburg was known in the 1930s] demanding bread that heralded the Russian Revolution. Is the Rhondda woman's blood thinner that they leave it all to the men? Rhondda women get about your own business. Let the world know about your suffering, about your continuous poverty. Join together to put things right. Organise in groups from your streets, villages, towns, valleys; join the men in the demonstrations. Let the National Government know that you will not permit your menfolk to take this lying down, and that you yourself will enter the fray side by side with the men to bring about the downfall of the capitalist system and the setting up of a Workers' Soviet rule.[58]

Gwen Ray Evans's Soviet-inspired feminism was echoed by appeals in the *Daily Worker* for stronger organisation of women, made by Mavis Llewellyn. Writing in 1932, she reminded readers of Lenin's view that 'there is no mass movement without women'.[59] She added,

> Our method of attacking this task was 'lamentably weak'; no concrete plans laid; no slogans around which women could be rallied. No mention of work among the hundreds of thousands of unorganised housewives. Fruitful work has doubtless been done among women in industry, but let us not underestimate the influence of the other wives and mothers ... Let us now go forward with definite tasks, let us lead these women in their activities, let us have a paper where

these activities will be reported, the reading of which will spur us on to greater activities.[60]

As a young woman, Mavis Llewellyn had been a member of the Labour Party and active in the women's section in Nantymoel. Her father was a coal miner, her mother a prominent member of the Women's Co-operative Guild, Mavis herself was a qualified schoolteacher. In this sense she was typical of those who were at the forefront of the Labour Party's interwar women's movement. She was also indicative of those who moved left politically in the aftermath of the 1926 miners' lockout and the rising tide of unemployment in the second half of the 1920s. She joined the Communist Party in 1931, having come to the view that 'the Labour Party was wrong in asking us to accept [the means test] as a lesser evil because it was a most diabolical thing'.[61] She continued,

> I can remember feeling a plague on all your houses, you're one as bad as the other. You know you were so let down, I'd been so confident that the Labour Party was the Party that was going to solve all our problems: they were the socialists, I was a socialist, and I was so disappointed, that I think for a time I [wanted to] get away from it all. Didn't believe any of them. But you can't live in a vacuum can you.[62]

Mavis Llewellyn's clarion call coincided with the creation of a new movement, ostensibly at arm's length from the main Communist Party machine: the working women's guilds. These were deliberately designed to build a united front, to circumnavigate the Labour Party's rules about working with communists, and to develop a mass movement of working people. During the 1930s, there were at least half a dozen of these guilds in existence, in communities such as Abertillery, Bedlinog, Cardiff, Nantymoel, Nantyglo and in the Rhondda – a network Mavis Llewellyn recalled many years later when she told Hywel Francis that working women's guilds were 'all over South Wales, they were'.[63] But the appeal of the guilds to members of the Labour Party was limited. As the organiser of the Nantymoel Working Women's Guild, Mavis Llewellyn noted that it was comprised 'mainly [of] members of the [Communist] party, and other women who were sympathetic'.[64] Given that almost none of the work of the working women's guilds was ever reported in the mainstream press and nothing so formal as minutes were ever taken – let alone survived – it is not surprising that historians have tended to cast doubt on oral testimony.[65]

Careful examination of the communist press, usually the only outlet for these groups, together with other extant campaign material, suggests that Mavis Llewellyn was broadly accurate in her recollection. Hannah Gabriel, the secretary of the Ferndale Working Women's Guild, was included as a co-signatory of Harry Pollitt's election literature in 1935, for instance. Across the coalfield the guilds were responsible for organising International Women's Day, the 1935 Peace Pageant in Abertillery, a women's march to protest the visit of George V to Cardiff, the women's hunger march of 1934, and entertainments for the unemployed.[66] The combined membership of the guilds was never large. Yet neither was it insignificant, especially in those parts of the coalfield where communist women were a visible force on the streets. Betty and Esther Sweet, Ceridwen Brown and Ma Lloyd, Nellie Paddock and Elizabeth Collingbourne were known figures in their localities, not only because they appeared in the court columns of the newspapers so often, but also because they were actively contributing to politics as an arena for working-class women. Gwen Ray Evans and Mavis Llewellyn gave that work an intellectual and journalistic gloss, and in the case of the latter enabled a successful electoral campaign.

*

The lasting contribution of communist women to the women's movement was to ensure the annual celebration of International Women's Day (IWD) in Wales. Although in the second half of the twentieth century, events on 8 March would become non-political, in the early part of the century IWD was closely associated with the labour movement and marked chiefly by socialists and communists. In the Soviet Union, it was even a national holiday. This communist influence was evident in Abertillery in 1938, at Maesteg and Caerau in 1942, and in Neath in 1944.[67] During the Second World War, the festival gained a broader resonance, marking the contribution of women to the allied war effort and subsequently to the manifestation of global peace once allied victory was assured, although in practice most of its adherents still tended to be members of either the Communist Party, the Women's Co-operative Guild, or the Labour Party.[68] In 1943, for example, Olive Annie Wheeler, by then professor of education at the University College of South Wales and Monmouthshire in Cardiff, used her address at an event in Swansea to pay tribute to 'the women of Wales working in the Services, factories, hospitals, and in many other forms of employment where their labours had freed men for the fighting forces'.[69]

After the war, there was cross-party consensus on the need to celebrate IWD, in line with the aspirations of the United Nations Charter and the 1948 United Nations Declaration of Human Rights. Megan Lloyd George was even appointed president of the

British organising committee; a role from which she resigned in 1948, just as the Cold War was getting under way. In her public letter sent to the committee chair, Leah Manning MP (Labour, Epping), the Liberal MP for Anglesey, complained that the movement had 'increasingly come under extreme Left and Communist influence', adding that she had

> received a growing number of complaints – both from women's Liberal Associations and from individuals in many parts of the country – that International Women's Day, which started as a non-political body of women, basing their activities on the charter to which we pledged ourselves at the Albert Hall meeting in 1945 ... can no longer claim to be non-political.[70]

Megan Lloyd George's high-profile resignation prompted some debate as to the purpose of the annual IWD celebration and the possibility of non-political and non-partisan organisation. From Pembroke Dock came the insistence that 'our local committee is a representative body of women of all parties – and of none – and is not and never has been under the domination of any one party'.[71] Similar points were raised by the Swansea organising committee.[72]

Given the origins of International Women's Day, Megan Lloyd George's lament was not entirely groundless. In Abertillery, organisers *were* members of the local Communist Party branch, or fellow travellers, and they used an event in March 1949 to 'urge the Government to promote international peace [between] the USSR and [the] USA'.[73] The Cardiff Committee, which was technically non-partisan and had been chaired by the city's mayoress on its foundation just after the war, likewise showed signs of fellow travelling.[74] In 1949, they arranged for a 'peace bus' to visit the city – the speeches delivered were laced with pro-Soviet ideas. The *Western Mail* reported that 'most of the speakers referred to Russia [as] a misunderstood nation'.[75] A year later, several women's day committees in South Wales, including in Cardiff and the Rhondda, hosted a small Soviet delegation, consisting of a schoolteacher and a scientist who were taken on trips to factories, schools and to the weekly meeting of the Gabalfa Old Age Pensioners Committee – all to gain an insight into the western way of life.[76] Those who marked IWD emphasised the contribution of women to society, to culture and to intellectual endeavour. They spoke of peace and prosperity. They dreamed of a world in which women no longer faced discrimination and were regarded as equals.

Writing women back into the history of interwar Welsh communism, and communism into the Welsh women's movement, helps to make sense of the lives of those such as Ceridwen Brown, Betty and Esther Sweet, Nellie Paddock, Elizabeth Collingbourne, Mavis Llewellyn and Gwen Ray Evans, who were ever present in the street politics of the period. In the aftermath of the Second World War there was a decline in that kind of activism, as wealth and economic opportunity was better redistributed, unemployment fell, and the need for an anti-fascist movement waned. In its absence, the Communist Party turned towards electoral politics and winning control of trade union officerships, a direct echo of the Labour Party. In 1979, more than forty years after the hunger marches and her first forays into organised street politics, and fifty years after Ceridwen Brown first stood for election as a communist woman in Aberdare, Annie Powell was invested as mayor of the Rhondda. She was 73. In an interview with the BBC, she told reporters that she had joined the Communist

Party because 'they knew what they wanted to do: they wanted to change the old way to a new way'. Her aim, she said, was to 'create hope that the Rhondda has a future, that it isn't dying'. It was as if the 1930s were happening all over again.

Notes

1. Hywel Francis and Dai Smith, *The Fed: A History of the South Wales Miners in the Twentieth Century* (London, 1980), p. 260.

2. Parts of his story are detailed in Hywel Francis, *Miners Against Fascism: Wales and the Spanish Civil War* (London, 1984); for a description of his funeral see Gwyn A. Williams, *Fishers of Men: Stories Towards an Autobiography* (Llandysul, 1996).

3. *AL*, 9 February 1935; cited in Francis and Smith, *The Fed*, p. 259.

4. Gail Baylis, 'Metropolitan Surveillance and Rural Opacity: Secret Photography in Nineteenth-Century Ireland', *History of Photography*, 33/1 (2009), 26–38; Linda Mulcahy, 'Docile suffragettes? Resistance to police photography and the possibility of object-subject transformation', *Feminist Legal Studies*, 23/1 (2015), 79–99.

5. Hywel Francis, 'notes of interview with Ceridwen Brown, 23 April 1970'. I am grateful to Hywel for a copy of these notes and his insights. They are otherwise contained in volume two of his doctoral thesis, D. Hywel Francis, 'The South Wales Miners and the Spanish Civil War: A Study in Internationalism' (unpublished PhD thesis, University College Swansea, 1979).

6. TNA, War Office Records, WO/363: Attestation papers for Edward Brown, Aberaman, service number 28314, 24 March 1915; TNA, WO/363: Discharge papers for Edward Brown, Aberaman, service number 28314, 12 September 1915.

7. Ronald Brown (1916–66) served in the International Brigade as a truck driver. He arrived in Spain in June 1937 and was repatriated in December 1938.

8. Francis, 'Ceridwen Brown Interview'; *AL*, 17 May 1913.

9. The role of family in the creation of communist activists in Britain is now a well-recognised feature. Kevin Morgan, Gidon Cohen and Andrew Flinn, *Communists and British Society, 1920–1991* (London, 2007); Linehan, *Communism*.

10. *MPn*, 16 March 1918; the wider history of this period is told in Leeworthy, *Labour Country*, pp. 311–412.

11. *MPn*, 15 March 1919. Secretary of the group was Will Dyer, 38 Thomas Street, Robertstown, Aberdare; *AL*, 12 April, 19 April, 6 December 1919.

12. *WM*, 13 March 1929.

13. *WM*, 13 October 1931; 16 October 1931.

14. Her daughter, Beth Winter, was elected to parliament as the Labour MP for Cynon Valley in December 2019.

15. This anecdote was related to me by the late Hywel Francis.

16. Annmarie Hughes, *Gender and Political Identities in Scotland, 1919–1939* (Edinburgh, 2010), p. 48.

17. Bruley, *Women and Men*, p. 98.

18. Linehan, *Communism in Britain*, p. 11.

19. Bruley, *Leninism*, p. 164. The list of names given was: Ceridwen Brown, Ethel Horner, Mrs Williams, Daisy Tanner, Dora Maslin, Lil Price, Mrs Tudor, Essie Murphy, Mrs Lawrence and an unidentified woman from Ferndale.

20. RGASPI, 495.14.261: 'Registration of Party Membership in South Wales', undated but April 1938.

21. RGASPI, 495.14.156: 'Registration of Party Membership in South Wales, February 1937'.

22. RGASPI, 495.14.261: 'Communist Party of Great Britain, District Report for South Wales', undated but April 1938, p. 2.

23. RGASPI, 495.14.239: 'Membership Reported, April 1937'.

24. For instance, in Abertillery. RGASPI, 495.14.156: 'Communist Party of Great Britain, Abertillery Branch Report', undated but *c.*1936. Two of the twelve members of the Local Party Committee were women: Mrs Davies of Six Bells and Mrs B. Lloyd of Cwmtillery.

25. 'District Report for South Wales', p. 9.

26. 'Valleys Loved Him', *DW*, 11 July 1960.

27. *WM*, 5 April 1932. Harcombe secured 1,751 votes to Paddock's 403.

28. *WM*, 31 July 1936.

29. Francis, *Miners*, pp. 94–5.

30. *WM*, 14 December 1936; *DW*, 31 May 1937.

31. *WM*, 24 December 1936.

32. *WM*, 4 March 1930. The others arrested were Ada Symonds, Ann Townsend and Christmas Randall of Trealaw; Margaret Lloyd of

Edmundstown; Samuel Wilkinson of Williamstown; Dewi Chubb of Tonypandy; Arthur Griffiths of Clydach Vale; and John Benjamin of Blaenclydach. Ada Symonds was the secretary of the women's section of the Minority Movement in South Wales.

33. *Yorkshire Evening Post*, 29 May 1930; *DW*, 31 May 1930.

34. *WM*, 6 June 1930. Her co-defendants were Albert Payne (her brother), Arthur Griffiths, John Benjamin, Samuel Paddock, Ebenezer Thomas, Isaac Lewis and Betty Ford.

35. *WM*, 14 December 1936.

36. *WM*, 4 December 1931, 20 February 1932, 24 February 1932.

37. *WM*, 25 February 1932.

38. *WM*, 7 April 1933.

39. SWML, AUD/172. Interview conducted with Mrs John Morgan Evans [i.e. Velinda Tudor], Maerdy, 11 June 1973. Mrs Evans was Helen Tudor's daughter; Francis and Smith, *The Fed*, pp. 180–2.

40. *WM*, 19 February 1932.

41. *WM*, 25 February 1932.

42. *WM*, 15 June 1928.

43. *WM*, 6 June 1928.

44. Horner, *Incorrigible Rebel*, p. 118.

45. *WM*, 3 August 1928.

46. GLA, D1006/2/4, Pontypridd Women's Co-operative Guild, Minute Book, 1933–7, entry for 25 September 1936; D1006/2/5, Pontypridd Women's Co-operative Guild, Minute Book, 1937–44, entries for 8 June 1937, 17 October 1939; hostility had been evident since 1921. D1006/2/1, Pontypridd Women's Co-operative Guild, Minute Book 1919–22, entry for 27 September 1921.

47. Leeworthy, *Labour Country*, pp. 366–8; RGASPI, 495.14.178: 'Report and Recommendations of the EC to Rhondda Borough Labour Party', undated but *c.*1936.

48. *WM*, 19 February 1929; *SWG*, 22 February 1929.

49. RGASPI, 495.14.239: 'Report of Visit to Rhondda Area, October 1937'.

50. RGASPI, 495.14.239: 'Analysis of Party Membership for South Wales, August 1937'. The list was as follows: one member in each of Gwaun-Cae-Gurwen and Ogmore, three in Abertillery and four in Cardiff.

51. RGASPI, 495.14.156: 'Summary of Speech Given by Idris Cox to South Wales Communist Congress, 20 February 1937'.

52. Bruley, *Leninism*, p. 163.

53. RGASPI, 495.14.156: 'A Guide for the South Wales Delegates to Report on the National Congress, June 1937'.

54. RGASPI, 495.14.239: 'Report of South Wales District, October 1937'.

55. *GG*, 25 September 1936.

56. D1006/2/4, Entry for 19 February 1935; 'Progress of the Peace Ballot', *Ocean and National Magazine*, 5 (May 1935), 184; Martin Ceadel, 'The First British Referendum: The Peace Ballot, 1934–5', *English Historical Review*, 95/377 (October 1980), 810–39; Helen McCarthy, 'Democratizing British Foreign Policy: Rethinking the Peace Ballot, 1934–1935', *Journal of British Studies*, 49/2 (April 2010), 358–87.

57. D1006/2/4, Entry for 9 October 1934; for local hostility to white peace poppy sales see: *WM*, 20 November 1933, 11 June 1935, 22 October 1936, 29 November 1937; *PTG*, 1 December 1933, 21 April 1937.

58. *DW*, 26 January 1935.

59. The original phrase was taken from an interview with Lenin conducted by Clara Zetkin, the veteran German communist, in 1920.

60. LHASC, CPA, CP/CENT/CONG/03/03: Pre-Congress Discussion and Congress Reports, 1932.

61. SWML, AUD/98: Mavis Llewellyn Interview, 16 May 1974.

62. SWML, AUD/98: Mavis Llewellyn Interview, 16 May 1974.

63. SWML, AUD/98: Mavis Llewellyn Interview, 16 May 1974; *DW*, 14 March 1930, 18 February 1931, 10 September 1931, 23 October 1931, 5 December 1931, 9 March 1932, 19 September 1932, 24 December 1932, 28 March 1933, 15 July 1933, 29 July 1933, 6 June 1934, 4 August 1934, 4 February 1935, 23 February 1935, 19 April 1938, 9 March 1948.

64. SWML, AUD/98: Mavis Llewellyn Interview, 16 May 1974.

65. For instance, David Selway, 'Collective Memory in the Mining Communities of South Wales' (unpublished PhD thesis, Sussex University, 2017), p. 63; Stephanie Ward, *Unemployment and the State: The Means Test and Protest in 1930s South Wales and North-East England* (Manchester, 2013).

66. RBA, SWCC, SC49, Irene Paynter Papers: International Women's Day, 1938; *SWG*, 14 December 1934, 28 December 1934, 13 September 1935, 4 October 1935; *DW*, 7 July 1936.

67. *SWG*, 11 March 1938, 18 March 1938; *GG*, 13 March 1942; *GA*, 13 March 1942; *NG*, 3 March 1944, 24 March 1944.

68. *NG*, 16 March 1945.

69. *WM*, 25 March 1943.

70. *WM*, 6 March 1948.
71. *WM*, 8 March 1948.
72. *WM*, 12 March 1948.
73. *SWG*, 18 March 1949.
74. *WM*, 3 March 1947.
75. *WM*, 25 July 1949.
76. *WM*, 16 March 1950; *PO*, 18 March 1950.

5

Raising Consciousness

In December 1940, members of the North Wales Labour Women's Advisory Council gathered in Llandudno for their quarterly meeting. On the agenda were two items: the opening of day nurseries to support women working in support of the war effort, and food supplies. Elizabeth Andrews was in attendance as guest of honour. A motion was passed in favour of day nurseries.[1] A few months later, similar motions were passed by women's sections in Bridgend, Maesteg, Abertillery and the Monmouthshire Labour Women's Advisory Council.[2] The latter stated that nurseries were 'the only satisfactory solution created by the call to women to enter industry'. Delegates added that 'factory life, with women playing an important part, had come to stay in South Wales'.[3] In the absence of traditional party politics and elections, which were suspended for a significant portion of the Second World War, motions of this kind were vital in the maintenance, not only of the parties themselves, but also of local democracy. Within the Labour Party, especially, women's section activity expanded, with work parties and knitting circles producing garments and other materials for the forces, evacuees, refugees and liberated families.[4] Sections also took opportunities to nominate members to wartime committees, such as those which eventually administered day nurseries and which looked forward to post-war housing provision.[5]

Wartime conditions renewed the debate about the role of women in politics, particularly considering their new earning potential and the lack of public facilities designed to support women in work. Long-standing arguments about men as bread-winners were temporarily muted, too. In the summer of 1941, the launch of the London Women's Parliament, by co-operators, trades unionists and those close to (or in) the Communist Party, saw demands for 'the fullest use of the practical experience of working-class housewives'.[6] Over the next few months, wom-en's parliaments were launched in Yorkshire (in September 1941), Lancashire (in April 1942), the north-east of England (in October 1942), Scotland and Wales.[7] The South Wales Women's Parliament (as it was known) was launched in Cardiff in August 1942, with Rhondda's Annie Powell in the chair. Several of the delegates were drawn from the ranks of the women's sections of the Anglo-Soviet Friendship Council.[8] Both were an indication of the communist link to proceedings. Amongst the demands debated in the augural meeting was the need for twenty-four-hour nurseries to enable women to work around the clock without having to disrupt the lives of their children. Subsequent ses-sions considered the post-war world, including the terms of the Beveridge Report.[9] Local branches of the South Wales Women's Parliament were subsequently formed in Abertillery and Neath.[10]

The Women's Parliaments were intended to give voice to the material concerns of working-class women and to build a women's movement for economic and social change. They were not the platform to build the case for increased parliamentary representation. That came in the form of the Women's Publicity

Planning Association's 'Women for Westminster' campaign, which launched nationally in January 1942. It aimed at convincing all political parties to adopt more women candidates for parliamentary elections. Welsh conferences were held at Swansea's Guildhall, at the Engineers' Institute in central Cardiff, and in Barmouth, early in 1943.[11] Much of the political support for the campaign came from the Liberal Party: Conservatives withdrew their support when it became clear that Women for Westminster activists had allied themselves to Jennie Lee's by-election campaign as an independent in Bristol Central in 1943. She was seeking to take the seat from the Conservative Party's Violet Apsley. The latter was eventually returned to parliament. It is worth noting that the Conservatives were not alone in their anxiety. Labour had also withdrawn its support, fearing that the Women for Westminster campaign was either a Communist-led initiative from the left, or a move from the right to sustain permanent electoral coalitions.[12]

Labour had its eye on the bigger prize: government. As early as 1943, members of the women's sections were being encouraged to dedicate themselves, in the words of Bella Burke of Abertillery, 'to the establishment of socialism' and a parliamentary majority, 'knowing that as women we have the opportunity and the power within our grasp'.[13] They joined with the rest of the grassroots Labour Party to call for an end to the wartime electoral pact and to push for implementation of the proposals contained in the Beveridge Report.[14] The distinction was between a single-issue campaign, however important on principle, and the pragmatic politics which would achieve meaningful reform. Indeed, there was an air of possibility and change. When Monmouthshire Labour Women's Advisory Council celebrated its twenty-fifth anniversary (a few months early) in September

1944, members readily congratulated themselves on how far they had come at all levels of government and as a women's movement, and agreed on the need never to go back to the locust years of the 1930s. Then Elizabeth Andrews took to the stage to deliver her address. In three years, she said, 'I will have to retire as your organiser. I will be a rank and filer. Times have changed and they call for new people'.[15]

*

True to her word, Elizabeth Andrews retired from her role as women's organiser for Wales in the spring of 1948. She was 65 and, after almost thirty years in post, was widely feted, including with an OBE as part of the King's Birthday Honours List.[16] However, there was also a sense that Elizabeth Andrews was not best placed to renew the Labour Party's appeal to women in the aftermath of the Second World War. Her views were traditional, typical of the older idea of the Labour woman, and she worked best with her own cohort: those who had joined the party in the surge of organisational enthusiasm in the 1920s. In an indicative interview given shortly before leaving her post, Elizabeth Andrews explained to the *Western Mail* that, in her view, 'bad housekeeping' was leading to an increase in broken marriages and failed relationships. In the Rhondda, she said, the new factories 'took girls from their homes straight from school', and therefore 'girls were not taught the elements of good housekeeping and when they fell in love and married, their limitations proved disastrous'. She concluded that girls should be provided with 'domestic training' to fit them for married life.[17] It was language akin to the nostalgia which had prompted the *South Wales Echo* to ask in January 1946 whether 'it is time to return to the old-fashioned view that it is the man's job to go out to earn the family's income'.[18]

But this was ill-suited to a world in which more women worked and in which material questions of equal pay and employment rights were increasingly to the fore, to say nothing of domestic violence, demographic diversity, and consumerism. By the 1950s, observers 'noted a growth in the number of married women workers, the decrease in family size, the increased companionability of working class marriages, and the emergence of an apparently reformed working class masculinity'.[19] With working-class identity itself beginning to change in the aftermath of the Second World War and in the wake of declining unemployment, declining industrial strife in the now nationalised coal industry, and a move away from heavy industry as a staple employer, there was less acceptance of older perceptions. But the disregard was not a total one. Nostalgia found itself embedded in the way in which Britain's workers were popularly conceptualised.[20] And against the apparent 'softening' of men who no longer worked underground or in the raw heat of the steelworks was projected the 'angry young man' – whose source of aggression lay in frustration at the absence of the certainties of class and gender afforded to earlier generations. To this we might also add frustration at the gap between professed social mobility and its relative absence in working-class communities.[21]

Labour's change of women's organiser in the post-war period provided at least the means of avoiding too great an emphasis on nostalgia and on past achievement. Ismay Hill, a native of Monmouthshire, who was Elizabeth Andrews's immediate successor, conveyed a striking generational change both in attitude and age. She was then in her twenties, a dynamic character who had previously stood for Labour as a council candidate in Cwmbran and who was recognised immediately as someone 'destined to leave her mark on any task she was set'.[22] Her vision was of a modernised women's movement which would take advantage of Labour's parliamentary victories all over Wales. She faced a complicated challenge: by 1950, membership of the Welsh women's sections was demographically uneven, with just over ten per cent under the age of 30 and more than forty per cent aged over 50.[23] Many of the latter cohort had been members for a long time, often as founders of sections, and occupied many of the administrative and executive posts. They were especially prone to reflection. To revitalise the women's movement, particularly in rural constituencies, where the Conservative Party appeared to have the upper hand in its appeal to women voters, Ismay Hill set in train the development of new federations bringing together ward-level sections and activists on a larger scale.

There was early success in Brecon and Radnorshire in the summer of 1950, but Ismay Hill's resignation a few weeks later, prompted by an impending move to Sudan, where she was to become senior lecturer at the Girls' Training College in Omdurman near Khartoum, curtailed further efforts.[24] The work of refitting the women's sections for the new decade was instead undertaken by Megan Roach, also from Monmouthshire, who was appointed as women's organiser in the autumn of 1950.[25] She found the party split in two geographically, with greater efficacy and presence in southern constituencies compared with northern ones – an indication of what Andrew Edwards has referred to as Labour's 'fragility' outside of its southern heartland.[26] The regional distinctions could, at times, be striking. The joint annual meeting of the South Wales and Monmouthshire Labour Women's Advisory Councils in June 1952, for instance, attracted more than 1,000 delegates.[27] By 1955, as recorded in the party's annual reports, women formed the majority of individual party members in Glamorgan and Monmouthshire, although their influence was limited in practice by the dominance of the industrial trades unions, whose membership was overwhelmingly male. In the north, where in some constituencies women's sections ceased to function during the early 1950s, the party's presence was generally uneven.[28]

Much of that imbalance reflected electoral success at a parliamentary level: where Labour held the seat, such as in East Flintshire or Conwy, both of which were created for the 1950 general election, the party experienced a degree of momentum.[29] There was, for instance, considerable activity in Bangor and Llandudno in the 1950s and 1960s, with high-profile national figures such as Liverpool's Bessie Braddock attending women's section meetings.[30] Likewise, the appointment of Joan Clark as chair of Conwy Borough Labour Party in 1951 came just a year after the constituency party's new women's section was formed. She joined an executive which was evenly split between men and women.[31] The Conwy women's section became a federation in 1965 and was championed as 'remarkable' and 'buoyant' and 'an inspiration to local Labour parties throughout the constituency'.[32] But in those constituencies held by the Conservatives, such as Denbigh and Flintshire West, Labour struggled to maintain its coherence. By 1955, the party had been pushed into third place in Denbigh – behind the Conservatives and Liberals – and that decline was mirrored in the relative collapse of the local women's movement. There were fewer than half the number of women's sections at the start of the 1960s that there had been in 1945.

Labour's challenge in a period of significant social and economic change, albeit one defined by political stability, which favoured the Conservatives in Westminster and the Labour Party in Wales, was translating membership and organisation into successful appeals to women as independent voters. At a parliamentary level, historians have noted, the party struggled with the Conservatives developing a contemporary message which directly appealed to women as consumers and as citizens.[33] This 'gender gap' was evident in national voting habits. Between 1945 and 1970, Labour attracted a majority of women only twice: at the general elections of 1945 and 1966.[34] There was much greater nuance in voting habits at the local government level, however, where Labour was much more successful, both in attracting women as voters and in presenting women as candidates. By the end of the 1950s, the phrase 'first woman chair' became, increasingly, a thing of the past; more women were elected to district and county councils under the Labour banner and took charge of major committees on education and health, and ultimately of the authorities themselves. The career of Rose Davies, the Aberdare-born Labour councillor and alderman, who led Glamorgan County Council during the 1949–50 session, is well known, and is mirrored in the parallel experiences of Dorothy Rees, who chaired Glamorgan County Council in 1964.[35]

There were limits to progress, of course, though these were indicative of the discrete circumstances which local government provided. Some district councils, usually not controlled by the Labour Party, such as Llandudno Urban and Neath Rural, elected just one woman to the chair during their entire existence from 1894 until 1974, and typically after the Second World War. A Labour-controlled authority such as Pontypridd Urban District elevated three women to the chair, although the gap between each term was sizeable. Blodwen Randell, the first, served in 1950–1; Gwladys May Williams in 1963–4; and Mary Murphy in 1971–2. In all cases these women emphasised the historic importance of their role.[36] Labour's Elizabeth Somers, the first woman to chair Bridgend Urban District Council, speaking after her election in 1959, was clear. 'I shall not fail the council neither shall I fail the women', she said,

> because I am determined to carry out my duties with inter-est, enthusiasm and perseverance in order that should there be a similar occasion in the future when a woman may be appointed chairman, then no one shall be in a position to say that on the last occasion the job was not carried out properly.[37]

Her year in office came just twelve months after the Labour Party won control of Bridgend council from the Conservatives.[38]

An atypical example of the post-war period was Caerphilly Urban District. In 1945, the council had eight wards, each rep-resented by three members. Of the twenty-four councillors in office at the end of the war, four were women: Ethel Sargent in Ystrad Mynach, Elizabeth Jones in Trecenydd, and Gwen Jones and Isabel Harris in Senghenydd.[39] In the latter, women formed the majority of local representation, a situation which prevailed from the mid-1940s until the early 1960s. The longest-serving councillor was Isabel Harris, who first stood as a Labour candi-date in 1932.[40] By 1938, she was returned unopposed.[41] To mark her tenth anniversary on the council, Isabel Harris was elected vice chair in 1942 and proceeded to become chair of Caerphilly Urban District in 1943, the first woman to do so.[42] That was not an unusual step: the late 1930s and early 1940s saw women step into leadership roles in Welsh local government, particu-larly in the southern coalfield. Women became chairs of local authorities, in part, because of the happenstance of seniority and rotation; after a certain length of service they were in line for that position. What made Caerphilly distinctive was that each of the other women councillors, all of them Labour Party members, Ethel Sargent, Elizabeth Jones and Gwen Jones, served as chair of the council successively (and in that order) from 1952 until 1955.

*

Someone who has garnered little historical attention, but who is nevertheless illustrative of how women sought to navigate the immediate post-war period and to develop a Labour politics which spoke to contemporary conditions, is Lily Jones (née Plummer), who chaired Monmouthshire County Council in 1964–5. Lily Jones's achievements as a county councillor have tended to be overshadowed by historians' collective interest in the careers of Elizabeth Andrews and Rose Davies, figures identified both as indicative examples of women at the apex of Welsh politics and as unusually prominent activists. But as more research is undertaken on sub-parliamentary politics, and the involvement of women more especially, and moves away from the personal records that Elizabeth Andrews and Rose Davies left behind, it is apparent that they were not atypical. Rather, they were part of a cohort of dozens of Labour women who shaped twentieth-century Welsh life through the often dull, quotidian, but necessary, work of public administration. And the cohort was itself diverse, as the example of Elvira Gwenllian Payne (née Hinds, 1917–2007), Wales's first woman of colour to be elected as a councillor, demonstrates. In 1979, standing on the Labour platform, she was elected on to the Vale of Glamorgan Borough Council for the Baruc ward in Barry.[43] She was followed, in Butetown, in 1983, by Labour's Gaynor Legall.

These local nuances are important because they challenge the impression given by parliamentary elections that the

Conservatives, for much of the immediate post-war period, were the natural party of women and better spoke the language of gender – even in Wales. At the grassroots, women in office tended to come from the Labour Party and that itself was a signal of which political party provided more opportunities for women to effect change in their own communities. As Megan Roach explained to the press in 1959, women 'feel most strongly about food prices and anything affecting their children'.[44] Such detail is illustrative of 'valence voting' – decisions made based on which party or candidate seems the most competent on issues of importance, be they schools which are locally governed, or macroeconomics and the cost of living which are reserved to parliament. In her interview with the press, Megan Roach added that in 'a sign that their [women's] interests take in more than domestic issues is their great concern in recent years over the conditions in under-developed countries'. The launch of the Boycott Movement in June 1959, which aimed at levelling western pressure on apartheid South Africa, provided one means of expressing that interest in international affairs. It became the Anti-Apartheid Movement nine months later, in the aftermath of the Sharpeville massacre.

Each of these themes was evident in Lily Jones's career. She was born into a mining family in Six Bells, where she grew up; she won a scholarship to study at grammar school in nearby Abertillery and then entered the teaching profession.[45] Marriage in the mid-1920s, to schoolmaster Henry Jones, brought an end to her teaching career, but not to her public life. She remained active as a preacher in the primitive Methodist church in Six Bells, and in the Labour Party. During the fateful year of 1926, she was secretary of the local women's section and assisted the organisation of that body's efforts to maintain food supplies during the general strike and the miners' lockout. That work propelled her to the front rank of Abertillery Divisional Labour Party – eventually as its chair – and the Monmouthshire Labour Women's Advisory Council, which she chaired twice in the 1950s.[46] It was in the 1930s that she began to be considered as a potential councillor, not least by herself. In 1934, she told the *South Wales Gazette* that, in recognition of the multifaceted role women play in public life, the district council should have women members.[47] In the event, during the autumn of 1940, she was instead elected to Monmouthshire County Council.[48]

It took nearly a quarter of a century for Lily Jones to rise through the ranks to become council chair, the same length of service given in neighbouring Glamorgan by Rose Davies and Dorothy Rees. Both authorities, the most powerful councils in Wales, had internal systems of patronage, which favoured influential councillors and which all three women learned effectively to navigate. Lily Jones's rise began in the early 1950s, although by then her record was already celebrated as 'second to none'.[49] Her first chair was that of Monmouthshire special services committee; in 1952, she was appointed as a magistrate. In 1956, she moved to chair the children's committee, and in 1963 was elected chair of the education committee as well as vice chair of the county council.[50] During her tenure, she focused on the provision of youth services and maintaining the system of community-based adult education classes, which were an important lifeline for women. She also had oversight of the abolition of the eleven plus examinations in Monmouthshire, gifting the power to determine places at the county's grammar schools to teachers instead – a precursor to the creation of the comprehensive system.[51] Such action earned praise from local commentators, who thought the committee, as chaired by Lily Jones, 'undoubtedly one of the foremost and most liberal-minded authorities in the country'.[52]

Education policy was a traditional area in which Labour women took a significant interest, of course, but the context was such that councillors were making decisions, not just about the shift from grammar schools to comprehensives, which was substantial enough, but also about international affairs and about changing social dynamics. In 1962, during her tenure as vice chair of the education committee, Lily Jones had helped to steer the council's response to the selection of Monmouthshire teachers for the British and Irish Lions tour of South Africa. The committee vigorously denounced the apartheid regime and its colour bar, and refused to pay any teaching staff who chose to take up their selection. They would have to take unpaid leave instead. To pay them, committee members argued, would be to provide financial support, by proxy, to racism.[53] A similar stance was taken two years later in response to the Welsh Rugby Union's controversial tour of South Africa.[54] And in 1964, following an approach by the Anti-Apartheid Movement, Monmouthshire County Council, as chaired by Lily Jones, signed up to the widening boycott of South African goods – the first county council in Wales to do so.[55] This followed the similar decision of the county borough councils in Cardiff and Merthyr Tydfil.[56] Glamorgan joined the boycott in 1965.[57]

The anti-apartheid movement dominated Welsh anti-racist activity throughout the post-war period, with local councils, political parties and trade unions, all adopting a hostile stance towards the South African government. By the mid-1960s, there were local anti-apartheid groups, such as the Afan Valley Anti-Apartheid Committee near Port Talbot and the Swansea co-ordinating committee, interventions from trades councils such as Neath, and thirty-eight local authorities were active in the boycott of South African goods by 1966.[58] With the exception of Wrexham Borough Council, all were situated in the south. Women took an active role, as Glenys Kinnock recalled in an interview for the Forward to Freedom project in 2013,

> I was very active as a student [in the 1960s] in the Anti-Apartheid Movement and was a supporter of the South African Black Sash movement ... at the annual South Wales Miners' Gala, we would join the procession. This was a huge event with busloads of people coming down from the South Wales Valleys to march, and women students organised the Black Sash part of the march. We wore black sashes and we would carry our anti-apartheid banner.[59]

The Black Sash, a white women's civil rights organisation, had been founded in May 1955 as protest against the removal of constitutional and voting rights from black South Africans in the Cape. It later grew into a much broader campaign group and, together with the students' union, was the most significant white South African opposition to the apartheid regime. Women seen wearing the black sash in public in Cape Town or Johannesburg, for example, especially alone, ran the risk of being violently attacked. The confrontations between the anti-apartheid movement and the National Front in Cardiff and Merthyr brought home the parallels between racist South Africa and a Britain – indeed, a Wales – which was by no means free of the same forces.

The 1960s saw the creation of new legislative frameworks, introduced by Harold Wilson's Labour government to tackle racism. In 1965, the first Race Relations Act banned discrimination in public places and made race hatred illegal. It was followed three years later with the 1968 Race Relations Act, which extended the ban on discrimination to housing, employment and public services. Both pieces of legislation were replaced with the more comprehensive 1976 Race Relations Act, which also established the Commission for Racial Equality. But the law could not stamp out racism entirely, nor did it prevent the persistence of far-right politics and white supremacism, including the growth of the National Front across Britain. Grassroots anti-racism was well organised, especially in Cardiff and Barry, although it took several years for groups outside the Anti-Apartheid Movement and the far left (including the Communist Party) to coalesce. The anti-racist movement which emerged in the second half of the 1970s comprised several elements (and varying left-wing orientations): the Anti-Nazi League and associated spin-offs, such as School Kids Against Nazis, Student Campaign Against Nazis, Football Fans Against Nazis, Teachers Against Nazis; the Welsh Committee Against Racialism; the Wales Anti-Apartheid Movement; the Newport Anti-Racist Group; and the Cardiff Committee Against Racialism (CCAR).

The origins of the CCAR, which was formally established in 1978, lay in a suggestion made to members of the Welsh Committee Against Racialism the previous year, namely that there should be a dedicated group to deal with discrete circumstances in the city.[60] It drew on the resources of the labour movement and was led by three women: Ann Clwyd (as chair), Eileen Keane (as treasurer), and Joanne Richards (as secretary). The role of vice chair was taken by Dai Francis, the communist former general secretary of the South Wales NUM and inaugural president of the Wales TUC. Most of CCAR's organisational work was undertaken by Joanne Richards, who was herself a prominent member of the Communist Party.[61] Similar anti-racist work was undertaken in the north by Manny Cohen, the party's regional secretary, who spearheaded protests when

National Front leaflets were found in a comprehensive school in Abergele.[62] Once formed, the CCAR was active in organising street protests and demonstrations, picketing outside meetings addressed by figures such as Enoch Powell, leaflet campaigns and direct action, such as painting over racist graffiti, under the umbrella of 'Women Against Nazism', the Cardiff Carnival Against Racialism, and conferences tackling themes such as racism at work. The latter was held early in 1979. The CCAR also enjoyed the prominent support of Neil Kinnock, then the rising star of the Labour left, who memorably addressed the Cardiff carnival.

The Cardiff Carnival Against Racism, which was held on 15 July 1978 and concluded with a rock concert, was largely modelled on the Rock Against Racism movement established in 1976. It mirrored two large events held in London in the spring and summer of 1978, and in other cities around the country, including Coventry, Edinburgh, Leeds and Manchester.[63] There were also contemporary local influences. These included Cardiff city council's 'international carnival', established in the 1960s as part of an amelioration of the disruption caused by slum clearance and reconstruction, and the community-based Butetown Carnival, which began in 1977 as a reaction to ongoing racism in the city. By the mid-1980s, the latter event was attracting crowds of 50,000 people.[64] Organisers of the Cardiff Carnival Against Racism approached bands whose politics aligned with the anti-racism campaign, and with the left more generally. These included the Cimarrons (a reggae band formed in Birmingham in 1967), Rikki and the Last Days of Earth (an early punk band from London formed in 1976), and the Sunsets – the rock and roll band formed in Cardiff in 1969 and fronted, until 1977, by Shakin' Stevens. The latter were managed by

Blackwood-born but Penarth-raised Paul Barrett, who was himself a card-carrying communist and well connected to members of the CCAR.[65]

Amongst the other anti-racist organisations in Wales, such as the Anti-Nazi League, women were less prominent at the organisational level. Of the eighteen members elected on to the Cardiff branch committee in 1979, for example, just five were women. All the branch officers were men.[66] Outside Cardiff, where the distinction between being a committee member and an ordinary activist was thinner, women took part in the full range of anti-racist activity and ran the risk of being intimidated, even assaulted. In Merthyr Tydfil, for instance, towards the end of the 1980s, it was reported that one local woman was spotted by members of the National Front covering fascist propaganda with 'Free Nelson Mandela' stickers. 'After swearing at her', recorded the Cardiff student newspaper *Gair Rhydd*, 'they threw her to the ground, bruising her and ripping her clothes, and stole her bag containing confidential documents'. Another woman was attacked in the town returning home alone from an anti-apartheid meeting.[67] Such attacks took place in the context of the women's liberation movement's Reclaim the Night protests and campaigns against domestic violence, and prompted some to begin to think in terms which would be described later as intersectional. Namely that race and gender, especially, but social class, sexuality and other identities also, intersect each other in systems of discrimination, inequality and injustice.[68]

*

Anti-racism was one of several themes, including provision of facilities and services on new housing estates, the environment, and the campaign against nuclear weapons proliferation, which emerged in the 1960s and early 1970s, and which served to activate a new generation of women. In 1974, for example, members of Neath Labour women's section spoke out against recent nuclear tests by the Wilson government, demanding that instead they work towards an international treaty banning all nuclear weapons.[69] The perennial issue of organisation within the women's movement remained a live matter, of course, although Megan Roach, speaking in Conwy in 1965, reminded party members that 'it mattered little whether women met as small groups in each other's houses, formed supper clubs, held sherry parties, coffee mornings, or organised traditional Labour Party women's sections. Whatever programme they adopted, it would help'.[70] Indeed, she was quick to stress that the number of women's sections in Wales was by proportion the largest in the country, although it fell into second place just a year later, in the aftermath of the 1966 general election.[71] Top of the Welsh list through the early part of the 1960s, with an active membership of around 100, was the Velindre women's section in Port Talbot, which had formed in 1947.[72]

Then, in 1970, the women's movement was shaken by the loss of Wales's remaining woman MP, Eirene White, who retired from the Flintshire East constituency at the general election. For the first time since Megan Lloyd George's election as MP for Anglesey in 1929, Wales's entire parliamentary cohort was male. For all the possibilities of the 1950s and 1960s, certainly at the grassroots, that one fact seemed to put the limitations of equal representation into context and provided some of the background against which the Labour Party was cast by the Welsh women's liberation movement. So serious was the concern within the party that women's officers expended considerable effort to grow the membership of their sections and to ensure that their activities were politically effective.[73] Local government reorganisation in 1974 provided an opportunity to project an image of strength and to remind the party of the presence of women below the parliamentary level. Edith Letts, the inaugural mayor of Afan Borough Council, which included Port Talbot and Aberavon, for instance, drew attention to her work for the Labour Party's women's sections at all levels, including as chair of the West Wales Labour Women's Advisory Council and as chair of the Port Talbot Labour Women's Section, as a testament to her dedication to the community.[74]

Early in 1976, Megan Roach retired from her role as women's organiser for Wales. Her successor was Anita Holmes (later Baroness Gale) from the Rhondda, who was appointed that June. At a meeting of the South Wales Labour Women's Advisory Council in October 1976, Anita Holmes dealt with the absence of Welsh women in Westminster. 'There are', she said, 'no parliamentary Labour women candidates or MPs [and] this situation could remain the same for about fifteen years if we do nothing about it'.[75] She proposed new systems of training and the possibility of further structure reform, all with a view of bringing on women as potential candidates at all levels of government. This was not a uniquely Welsh or Labour problem, but one which reflected ongoing challenges across Britain and for all parties: in 1979, despite the election of Margaret Thatcher as Britain's first woman prime minister, there were just four more women members of parliament than there had been in 1931. In fact, the 1979 general election marked the lowest return of women since 1951. Only the first direct elections to the European Parliament, held on 7 June 1979, provided Wales with female representation outside of local government. Of the four MEPs elected, two were women.[76]

That record has prompted some to observe that 'a radical feminist would duly convict the [Labour] party at the bar of discriminatory attitudes', given the party's overall commitment to equal representation.[77] But it would be an unfair conviction in many respects. Indeed, no other political party in Wales has succeeded in getting as many women elected, at all levels of government, as has Labour – although most of its parliamentary candidates were nominated after 1979, largely because of concerted efforts to improve selection processes. Those efforts would culminate in the all-women shortlists of the 1990s. Moreover, the party's adaptation to second-wave feminism, which emerged in the 1960s and 1970s, was impressive. As Amy Black and Stephen Brooke have noted, by the end of James Callaghan's period as prime minister, 'most of the demands adopted by the inaugural women's liberation conference meeting at Oxford in 1970 (equal pay, equal education and opportunity, twenty-four-hour nurseries, free contraception, and abortion on demand) had found their way into Labour's policy discussions'.[78] Legislation including the Abortion Act (1967), the Equal Pay Act (1970) and the Sex Discrimination Act (1975), all of which were passed by a Labour government, were also indications that the party was taking such matters seriously.

Indeed, by 1980 there was a strong sense within the party in Wales that a separate women's movement had achieved its aims and could be abolished. Conwy Constituency Labour Party argued, in response to an internal review conducted in 1979, for example, that 'women party members [should be] encouraged to take their rightful place within the main party structure'.[79] But such a view was premature. Instead of abolition, there were to be new innovations, including all-Wales Labour women's conferences, which were held for the first time in 1980. In contrast to the impression a review of structures might have conveyed, there was no sense that the women's sections were in terminal decline, either. More than 500 women members attended a rally at the Afan Lido in 1977, where they were joined by Prime Minister James Callaghan and his wife Audrey – who was the guest of honour.[80] By 1980, there were as many as 110 sections in Wales – an increase from the mid-1960s – and twenty-five constituency councils, although that still left eleven constituencies without representation. Those sections which thrived, such as in Neath and Port Talbot, engaged with a range of diverse subjects: racism, inequality, unemployment and job creation schemes.[81] In the case of the Briton Ferry women's section, issues such as educational psychology, healthcare, Ireland, co-operation, micro-technology and women's liberation were all on the agenda.[82]

And yet for all of Labour's gains over the course of the post-war period, the failure to achieve absolute equality, which the absence of parliamentary representation signalled more than anything else, provided the context in which the Welsh women's liberation movement emerged. In an era of liberationist politics, whether focused on race, sexuality or gender, Labour women's sections which gathered to listen to members tell of their journeys to the Soviet Union, for instance, seemed old-fashioned or unsuited to the challenges of the modern world – at least to radical campaigners.[83] Lesbian and trans women, especially, found little discussion of their own fight for equality and so turned to liberationist movements to build a different kind of pressure. The non-political-party environment of the women's liberation movement (as will be discussed in the next chapter) was often preferred – and certainly more comfortable – than the traditionally male-dominated parties. But as struggles for legislative change coalesced over the course of the 1970s, some began to think carefully about working within political parties and then potentially in government. As Jane Hutt has recalled,

> we had to influence government in terms of women's issues and women's needs [and] to me it became more and more obvious that one had to make the decision ... and I suppose that is the step I made, and I am certainly not the only one.[84]

By the early 1980s, that migration was sufficient to kick-start the growing influence of women within the Labour Party, which was seen (and experienced) as 'macho'.[85] In 1984, Anita Gale (as Anita Holmes was then known) was appointed general secretary of the party in Wales, moving from an assistant's role – as the women's post had been – to the principal organiser. At a national level and in urban centres, radical groups such as the Labour Women's Action Committee (formed in 1980), Labour Movement Lesbians, and the Labour Campaign for Lesbian and Gay Rights, served to amplify left-feminist and lesbian feminist perspectives.[86] Together with the Labour Women's Network, which launched in 1988, the shadow ministry for women created in the aftermath of the 1983 general election, and revitalised women's sections, these groups worked to build the case for affirmative action and to illustrate to members and voters alike that the arc of the women's liberation movement bent towards, rather than away from, Labour.[87]

Notes

1. *NWWN*, 12 December 1940.
2. *GG*, 21 March 1941, 9 May 1941; *SWG*, 25 July 1941.
3. *SWG*, 2 May 1941.
4. Andrew Thorpe, *Parties At War: Political Organization in Second World War Britain* (Oxford, 2009), p. 195.

5. *PO*, 23 March 1946; *NWWN*, 23 November 1944.

6. *Northern Whig*, 14 July 1941.

7. *Bradford Observer*, 15 September 1941; *DM*, 13 April 1942; *Newcastle Evening Chronicle*, 10 October 1942; *Dundee Courier*, 6 June 1942; *Aberdeen Evening Express*, 9 March 1942; *WM*, 14 August 1942.

8. *SWG*, 21 September 1942, 22 January 1943.

9. *NG*, 29 January 1943.

10. *SWG*, 4 September 1942; *NG*, 30 October 1942, 20 November 1942.

11. *WM*, 20 March 1943, 31 March 1943, 28 August 1943.

12. Thorpe, *Parties at War*, p. 88.

13. *SWG*, 23 March 1943.

14. *NG*, 26 February 1943.

15. *SWG*, 29 September 1944.

16. *WM*, 10 June 1948; *GG*, 16 July 1948.

17. *WM*, 10 February 1948.

18. *SWE*, 29 January 1946.

19. Stephen Brooke, 'Gender and Working Class Identity in Britain during the 1950s', *Journal of Social History*, 34/4 (2001), 773–95, p. 775. The wider theme of community and post-war change is usefully considered in Jon Lawrence, *Me, Me, Me? The Search for Community in Post-War England* (Oxford, 2019), and in Florence Sutcliffe-Braithwaite, *Class, Politics and the Decline of Deference in England, 1968–2000* (Oxford, 2018). For a sense of the observers, Laura Carter, *Histories of Everyday Life: The Making of Popular Social History in Britain, 1918–1979* (Oxford, 2021), and Lise Butler, *Michael Young, Social Science and the British Left, 1945–1970* (Oxford, 2020).

20. Chris Waters, 'Representations of Everyday Life: L. S. Lowry and the Landscape of Memory in Postwar Britain', *Representations*, 65 (1999), 121–50; Chris Waters, 'Autobiography, Nostalgia, and the Practices of Working-Class Selfhood', in George K. Behlmer and Fred M. Leventhal (eds), *Singular Continuities: Tradition, Nostalgia, and Identity in Modern Britain* (Stanford, 2000), pp. 178–95.

21. Selina Todd, *Snakes and Ladders: The Great British Social Mobility Myth* (London, 2021). This is a development of parts of the argument present in Selina Todd, *The People: The Rise and Fall of the Working Class, 1910–2010* (London, 2014).

22. James Callaghan, 'Foreword', in Graham Thomas (ed.), *The Sudan Journal of Ismay Thomas* (London, 2000), p. xi; NLW, NLW ex 1463, Ismay Thomas Scrapbook, 1946.

23. *WM*, 12 June 1950.

24. *MEx*, 15 July 1950. Her husband, Graham, who stood in 1950 as the Labour parliamentary candidate for Monmouth, had been appointed to the Sudanese civil service. For a sense of his career see *GG*, 6 May 1949.

25. *WM*, 23 November 1950.

26. Andrew Edwards, *Labour's Crisis: Plaid Cymru, The Conservatives and the Decline of the Labour Party in North-West Wales, 1960–74* (Cardiff, 2011), pp. 3–5.

27. *GA*, 20 June 1952.

28. Evans and Jones, 'Women in the Labour Party', p. 230; *NWWN*, 17 November 1955.

29. *NWWN*, 16 March 1950, 13 April 1950, 27 April 1950, 14 May 1953.

30. *NWWN*, 5 September 1963.

31. *NWWN*, 15 February 1951.

32. *NWWN*, 7 October 1965, 4 November 1965. The latter observations were made by Ednyfed Hudson Davies (1929–2018), who served as member of parliament for Conwy between 1966 and 1970.

33. Amy Black and Stephen Brooke, 'The Labour Party, Women and the Problem of Gender, 1951–1966', *Journal of British Studies*, 36/4 (1997), 419–52, p. 420.

34. Ina Zweiniger-Bargielowska, 'Explaining the Gender Gap: The Conservative Party and the Women's Vote, 1945–64', in Martin Francis and Ina Zweiniger-Bargielowska (eds), *The Conservatives and British Society* (Cardiff, 1996).

35. The first woman to chair a Welsh county council after the Second World War was Elsie Marks (née Edge, 1871–1958), who was elected to the chair of Caernarfonshire County Council in 1945. She was 74. Born in Preston, she moved with her parents as a baby to live in Llandudno, where her father established the town's first photography studio. She married the locally prominent Liberal solicitor and councillor James Marks in 1899. Active in the women's suffrage movement, she was elected to represent Llandudno's West Ward in 1936. She held the seat for the next two decades, retiring in the autumn of 1957. She made history in 1942 when she became the first woman in Britain to chair a standing joint committee – the forerunner of police authorities. *Llandudno Advertiser*, 2 March 1900; *NWWN*, 26 June 1958.

36. *PO*, 27 May 1950.

37. *GA*, 29 May 1959.

38. *WM*, 9 May 1958.

39. Ethel Sargent and Elizabeth Jones were sisters, as reported in *WM*, 24 May 1951.

40. *MEx*, 26 March 1932, 9 April 1932.

41. *Mex*, 23 March 1935, 30 March 1935, 6 April 1935, 9 April 1938.

42. *MEx*, 25 April 1942, 24 April 1943.

43. Elvira Payne's brother, John Darwin Hinds, was the first black councillor in Wales when he was elected to Barry Borough Council in 1958. Brother and sister served as mayor and mayoress of the Vale of Glamorgan between 1975 and 1977, the first black civic leaders in Wales. *Belfast Telegraph*, 8 January 1975.

44. *WM*, 30 September 1959.

45. *SWG*, 15 May 1953.

46. *SWG*, 14 July 1961.

47. *SWG*, 28 December 1934.

48. *WM*, 23 October 1940; *SWG*, 1 November 1940.

49. *SWG*, 8 June 1951.

50. *SWG*, 1 March 1957, 5 April 1963.

51. *SWG*, 28 September 1962.

52. *SWG*, 25 October 1963.

53. *Birmingham Daily Post*, 4 April 1962; *SWG*, 13 April 1962.

54. *Birmingham Daily Post*, 2 April 1964.

55. Roger Fieldhouse, *Anti-Apartheid: A History of the Movement in Britain* (London, 2005), p. 363.

56. Anti-Apartheid Movement, *Annual Report* (London, 1964), p. 6.

57. United Nations Centre Against Apartheid, *Local Authority Action Against Apartheid* (Sheffield, 1985), p. 47.

58. *PTG*, 11 September 1964, 30 October 1964, 200 November 1969; *NG*, 4 December 1969; United Nations Centre Against Apartheid, *Local Authority Action*, p. 47.

59. Forward to Freedom Project, 'Transcript of interview with Glenys Kinnock conducted by Jeff Howarth, 20 November 2013'. Available online: *https://www.aamarchives.org/archive/interviews/baroness-kinnock-of-holyhead.html* (accessed 7 January 2021).

60. Welsh Committee Against Racialism, Minutes of Meeting, 14 April 1977.

61. Joanne Richards (née Roxborough) was involved in the revision of 'The British Road to Socialism' – the party's programme – in 1977–8 and was a member of the party's Internal Democracy Commission. The relationship

between the Communist Party and matters of race are considered by Evan Smith in his *British Communism and the Politics of Race* (Chicago, 2018).

62. *NWWN*, 2 March 1978.

63. Ian Goodyer, *Crisis Music: The Cultural Politics of Rock Against Racism* (Manchester, 2019); Matthew Worley, *No Future: Punk, Politics and British Youth Culture, 1976–1984* (Cambridge, 2017).

64. *The Stage*, 31 January 1985.

65. Paul Barrett and Hilary Hayward, *Shakin' Stevens* (London, 1983).

66. *Anti-Nazi News* (Newsletter of Cardiff Anti-Nazi League), 24 (14 June 1979); the most useful history of the Anti-Nazi League is by David Renton. David Renton, *Never Again: Rock Against Racism and the Anti-Nazi League, 1976–1982* (London, 2019) and Smith, *British Communism*, pp. 193–8.

67. *Gair Rhydd*, 18 November 1987.

68. 'Intersectionality' was first coined by Kimberlé Crenshaw, an American lawyer, in 1989. Useful guides on its academic practice can be found in Patricia Hill Collins and Sirma Bilge, *Intersectionality* (Cambridge, 2016); Patricia Hill Collins, *Intersectionality as Critical Social Theory* (Durham, NC, 2019).

69. *NG*, 5 July 1974.

70. *NWWN*, 1 July 1965.

71. East Glamorgan Labour Women's Advisory Council, Minutes, 14 May 1966.

72. *NG*, 4 November 1960; *PTG*, 5 November 1965.

73. *PTG*, 29 November 1974.

74. *PTG*, 8 March 1974.

75. GLA, D817/10/1/2, Labour Party Women's Advisory Councils (North and South Wales), Minute Book: 'Annual Meeting of South Wales Labour Women's Organisations, 16 October 1976'; for a note on her appointment see Labour Party, *Report of the Fifty-Second Annual Conference of Labour Women* (London, 1976), p. 4.

76. Ann Clwyd (Labour, Mid and West Wales); Beata Brookes (Conservative, North Wales).

77. Evans and Jones, 'Women in the Labour Party', p. 236.

78. Amy Black and Stephen Brooke, 'The Labour Party, Women and the Problem of Gender', *Journal of British Studies*, 36/4 (1997), 419–52, p. 424.

79. Cited in Evans and Jones, 'Women in the Labour Party', p. 231.

80. *PTG*, 16 June 1977.

81. *NG*, 10 November 1977; *NWWN*, 22 September 1977; *PTG*, 8 June 1978.

82. *NG*, 25 October 1984, 15 November 1984, 25 November 1984.
83. *PTG*, 3 February 1977.
84. BL, Sound Archive, C1420/41, 'Interview with Jane Hutt conducted by Margaretta Jolly, 1 June 2012'.
85. Labour Women's Network, *Uphill All The Way: Labour Women Into Westminster* (London, 1994).
86. Joni Lovenduski and Vicky Randall, *Contemporary Feminist Politics: Women and Power in Britain* (Oxford, 1993), p. 140.
87. Joni Lovenduski, 'United Kingdom: Male Dominance Unbroken?', in Drude Dahlerup and Monique Leyenaar (eds), *Breaking Male Dominance in Old Democracies* (Oxford, 2013), pp. 77–8; Sarah Perrigo, 'Gender Struggles in the British Labour Party from 1979 to 1995', *Party Politics*, 1/3 (1995), 407–17.

6

Women's Liberation, Now!

On 10 November 1975, at precisely a quarter past eight in the evening, BBC Wales broadcast its annual radio lecture, that year called 'Women and Society'. For the first time since the inauguration of the series in the 1930s, the lecturer was a woman. 'I imagine', said the playwright and television dramatist Elaine Morgan,

> the reason I was offered this subject to talk about – and probably the main reason I am here at all – is that this is 1975 and International Women's Year. I don't know how much impact it's made on you to date. I get the impression that in most parts of Wales we haven't hung out a great many flags to celebrate the occasion.[1]

The other reason, which she knew only too well, was that Wales in the 1970s lacked many alternatives: her voice was almost alone in a public sphere dominated by men. In politics, as well as education, business, media and the arts, women were absent from the corridors of power. Midway through her lecture, Elaine Morgan turned her attention to women's liberation, which was then at its height. 'In the more self-conscious suburbs where people keep themselves to themselves', she said,

> women sometimes get together in consciousness-raising groups and steel themselves to the point of rebellion. In working-class areas in places like Wales where the words women's lib are hardly ever uttered you might imagine that nothing of the kind goes on. Don't you believe it.[2]

The raising of women's consciousness took place in the factory canteen, the supermarket, on the streets, in the chapel and in the home. In drawing attention to the formal and informal mechanisms for organisation and liberation, Elaine Morgan laid stress on pragmatism. 'There will, no doubt, be times and places when it will still be relevant to shout the exhilarating old slogan of "Male Chauvinist Pigs Out"', she told listeners, 'but there will be other areas where we may have to adopt a more reasonable and exacting motto, more on the lines of "The Buck Stops Here"'. Much of what was discussed in those informal settings – in canteen or supermarket chats, for example, or on the doorstep – was never captured and is now largely lost. Occasional snippets made it into the newspapers.[3] Yet as recently as 2003, as Avril Rolph observed, the fact that women's liberation existed in Wales at all was 'a source of surprise to many people'.[4] Not least to other (male) historians. 'There is scant evidence', wrote Kenneth O. Morgan dismissively in 1981, 'that the more aggressive or misanthropic forms of "Women's Lib" made much impact in a friendly country like Wales'.[5] Another added that he hoped women's liberation did not want to see a unisex world. 'Where will it end?', he mused, 'I still believe there are some things which can be done better by men'.[6]

The contours of the women's liberation movement are easily mapped, mirroring, as they do, the parallel growth of feminist activity elsewhere in Britain. What came to be recognised as the national women's liberation movement was founded in February 1970 at Ruskin College, Oxford. Several hundred delegates gathered to debate and to formalise the movement's four demands, which were issued as a product of the conference. These were: equal pay, equal educational and job opportunities, free contraception and abortion on demand, and free twenty-four-hour nurseries. Welsh women played their full part, and on their return women's liberation groups were established. In general, the movement was 'at its strongest in the south', but had a 'widespread presence', stretching from Bangor in the north-west to Newport in the south-east.[7] Although the groups often worked together, shared equivalent priorities, and a series of all-Wales women's liberation conferences were held, the first of which occurred in Aberystwyth in July 1974, there was little formality and certainly no established grounds for a 'national' women's liberation movement solely for Wales.[8] There was, as one contemporary directory put it, 'no one centre for the [Welsh] women's movement'.[9] Nor were all Welsh women content with 'our warlike sisters', as one northern commentator put it. She added,

> Why complain about a life which lets you go out when you feel like it, rush through your housework in an hour and go out for the day, or spend an afternoon pottering in the garden. All that washing and cooking and washing up is dull, but you don't have to clock in at nine o'clock on a fine summer's day and stay indoors till the evening![10]

A more practical approach to women's liberation was taken by

Mary Moule of Briton Ferry, who served as mayor of Neath in 1966, and was a long-standing Labour councillor and alderman. At the time she prompted front-page comment in the local press for refusing the title 'Mr Mayor', which was the established address for the role and had been adopted by the first woman to hold the mayoralty, Hilda Howells, in preference to 'Madam Mayor'. 'It has taken 134 years to get women mayors in the borough', she said, 'and I feel I must secure full credit for our sex'.[11] In an interview conducted in 1973, Mrs Moule reiterated her stance that it was right to protest about an office which had become seen as a male privilege, and explained further that whereas 'Women's Lib has become a very funny word ... it is only the lunatic fringe with their talk of burning bras that has given that impression – I think women have a great deal to give to politics'.[12]

*

The first formal women's liberation organisation established in Wales is generally regarded to be the Cardiff Women's Action Group (CWAG), founded in 1970. 'We're not so much a ball of fire', recorded the group self-consciously in 1976, 'more of a bunch of quietly glowing coals, shooting out sparks of activity into different groups'. Indeed, CWAG is best thought of as an umbrella for a variety of activities undertaken on themes such as women and health, housing, consciousness raising, education and women's aid. 'What we have in common', members concluded, 'is a concern for our society and each other as women within it'.[13] This loose structure corresponds with women's liberation groups in English cities, which themselves tended to be 'politically libertarian' and lacked the rigidity of more traditional political-party women's sections.[14] Bronwen Davies, one of those involved in CWAG, recalled that there were:

women who were feminists from quite a wide range of political backgrounds, such as some of the women were also members of the Labour Party at the time, some of the women were not in a political group. Some of the women were in political groups not parties that were too small but I guess what we had in common was a concern, we were feminists we were concerned with women's rights defending and extending them.[15]

The most formal feature of CWAG in its early years was the group's headquarters, in practice a rented office in Charles Street in Cardiff city centre. There members produced pamphlets, undertook the necessary administration to keep their activities going, and endeavoured to operate a telephone advice service three times a week by the end of 1973.[16]

The women's liberation group in Swansea had slightly different roots. There women were active in street campaigns, thought carefully about how to articulate their experiences of social class, were involved in leftist politics and in working-class organisational culture. One of the group's founder members and its most high-profile participant, Jenny Lynn, described in a 2011 interview that she had moved to the city in the aftermath of the 1972 miners' strike and soon joined the International Socialists (the forerunner of the Socialist Workers Party).[17] Through that activism, she was introduced to – and became active in – the city's Claimants' Union, whose primary purpose was to assist with social security applications. It acted as an alternative advice bureau for the unemployed and the vulnerable and agitated for a universal basic income. Members produced a weekly newsletter, the *Dole Express*, with those aims in mind.[18] One of the women Jenny Lynn met was Rose Barnes. From Bonymaen, in the east of Swansea, where she lived with her five children in difficult circumstances, Rose Barnes was part of the 'cutting edge hit squad' and was often at the forefront of direct action – not least leading sit-ins at the dole office in the city centre.[19]

Like many women, Rose Barnes also lived under constant threat of domestic violence, which made her wary of official sources of help. After failing to get help from social services, she planned to commit suicide as a last resort, but her example led women members of the Claimants' Union to rethink and to widen their approach. They began to meet in a house in the Uplands district to discuss how to respond to poverty and to domestic violence, and to raise their consciousness as women. Topics debated ranged widely, from childhood and parental care to sexuality, all with the intention of producing material on these matters for the *Dole Express* and a separate series of leaflets which they distributed around the city – outside schools, in launderettes, and in other places where women were likely to gather without men being present. The leaflets came to be known as *Women Come Together*.[20] The women who worked on the leaflets and the articles for *Dole Express*, initially a small cohort of just six, formed Swansea Women's Liberation Group (SWLG) at the end of 1972.[21] At first, an organisation separate from the Claimants' Union and the International Socialists had not been the intention; members had instead wanted to incorporate women's liberation ideas, but they faced hostility from the predominantly male membership.

Those men did not regard women's liberation as important, overall, at least not in comparison to class conflict and industrial disputes, and so refused to countenance the inclusion of a women's liberation campaign into their work. Although that was a blow, Jenny Lynn, Rose Barnes and the other activists who formed the SWLG did not abandon their radical politics, and remained committed to – and endowed the new group with – the anti-authoritarian 'us not them' attitudes of the International Socialists and the anti-social services habits they had absorbed from their Claimants' Union work. As in Cardiff, core women's liberation activity in Swansea soon generated other work and allied groups. One such was the Battered Wives Action Group, which formed in the east end of Swansea in July 1974, and comprised several members of SWLG as well as other working-class women who did not entirely trust official channels. The Battered Wives Action Group led protests in support of victims of domestic violence and picketed local courts.[22] Some members also organised a squat for women and children left homeless after fleeing violent partners – the unofficial basis for the city's women's refuge which opened, eventually, in 1977. The city's women's centre followed two years later, after a long search for suitable premises – a search which began early in 1975.[23]

As befitted its origins, SWLG was chiefly oriented towards the working-class population in the eastern wards of the city and to identifying and ameliorating the problems which existed for those women. Consequently, Swansea had two women's liberation groups, the second being based at the university college, although they worked closely together on a range of local campaigns.[24] At the start of 1970, women students at the university's single-sex Beck Hall residence went on strike, demanding autonomy and an end to discriminatory rules and regulations in operation on campus. Fifteen students were suspended from their studies after refusing to back down, prompting the Student's Union to call a general strike in solidarity – more than sixty per cent of the student body joined in the two-week-long protest, a figure which rose to nearly ninety-five per cent before the strike ended.[25] Women on campus, as in the city itself, faced wide-ranging discrimination, from being unable to be served in many pubs and bars, to the lack of a campus crèche until 1981, to the general atmosphere of danger in the streets and parks after dark. 'Watch yourselves', recorded the university newspaper in the early 1980s, 'Swansea seems to be the Sexual Perverts Centre of the western world'.[26]

The distinct origins of the Cardiff Women's Action Group, which tended towards the non-political, and the Swansea Women's Liberation Group, which was firmly rooted in grass-roots radical politics, illustrate the challenges of providing a single definition for women's liberation. Diversity of organisation and activity, as well as membership, was typical of the movement. Depending on where an individual activist or participant found themselves, or what they did as members, made for a different sense of things, even when the principal focal points of group campaigns – reproductive rights, family planning, domestic violence, equal pay, social services, housing, education, and consciousness raising – were common across the movement. 'Women pursued feminist campaigns', writes the historian Sue Bruley of this universality, they 'challenged sexism and built feminist counter cultures in their own communities'.[27] Nevertheless, for all that the movement was 'about working-class women as well as middle-class women', for Jenny Lynn it was the battered women like Rose Barnes who were the 'radical feminists' and at the forefront of creating social change.[28] 'Rose believed passionately', wrote Jenny Lynn in an obituary for her friend published in the *Guardian*, 'that if people got together to organise and campaign, they could really get things done'.[29]

Central to feminist campaigning was a woman's right to choose. The 1967 Abortion Act marked a turning point in the struggle for self-determination, but was far from the end of the struggle. Abortion services, although legalised, were difficult to access, and women faced a long battle to convince doctors and health administrators to act in accordance with the law. Six years passed before the first Welsh lunchtime abortion clinic was opened, at the Heath hospital in Cardiff in September 1973. Established ostensibly because of high demand and a shortage of hospital beds, the clinic was in fact little used: just six abortions were carried out there in the first three months of operation. It quickly became the focus of a local campaign to ensure that women were made aware of its services.[30] Campaigners from the Cardiff Women's Action Group discovered that part of the reason for lack of use was the habit of some general practitioners of sending patients to private clinics in London or Birmingham, rather than making use of the local NHS facilities. The health authority had itself also failed to advertise the clinic at the Heath hospital.[31] In 1976, CWAG published its landmark pamphlet *Abortion in Cardiff Now*, an indictment of the failure of Cardiff's NHS abortion services and the continued profiteering of private clinics.

Research undertaken by CWAG showed that whereas in Swansea nine in every ten abortions were carried out by the NHS, in Cardiff more than half were done privately.[32] In addition to a public information campaign and their pamphlet, both of which aimed at increasing knowledge of NHS services, CWAG utilised avenues of public scrutiny to press their case for abortion services. One mechanism was the Community Health Council (CHC), which had been established in 1974 as the voice of the public in the management of each health authority in England and Wales. The annual reports for Cardiff CHC in this period record the volume of pressure campaigners applied, with representations received regularly from women's organisations across the city.[33] Ongoing frustration led to the creation in 1978 of a women's health sub-group, which reported to the CHC. Two years later, the sub-group published its findings into the failure of the city's abortion services, arguing that any provision should be 'consider[ed] as a "matter of policy and resources"'.[34] One of those who went along to put the case for improving access to abortion and other healthcare services designed for women was Deirdre Beddoe, who was then a lecturer in history at the Polytechnic of Wales.[35]

Another of those to join, albeit in an officially appointed rather than voluntary capacity, was Jane Hutt. In oral testimony given as part of the Safe and Legal project in 2017, marking fifty years since the Abortion Act, she recalled that being a member of the Community Health Council had significant advantages, since 'I was then able to raise more formally the issue of our concerns and seek discussions, meetings [and] statistics'. But public scrutiny could not prevent the sudden closure of the daytime clinic at the Heath hospital in 1980, an event which coincided with the stormy passage through parliament of the Abortion (Amendment) Bill. Proposed by the Conservative MP John Corrie and supported on all sides of the Commons, with notably favourable interventions from Labour members such as Leo Abse, who was vigorously opposed to abortion on demand, the bill easily passed its second reading in July 1979, prompting a wave of protest. The largest, estimated at 50,000 people, took place on 28 October 1979 in London and was organised by members of the National Abortion Campaign and the Trades Union Congress. Local action took place as well, with a march of around 200 held in Cardiff in mid-October 1979, organised by the Cardiff Abortion Campaign.[36]

The Cardiff march was subject to police harassment, and women expressed concern 'about the attitude of police to demonstrations in Cardiff, in the light of harassment suffered by other groups'.[37] That alleged harassment, documented in other areas of public life by the Wales Campaign for Civil and Political Liberties in their newsletter *Writing on the Wall* and in a series of publications in the first half of the 1980s, did not deter members of the Cardiff Abortion Campaign from subsequent direct action. Efforts included a form of street theatre, featuring coffins and undertakers, which took place on the steps of the Welsh Office in Cathays Park in February 1982.[38] Such attention-drawing interventions were felt necessary partly because of the political situation and partly because of the growing organisational capacity and presence of the pro-life campaign. Offices of the anti-abortion charity Life opened in the centre of Cardiff and Newport in 1980, and they had had a presence at the Charles Street Carnival, targeting ethnic minorities with anti-abortion messaging.[39] Pro-choice campaigners picketed the carnival stall to minimise its efficacy, undertook protests outside the Life offices, and spent considerable time putting together 'tactics for dealing with Life'.[40] The tussle between the two movements – pro-choice and pro-life – continued through the 1980s.

*

The women's liberation movement had emerged alongside the gay liberation movement in the early 1970s, and together they provided for the development and public expression of lesbian feminist and trans identities. Organisationally, there was considerable cross-over, despite carefully guarded independence. In Cardiff, women's liberation, gay liberation, and lesbian and trans groups all used the same community hubs: the 108 Community

Bookshop in Cathays, and the Rights and Information Bureau in Charles Street. There was an equivalent cross-over in Swansea through the city's women's centre and the Neges bookshop, and in Bangor via Ty Gwydr/The Greenhouse, which functioned in part as the local women's centre and was home to the city's lesbian line. Although there was relatively little direct engagement with lesbian, queer or trans perspectives amongst the Welsh women's liberation groups, despite shared spaces, at the national level there was recognition of women's liberation as an umbrella movement for strands of feminism based on sexuality. The turning point was the sixth national women's liberation conference, held in Edinburgh in 1974, which added the right to a self-defined sexuality and an end to discrimination against lesbians to the movement's core list of demands. The plenary session at which the new clause was discussed was chaired by Jenny Lynn, who later recalled the impact on her own identity.[41]

Organisation of queer women took place in a context of misogyny, even within spaces and groups ostensibly reserved for queer people, and loneliness.[42] As one young woman explained in an interview with *Gay News* in 1976, 'there are two gay bars, one of which doesn't welcome women, and two clubs, one of which doesn't welcome women. You don't stand a chance'. As for the organised gay movement locally, namely the Cardiff branch of the Campaign for Homosexual Equality, which had fewer than a dozen women members, 'that's a lonely hearts club, isn't it', she added, 'I'd never dream of going there'.[43] The two bars were situated in the Royal Hotel and the Bristol Hotel, the latter being 'noticeably more popular with gay women', and of the two clubs – Sirs and Showbiz – the former admitted women only in the aftermath of the Sex Discrimination Act. Sirs was regarded by those who enjoyed the freer and more mixed environment of the

Showbiz club as a 'plastic place full of plastic people', the 'ultimate closet' where looking 'too gay' would bar you from entry. Its defenders insisted that it fulfilled 'a very overdue need'.[44] The absence of specific facilities for queer women prompted those who could travel to make the trip to Bristol, there attending bars such as the Moulin Rouge or events at the Bristol Women's Centre.[45]

There had been tentative attempts to provide public expression of lesbian sexuality in the 1960s, using the platform provided by the Minorities Research Group, which was founded in 1963 as Britain's first openly lesbian campaign organisation, and its national magazine *Arena Three*. The key contact was 'Mrs M.D.' of Swansea, a long-term subscriber to *Arena Three*, who maintained her anonymity partly because her family was prominent in the city and partly because she had yet to discuss her sexuality with her husband.[46] Nevertheless, she provided information and details of her own personal experience to the journalist and poet Mimi Josephson, when the latter wrote an article about lesbians for the *Western Mail* in August 1966.[47] The piece was designed to relate queer women to the debate around the Sexual Offences Bill, which was being sponsored through parliament by Mimi Josephson's cousin, Leo Abse. 'The worst thing', Mrs M.D. explained, 'is the loneliness, the feeling that one is unintegrated, unrecognised, outside society'.[48] One result of the publicity in the Welsh press was a rise in subscriptions to *Arena Three*, but, as Esme Langley, the magazine's founder and editor, lamented, 'no-one has offered to organise informal social gatherings for Welsh and West Country members'.[49]

The earliest known lesbian feminist organisation established in post-war Wales, as I have noted elsewhere, was the women's group created by the small group of women members of the

Cardiff branch of the Campaign for Homosexual Equality.[50] The leading member was Daphne Higuera (née Mogford), a married working-class woman from Caerphilly who was then in her forties.[51] The group began meeting at the Blue Anchor Hotel on St Mary Street early in 1973. Some of its members attended the first ever national women's conference on homosexuality in Manchester in 1974, for instance.[52] But outside CHE circles, it seems not to have been widely known, and by 1975 a survey of CHE branches found that in Cardiff 'women in the group don't want them', separate women's meetings, that is, and in Newport 'the women members are fully integrated'.[53] The contemporary 'West County Three', which was allied to the Minorities Research Group, claimed to cover Cardiff but was in fact based in Bristol and had a geographical remit stretching from Gloucester to Taunton.[54] Unsurprisingly, in a letter to *Sappho* in 1973, 'R.S.' from Cardiff could stress that 'there are no organizations like yours in Wales which have regular meetings'. She added, pointing to the need for such groups, that there were 'only gay clubs which are mainly for boys and to my tastes distinctly sordid in so much as they are rough and cater for sensationalist minorities'.[55]

These points echo comments made in a private letter sent from Llanelli to CHE's national secretary in December 1973. The correspondent was one of very few women to join the Swansea-Carmarthen branch, and she found the experience disconcerting. 'The group is not really a very successful one', she wrote, 'the first meeting was held without its women members (the few as we are or were to my knowledge anyway) being notified of it'. She added,

> The next two meetings I was notified of, although the other
> girls said that they hadn't had any knowledge of any meetings

taking place when I met up with some of them later, so they asked me to notify them when next I heard of any meetings taking place, which I did. The first meeting I attended I was the only girl present amongst numerous boys. This I didn't mind in the least as I get on well with most of the lads but it would be nice to have a few girls there to talk and dance with as well. The second meeting would have been the same if it wasn't for the fact that I took two female guests along with me on this occasion.[56]

The letter continued in this vein, detailing occasions when 'the girls' had been excluded from branch organisation and social activities. 'CHE seems to have a good many male members', she concluded, 'but very few female ones'. Daphne Higuera levelled similar complaints at *Gay News*, noting in 1973 that it took her 'five minutes to read' because there was 'nothing of interest to myself being gay'. She added, 'we don't all want to know the details about cottaging' and appealed for a separate women's page, since 'there must be some news somewhere that would interest us'. The newspaper's editors offered a blunt rebuttal, 'there is little we can do about the one-sided balance in our pages'.[57]

Daphne Higuera's efforts to bring change to the Cardiff CHE branch were followed by a Sappho group in the city later in 1973, by the South Glamorgan Gay Women's Group, which was based in Barry, in 1975, and by a women's group within West Glamorgan CHE in 1976.[58] The Cardiff Sappho group seems to have had a limited range, with one woman from Carmarthenshire writing at around the same time that 'when I read in your magazine of all the groups that are going on up and down the country, I feel out of it down here, if you know what I mean'.[59] In the north, the lead was taken by Gwynedd CHE. At the group's main monthly meeting in Llandudno in February 1976, it was noted that 'there were no women present' and to generate interest they arranged a women's social a month later. The event was held in Llanfairfechan, halfway between Bangor and Llandudno, and drew interest from across the northern counties of Wales – several women from Denbighshire who were otherwise members of Chester CHE were invited to bolster turnout.[60] A women's group was formed as part of Gwynedd CHE by the end of 1976, and women from the branch were present at the National Organisation for Gay Women's foundation conference in Nottingham in November 1977.[61] As were women from Swansea.[62]

A second society, known as the North Wales Lesbian Group, based in Bangor, was advertised in the pink press from the summer of 1976 until the summer of 1978, although its relationship with the movements within CHE is not immediately clear from the surviving records.[63] What is apparent, however, is that the existence of these groups prompted local discussion, particularly in the women's columns of newspapers such as the *North Wales Weekly News*, of lesbian experience and enabled more women to begin the process of coming out. 'Sparked off by the women's lib movement', observed Pamela Rae for the *North Wales Weekly News*, 'the courage of lesbian women has ... extended to, as they put it, coming out of the closet ... [and] acknowledging their lesbianism openly'.[64] In the valleys, where women took the lead in organising the local branch of the Gay Liberation Front, there was more open discrimination, with women as the target. The co-chair of Aberdare GLF, Barbara Dudley, was denounced by one pub landlord as a prostitute, for instance, and GLF were barred from meeting in pubs in the Cynon Valley – they took refuge in the Red Cow in Merthyr Tydfil, which was widely known as the most gay-friendly pub in the area.[65]

Given the challenges of organising within the male-dominated gay movement, lesbian feminists found women's liberation much more comfortable, although they continued to reach out to lesbian organisations across Britain and internationally. Kath O'Driscoll from Cwmbran, who established a branch of Gemma, the disabled lesbian women's society, in the late 1970s, for instance, appealed for pen pals in *Focus*, the magazine of the Boston chapter of the American lesbian society, Daughters of Bilitis.[66] Women's liberation magazines provided space to advertise lesbian holidays, lesbian lines and other advice services, published personal advertisements, and pointed towards the various (though few and often part-time) women-only venues. But the relationship between the women's liberation movement and lesbian feminists was not always an easy one. By the end of the 1970s, there was a degree of conflict between those who felt gender and sexuality were separate issues and those, always the overwhelming majority, who felt they were closely and irrevocably connected. 'I often feel that even in the movement', wrote one Cardiff lesbian in the *Cardiff Women's Liberation Magazine* in 1981, 'I have to compromise myself ... I shouldn't have to compromise as much as I do'. She added,

Hundreds of times I've been asked about being a lesbian. Was it a sexual attraction? True love, at first? Your feminist politics? Basically, all the questions ask; why are you a lesbian? I don't mind answering because I think there is a very genuine interest when women ask. I also think 'coming out' is political – because society is heterosexist. Women are not brought up with the notion of choice around sexuality. Everything says 'you will be heterosexual'. Heterosexuality is assumed.

The article was symptomatic of an apparent division between women's liberation and lesbian feminism, and prompted one reader to comment that the true problem lay in the idea that there are 'only these two choices – bent or straight'. She appealed to readers to think about the possibility that human sexuality was fluid, that women can have 'different preferences, in different degrees or at different times of their lives', and urged members to be aware of 'our own form of feminist sexism, which is surely based on a lack of understanding, and therefore a lack of accept-ance of each other's right to choose'.

A Welsh trans liberation movement was considerably smaller by comparison with its lesbian and gay equivalents. For a long time, the movement lacked the advertising space afforded to lesbian feminist activism in the women's libera-tion magazines and newsletters, and there were sometimes sharp divisions, based on sexuality, between transmen, trans-women, those who would now be recognised as non-binary, and cross-dressers. To say nothing of the conflict with a distinct minority in the women's liberation movement in the 1970s who viewed trans people as 'traitors to the women's movement and to feminism generally'.[67] These more hostile attitudes have lingered, and provide some historic background to the fierce debates between trans-inclusive feminists and their biological-determinist opponents which have raged in Britain for several years. The Older Lesbian Network, the Welsh branch of which was formed in Cardiff in 1993, and which provided a women-only space for those aged over 35, considered the question of trans-inclusivity in a vigorous internal debate which culminated in a ballot in the spring of 2001 on the question of whether transwomen should be admitted into the network. The year before, as part of the discussions, the OLN's Welsh newsletter even considered whether (in the language then current) 'a trans-sexual [can] be a lesbian'.[68]

The earliest identifiable trans liberation organisation in Wales appears to have been the Transvestites National Group (variously called the Nationwide Transvestite Group), which was created in 1973 by Martina Rees, a transwoman from Bargoed.[69] For administration purposes, the group was headquartered at the Rights and Information Bureau in Cardiff, where it joined the other local elements of the LGBTQ+ civil rights movement and the women's liberation movement. A branch of the American Transsexual Action Organization (TAO), led by a transwoman called Kym, also existed in Swansea in the mid-1970s, although it seems to have been formed after the Cardiff group.[70] Swansea TAO joined with other branches around Britain and Northern Ireland in a loose network typically referred to by historians as TAO-UK (to distinguish from its more powerful American counterpart). As Susan Stryker has noted, 'TAO-UK was a short-lived group devoted to anti-sexism, anti-racism and peace campaigns that also specifically sought the right of self-determined medical treatment for transsexual people'.[71] By the end of the 1970s, both Swansea TAO and the Transvestites National Group in Cardiff had disappeared. Their effective successor, the South Wales TV/TS Group, came into existence in the 1990s, with Martina Rees at the helm.[72] It appears to have been known as Trans Wales by 1997.[73]

*

Viewed as discrete groups and societies, with different strands of feminism guiding activity, the women's liberation movement in the 1970s can seem quite fragmented in retrospect. But there were common themes and points of concern which united organised women, not least male violence. Welsh women joined in with the 'reclaim the night' campaign launched in the late 1970s against the backdrop of the Yorkshire Ripper murders and appeals from police for women to stay indoors at night. Sixty women marched through central Leeds in 1977 and their action was followed by a series of similar marches through central London and other major cities over the next few years. After much internal debate, the first reclaim the night march through Cardiff occurred in March 1979 and was attended by more than fifty women. Members used the opportunity to talk, to leaflet and, as one of those who marched recalled, 'to reach women who may have no contact with feminism'. She added,

> I am aware that one or a few such actions don't make it any easier next time we walk alone at night. We have to think of many more tactics. I see the main effects of this march as consciousness-raising for other women, and as strengthening for ourselves.[74]

Further reclaim the night activity occurred throughout the early 1980s, including just before Christmas 1981, when a group of thirty marched from the Student's Union building in Park Place, through St Mary Street, and on to the STAR leisure centre in Splott. Marchers chanted and leafleted but found the attitudes of the police and men on the street disconcerting and disorientating. 'They were flippant at first', recalled one of those present, 'but soon became threatening and aggressive'. Looking on the bright side, she concluded that 'the fact of their finding our presence disturbing did make me feel it was an important statement for us to make'. The jeering convinced those women on the 1981 march that feminist protest culture locally needed bolstering with songs and chants 'ones that everyone could sing'. The marchers suggested that 'the Women's Centre buys or gets hold of a ... songbook and we get into some communal singing, so we have got this shared knowledge/culture'.[75] A renewed activist culture was not easily implemented, of course. In May 1983, after a further reclaim the night march, the same issues recurred. 'Instead of filling me with a sense of strength and unity with my sisters', lamented one marcher, 'it left me feeling isolated and confused'.

The forty women who marched faced jeers and taunts; some men even deliberately stalked the march as it progressed through the streets. There was a palpable sense that the police were only too keen for violence to occur. 'Perhaps they were bored', thought one member, writing in the Cardiff women's liberation newsletter in the aftermath,

> or wanted to entertain us with a show of macho chivalry. But when they do that to <u>anyone</u>, it surely must be our concern. Police brutality can and frequently is turned against women, lesbians in particular, and black people. I don't want to live in a world where oppressive men are kept at bay by an equally oppressive (male) police force.[76]

The frustrations felt by those who sought a more vigorous programme of direct action were balanced by the feelings of those who believed that there was a need to be more pragmatic and less boisterous. 'The image of the outraged, placard-waving feminist is very off putting', suggested the organisers of Swansea Women's Festival in the summer of 1980, 'and we wanted to show that women can generate terrific warmth and laughter and that we need that supportive and friendly atmosphere to find the strength to carry on the fight'.[77]

This appeal for pragmatism and, as was seen in the previous chapter, the contemporary shift towards more formal political activity, as members of the women's liberation movement migrated into the Labour Party, provided some of the response to Thatcherism in the 1980s. To the list of political activity, we can add the environmental and peace movements and the renewed campaign for devolution towards the end of the decade. The counterpart to politics lay in the rise of forms of direct action, such as the Greenham Common march and the women's peace camp, the women's support groups of the 1984–5 miners' strike, and the Women Against Pit Closures movement. This activism has been typically regarded as the catalyst for a 'new direction' for feminism and the women's movement.[78] But how much really changed? The main organisational themes remained reproductive rights, material conditions, domestic violence, housing, jobs, social security, peace and the environment. Direct action had always been part of the approach to campaigning. Both elements can be seen in the work of the Women's Rights Committee for Wales, formed in December 1974.[79] Its origins lay in a conference sponsored by the National Council for Civil Liberties and held in Cardiff the previous month, when 200 delegates debated equal pay, anti-discrimination, the relationship between women and trades unions, and the need for a working women's charter.[80]

'Our ideal is to help the whole woman to emerge from the shadows, liberated', the group explain in *Spare Rib* two years later, 'we work to persuade society to help women maintain their family roles, while making these compatible with working outside the home and taking part in political life'.[81] In 1975, the Women's Rights Committee for Wales became the first organisation from the United Kingdom to present a petition to the European Parliament – their demands included a revision to

the common market directives on work to ensure equal treatment for men and women. They were active in conducting and
disseminating research into contemporary social and economic
conditions, publishing pamphlets, and holding conferences on
topics such as women in work, industrial tribunals, equality and
the implications of the silicon chip. As a supplement to this policy discussion, and to ensure that the direct action roots of the
women's movement were not entirely lost, the Women's Rights
Committee for Wales also organised protests and marches,
including the March Against Women's Unemployment held on
4 September 1982.[82] Setting off in the morning from Pontypridd,
where participants were addressed by Dora Cox, a veteran of the
hunger marches of the 1930s, and the former communist mayor
of Rhondda, Annie Powell, the demonstration arrived at Cardiff's
city hall that afternoon. They were met by the lord mayor and
Jane Hutt, who had been elected to the county council in 1981.

What was most obviously different after 1979 was the
change of government and the arrival in Downing Street of
Mrs Thatcher, whose attitudes to gender and the role of women
in society seemed (at least to members of the women's liberation movement) reactionary: a clear indication that there was
a broad spectrum of views, not only about politics, but about
status and ultimately how to achieve equality. Thus, in the early
1980s, awareness of material conditions and the inequalities
exacerbated by government policies resulted in more frequent
discussions of social class. 'The women's movement has in general tried to avoid the question of class', observed one member of
the Cardiff Women's Action Group at the end of 1983, 'it could
incorporate women of all classes because it was a social movement although it had political demands ... today this seems no
longer possible'. She added,

> Thatcher is not unique, nor an exceptional phenomenon nor a puppet of men. She is one of a group of right-wing women. An increasing growing group ... [with] supporters in groups like the Northern Ireland Peace Women, Women for Life and the women of Newbury who attack the peace camps. What definitions can we use to distinguish between groups? I.e. some women in WFLOE [Women for Life on Earth – the organisers of the Greenham protests] do not agree with abortion, some left-wing groups do not support autonomous women's groups. Are these groups reactionary?[83]

Earlier in the year, a group of left-wing women had met to form a socialist-feminist group in Cardiff, prompted in part by the absence of political discussion in the women's movement, the uneven experience of joining the Labour Party, and a desire 'to have a means of crossing over the boundaries of Parties and of the issue-based groups within the women's movement to create a greater sense of unity and solidarity'. At the heart of socialist feminism, at least for the women who established the Cardiff group, was a consideration of the 'most effective ways to work to affect working class consciousness and mobilise working class women'.[84] The group met regularly throughout 1983 and into 1984.[85] In the summer of 1983, a separate working-class women's liberation group was formed by those tired of the absence of class discussion. 'Working class women have been conspicuous in the WLM by their absence', complained one member, 'this is no accident but is due to the particular forms that their oppression takes: lack of access to money, "free" time, information and many of the privileges that middle class women take for granted'.[86]

These articulations of a more radical, class-orientated feminism followed a socialist-feminist forum in Cardiff in June 1979, and a subsequent debate on class and classism held at Cardiff Women's Centre in June 1983.[87] Both took place in the after-math of Conservative victories at general elections. 'It is vital', stated the advertisement for the latter event, 'that we discuss the oppression of working-class women by middle-class women before the women who have the power divide us any further in this city'.[88] The outbreak of the miners' strike nine months later provided a practical demonstration of these debates, as working-class women across the coalfields of Britain organised to sustain their communities and their families and appeared to step into the public sphere for the first time, and women in cities such as Cardiff and Swansea organised to fundraise and provide other material support.[89] There was considerable cross-over of membership between the radical feminist groups which had sprung up in Cardiff immediately prior to the strike, for instance, and those focused on the strike itself, such as Cardiff Women Against Pit Closures and the Cardiff Miners' Support Group.[90] In the coalfield itself, anti-strike activism provided a strong sense of camaraderie and community, and a form of lib-eration from domestic duties. 'That's one good thing about it really', recalled Margaret Donovan, who was active in the Neath, Dulais and Swansea Valleys' Miners' Support Group, 'got me out of the house'.

For those working-class women who were activated by the strike, the events of 1984–5 proved a turning point in their lives and, by their own testimony, things were never quite the same again. But oral history can be misleading and there has been a tendency amongst historians of contemporary Wales to draw too sharp a distinction between the lives women led before the strike, and those which came afterwards, and too little recogni-tion given to the women's movement of earlier decades. It is better to think of the miners' strike, instead, as a large large-scale and practical exercise in consciousness raising, particularly about politics, about feminism, about community action, and about women's labour history. That raised consciousness was the most profound change of all. 'Whatever the miners' strike have done', observed one woman from Blaengwynfi, 'it have shown people can stay out, can stick together, and I think it have taught these kids something'. Another woman, who was from the Dulais valley, felt that 'my attitudes have changed through the strike. I thought I was a socialist before, now I know what socialism is – it's a whole way of life, and we're living it in our valley right now'. A third added, by way of agreement, that 'the socialists were the poorest of the poor ... [and] the poor had to keep together in order to survive'.

Those anticipating an upsurge in the women's liberation movement after the miners' strike were soon to be disappointed; by the end of the decade groups formed in the 1970s had fragmented and their magazines ceased publication. Cardiff women's liberation newsletter, indicatively, closed at the end of 1989. In publishing terms, the outstanding creation of the 1980s was Honno, the Welsh women's press. Its origins lay in a meeting of like-minded women in 1984, although it was not until 1986 that the press was launched as an independent co-operative. With financial backing from hundreds of shareholders and a European grant, Honno set out to deliberately challenge the patriarchy of the book industry by bringing back into print 'lost' classics by Welsh women in English or Welsh, publishing contemporary writing, and providing opportunities for women as writers.[91] The first title was Elizabeth Davis's autobiography, *Betsy Cadwaladyr: A Balaclava Nurse*, originally published in the nineteenth century. Three years after Honno's launch, the press achieved a notable success when Carol Ann Courtney's autobiographical novel *Morphine and Dolly Mixtures* (1989) was awarded Book of the Year by the Welsh Arts Council. It was adapted for television two years later by director Karl Francis and broadcast as part of BBC Two's *Screen Two* series.

Honno formed part of the institutional legacy of the Welsh women's liberation movement and was one of a series of new bodies, established in the mid-1980s, which were rooted in second-wave feminism and were sufficiently strong to survive into the changed economic and social landscape of the 1990s. The focus was to be on education and training suitable for a post-industrial world, thereby fulfilling the second aim of the women's liberation movement: 'equal educational and job opportunities'.[92] Some of those who had been active in the Neath, Swansea and Dulais Valleys' Miners' Support Group came together in the aftermath of the miners' strike to form the Valleys Initiative for the Employment of Women (VIEW) and to open two training centres: one in Banwen, at the head of the Dulais Valley, known as the Dulais Opportunity for Voluntary Enterprise (DOVE) Workshop, the other in Glynneath, at the head of the Vale of Neath, known as the Glynneath Training Centre.[93] Two years later, the launch of the Valleys Initiative for Adult Education at the DOVE Workshop pushed connections between lifelong learning and community development and regeneration one step further.[94] Finally, in 1993, the DOVE Workshop became the central node in the pioneering Community University of the Valleys, providing degree-level qualifications in a local setting in conjunction with University College Swansea and the South Wales Miners' Library.[95]

The DOVE Workshop mirrored the examples of Amman Valley Enterprises, which was created in 1987 by women who had been active locally during the miners' strike, and South Glamorgan Women's Workshop, which opened in central Cardiff in January 1984 with financial support from the local authority and the European Social Fund. Both were reactions to the 'increasingly urgent needs of women ... to gain marketable qualifications'.[96] In the case of South Glamorgan Women's Workshop, specialised in delivering classes in electronics and the use of computers to unqualified women over the age of 25, expanding the curriculum later in the decade to include subjects such as carpentry, plastering and business studies, all of which had traditionally been the preserve of men. Each of these training centres provided facilities, such as a crèche, designed to enable mothers and the unemployed to study and to train. In Cardiff, the teaching staff comprised women, too, illustrating that such career pathways were possible and sustaining the principle that this was a facility of and for women. As one former student of the DOVE Workshop recalled, it was 'a non-threatening environment within which I thrived and it gave me the confidence and flexibility to continue doing various courses over a period of years'. In that sense, and for all the challenges it faced, the Welsh women's liberation movement succeeded.

Notes

1. Elaine Morgan, *Women and Society* (Cardiff, 1975), p. 3; Elaine Morgan's life and career are detailed in Daryl Leeworthy, *Elaine Morgan: A Life Behind the Screen* (Bridgend, 2020).
2. Morgan, *Women and Society*, p. 14.
3. *NG*, 25 June 1971, 7 July 1972, 27 October 1972.
4. Rolph, 'A movement of its own', 87–95.
5. Kenneth O. Morgan, *Rebirth of a Nation: Wales, 1881–1981* (Oxford, 1981), p. 355.
6. *NWWN*, 14 October 1971. The speaker was Cyril R. Williams, lecturer in social history at Bangor.

7. Deirdre Beddoe, 'Women and Politics in Twentieth Century Wales', *National Library of Wales Journal*, 33/3 (2004), 341.

8. *SpR*, 23 May 1974.

9. Carolyn Faulder, Christine Jackson and Mary Lewis, *The Women's Directory* (London, 1976), p. 179.

10. *NWWN*, 28 June 1973.

11. *NG*, 1 April 1966.

12. *NG*, 13 October 1972.

13. Both quotes occur in 'On the Road', *SpR*, 52 (November 1976), 14.

14. Sue Bruley, 'Women's Liberation at the Grass Roots: a view from some English towns, *c*.1968–1990', in Laurel Foster and Sue Bruley (eds), *Historicising the Women's Liberation Movement in the Western World, 1960–1999* (London, 2018), p. 28.

15. 'Interview with Bronwen Davies for Safe & Legal Project, 15 September 2017'. Available online: *https://www.peoplescollection.wales/items/1152046* (accessed 27 March 2020).

16. Rolph, 'A movement of its own', p. 44; *SpR*, 19 (January 1974), 27; *Women's Report*, 1/6 (September–October 1973), 18.

17. BLSA, C1420/16: Interview conducted with Jenny Lynn by Rachel Cohen, 27–28 April 2011.

18. Annie Miller, Toru Yamamori and Almaz Zelleke, 'The Gender Effects of Basic Income', in Malcolm Torry (ed.), *The Palgrave International Handbook of Basic Income* (Basingstoke, 2019), pp. 139–40; Ian Bone, *Bash the Rich: True-Life Confessions of an Anarchist in the UK* (London, 2006), p. 59.

19. Bone, *Bash the Rich*, p. 61.

20. Jenny Lynn, 'Memories of Swansea Women's Liberation', talk delivered at Llafur Day School on Gay and Women's Liberation, March 2017. Notes in author's possession.

21. Rolph, 'A movement of its own', p. 47.

22. *Spare Rib*, 64 (November 1977), 10.

23. WGA, Jenny Lynn Papers, DWAW3: Letter from Swansea Women's Liberation Group to Swansea Council, 11 February 1975.

24. Rolph, 'A movement of its own', p. 48; Sam Blaxland notes similar initiatives: *Swansea University: Campus and Community in a Post-War World, 1945–2020* (Cardiff, 2020), pp. 216–17. Cardiff also had its own university women's liberation group.

25. Blaxland, *Swansea University*, pp. 167–8.

26. *Double Take*, 15 October 1982; cited in Blaxland, *Swansea University*, p. 216.

27. Sue Bruley, 'Women's Liberation at the Grass Roots: A View from some English towns, *c.*1968–1990', *Women's History Review*, 25/5 (2015), 724.

28. Lynn, 'Memories'.

29. Jenny Lynn, 'Rose Barnes', *The Guardian*, 7 October 2005.

30. 'Lunchtime abortion', *SpR*, 2 (August 1972), 31.

31. '& in England', *SpR*, 22 (April 1974), 27.

32. 'Secret Clinic', *SpR*, 49 (August 1976), 28; *Abortions in Cardiff Now* (Cardiff, 1976), p. 2. Available online: *https://www.peoplescollection.wales/items/860186* (accessed 26 March 2020).

33. Cardiff Community Health Council, *First Annual Report* (Cardiff, 1976), pp. 15–16.

34. Cardiff Community Health Council Women's Health Sub-Group, 'Discussion Paper on Day-Care Abortion Facilities in South Glamorgan, October 1980'. Available online: *https://www.peoplescollection.wales/items/860586* (accessed 30 March 2020).

35. Rolph, 'A movement of its own', p. 46.

36. *SWE*, 15 October 1979.

37. *SWE*, 29 October 1979.

38. *WM*, 10 February 1982.

39. Cardiff Abortion Campaign, Minutes of Meeting, 3 July 1980. Available online: *https://www.peoplescollection.wales/items/859906* (accessed 30 March 2020).

40. Cardiff Abortion Campaign, Minutes of Meeting, 7 August 1980. Available online: *https://www.peoplescollection.wales/items/860526* (accessed 30 March 2020).

41. BL, Jenny Lynn Interview.

42. LSE, Special Collections, Hall-Carpenter Archive, Albany Trust Records, 15/10, Social Worker's Files, Case Analysis, 1973–5. Reference here to 'Lonely Lesbian' living in Neath and a 'transsexual' living in Swansea, both of whom were referred to the Albany Trust for support and advice.

43. Keith Howes, 'Cardiff', *Gay News*, 4–11 November 1976.

44. Howes, 'Cardiff'.

45. The Bristol women's liberation newsletter, *Move*, maintained a list of friendly pubs and clubs of interest to its readers. These included the Cavern Club and King's Head Hotel in Newport, and the Showbiz in Cardiff. The list noted simply that 'Sirs is for men'. See, for instance: *Move*, 20 (July–August 1976).

46. *Arena Three*, 11 (November 1965); *Arena Three*, 3/7 (August 1966).

47. *Arena Three*, 3/8 (September 1966).

48. *Arena Three*, 3/8 (September 1966).

49. *Arena Three*, 3/8 (September 1966).

50. LSE, HCA/CHE/7/153: Letter from Chris Johnson to Paul Templeton, 11 October 1972.

51. Daryl Leeworthy, *A Little Gay History of Wales* (Cardiff, 2019), pp. 99–100. Daphne May Higuera (1930–2002) was the child of James Mogford (1890–1944), a railway signalman, and his wife Rose Louise (née Clavey, 1892–1976). Her husband, Manuel Higuera, was born in Butetown in 1932.

52. *Sappho*, 1/12 (1973), 14.

53. Campaign for Homosexuality, *CHE Bulletin*, 3/5, May 1975, Appendix B: Women's Meetings.

54. *Arena Three*, 9/2 (March 1972).

55. *Sappho*, 1/10 (1973), 6.

56. LSE, HCA/CHE/7/153: Letter from S. Howells, 1 December 1973.

57. *Gay News*, April 1973, 2. See also the response a few months earlier, in response to a letter from a woman called Betty appealing for more news about lesbians, which put the onus on women to provide news. *Gay News* (November 1972), 2.

58. *Sappho*, 2/1 (1973), 21; *Sappho*, 4/9 (1976), 33.

59. *Sappho*, 1/12 (1973), 7.

60. Gwynedd CHE, *Newsletter No. 3* (February–March 1976).

61. Gwynedd CHE, *Newsletter No. 19* (October 1977); *Gay News*, 103 (23 September–6 October 1976), 33.

62. *Sappho*, 3/8 (1975), 9–11.

63. *Gay News*, 124 (28 July–10 August 1976), 19; *Gay News*, 144 (1–14 June 1978), 21.

64. *NWWN*, 27 October 1977.

65. *Gay News*, 20 May–6 June 1976; *Lunch*, 21 (1973), 39; *Lunch*, 22 (1973), 32. *Lunch* was a London-based gay liberation magazine.

66. *Focus: A Journal for Lesbians* (July 1978), 2. See also her appeal in the New Jersey-based lesbian feminist satirical magazine *Albatross* (Summer 1978), 6.

67. *Gay News*, 19 October–1 November 1978.

68. Older Lesbian Network (Wales), *Newsletter*, May 2000.

69. *Lunch*, 22 (1973), 32.

70. Bishopsgate Institute, Switchboard Records, SB/5/1/1: Logbook for April–August 1975, entry for 9 June 1975. Other TAO groups noted were Belfast and Coventry.

71. Susan Stryker, '(De)subjugated Knowledges: An Introduction to Transgender Studies', in Susan Stryker and Stephen Whittle (eds), *The Transgender Studies Reader* (London, 2006), p. 6.

72. *Narcissus: TV/TS Magazine*, 4/1 (1992); *Transgender Tapestry*, 78 (Winter 1996), D18.

73. *Gay Times*, February 1997, 125.

74. Maggie Christie, 'Reclaim the Night March in Cardiff', *Cardiff Women's Liberation Newsletter*, 4 (April 1979), 4.

75. 'Reclaim the Night March', *Cardiff Women's Liberation Newsletter* (December 1981) (no pagination).

76. 'Clare', 'The Cardiff Reclaim the Night March – A Personal View', *Cardiff Women's Liberation Newsletter* (June 1983), 12–13.

77. *SpR*, 97 (August 1980).

78. Beddoe, *Out of the Shadows*, p. 163.

79. 'Women's Rights in Wales', *SpR*, 32 (February 1975), 27.

80. 'Shortlist', *SpR*, 28 (October 1974), 31.

81. 'On The Road', *SpR*, 52 (September 1976), 14.

82. Beddoe, *Out of the Shadows*, p. 162; 'Shortlist', *SpR*, 122 (September 1982), 30.

83. 'Women and Class', *Cardiff Women's Newsletter* (December 1983), 1–2.

84. *Cardiff Women's Liberation Newsletter* (May 1983), 9–10; Glamorgan Archives, Barbara Castle Papers, D1600/2/8, report of meeting to form a socialist-feminist group, 20 March 1983.

85. Glamorgan Archives, Barbara Castle Papers, D1600/2/9, Correspondence relating to socialist feminist group, 1983; D1600/2/12, minutes and notes relating to socialist feminist group, 1983.

86. 'Working Class Women's Group Seeks Funds', *Cardiff Women's Newsletter* (August 1983), 20.

87. *Cardiff Women's Liberation Newsletter*, 5 (June 1979).

88. 'Events', *Cardiff Women's Newsletter* (June 1983), 2.

89. That act of 'stepping out' is the main conclusion reached by Hywel Francis in his *History On Our Side* (London, 2015).

90. Glamorgan Archives, D1600/2/6, Cardiff Miners' Support Group Papers, 1984; D1600/2/7, Cardiff Women Against Pit Closures papers, 1984; DSWG, Women's Support Group papers; Cardiff University Special

Collections and Archives, Cardiff Trades Council Records, 321/16.45–46, miners' strike papers, 1984–6.

91. A. Howells, 'Honno: The New Welsh Women's Press Challenges the Publishing Patriarchy', *Radical Wales*, 11 (1986), 10.

92. Sonia Reynolds, 'Women and the regeneration of the South Wales Valleys', in Peter Alheit and Hywel Francis (eds), *Adult Education in Changing Industrial Regions* (Marburg, 1989), pp. 83–8.

93. Mair Francis, 'Dulais Opportunity for Voluntary Enterprise', in Sonia Reynolds and Hywel Francis (eds), *Learning From Experience* (Swansea, 1989)

94. Hywel Francis, 'The Valleys Initiative for Adult Education', in Alheit and Francis, *Adult Education*, pp. 89–96; Hywel Francis, 'Intellectual Property, First Time Around: The Reinvention of the South Wales Miners' Library', *Llafur*, 9/1 (2004), 27–31.

95. Mair Francis, *Up the DOVE! The History of the DOVE Workshop in Banwen* (Ferryside, 2008); Hywel Francis, *Do Miners Read Dickens: Communities, Universities and a New Beginning* (Swansea, 1994).

96. Ash Amin, Angus Cameron and Ray Hudson, *Placing the Social Economy* (London, 2002), p. 34.

Conclusion

B y the 1990s, the women's movement was at a crossroads. The spirit which had fuelled the women's liberation movement appeared to have gone into decline, and many of the groups which were established in the 1970s and early 1980s were disbanded. Indicatively, South Glamorgan County Council was the only local authority in Wales to set up a women's committee, a powerful mechanism for affirmative action, which it did in 1984. What remained was the infrastructure: women's centres, women's aid, lesbian lines, and the new women's training centres. The women's movement had evolved in previous generations, of course, moving from Chartism to co-operation, from suffrage to social democratic politics, and so women's liberation appeared to evolve into a more targeted campaign for devolution and into a feminist response to de-industrialisation. But what made the 1990s distinct was a crisis of knowledge – the historical memory of the women's liberation movement began to wane, and the ongoing absence of women's history either on the shelves or in the classroom meant that the achievements of Welsh women were not widely known or were easily stereotyped. The comforting symbols of the 'Welsh mam' or women dressed in the red flannel costume designed by Lady Llanover in the nineteenth century were otherwise thin disguises for historical understanding which focused almost entirely on men.

Deirdre Beddoe's *Welsh Convict Women*, the first modern work of Welsh women's history to be published, had appeared in 1979, and provided the catalyst for further historical and literary studies, community education courses, and film documentaries through the 1980s and early 1990s, although in practice the historical studies were fewer in number compared with the literary. In November 1981, Beddoe joined a co-operative of women film-makers to form the South Wales Women's Film Group. Over the next few years, they created several documentaries, including *Here Comes the Bride* (1982) and *Something Else in the House* (1985), detailing aspects of the collective experience of women in Wales. This was followed, in the aftermath of the miners' strike, which brought a new wave of members into the co-operative, by Red Flannel Films. Based at Chapter Arts Centre in Cardiff, Red Flannel developed a strong relationship with Channel Four, which provided funding for the company's work. Red Flannel's landmark documentary, *Mam*, was produced in 1988. *Special Delivery* followed in 1991. Both tackled the role of women in Welsh society, in both domestic and public settings, detailing the consistent sacrifices made over generations, all in favour of men. As one of the film-makers later recalled,

> There were a lot of tears, often from men, because they would say it's the first time they'd heard their mother's story or realised the work that women had put in to keeping the mining communities going ... there was always that feeling that women's role and contribution to history was up there on the screen.[1]

Red Flannel were part of a wave of community video production in the 1980s, much of it dedicated to documenting lives otherwise little seen. Community Video Workshop, which was also based at the Chapter Arts Centre, was especially prolific, putting together nearly two dozen films between 1981 and 1990, many of which focused on the mining communities of the valleys. Swansea Women's History Group, working in conjunction with the Department of Adult and Continuing Education at University College Swansea, likewise produced a series of notable films in the 1980s and early 1990s, including *Back of the Front Line* (1984), about women's work in munitions factories during the world wars; *Smiling and Splendid Women* (1986), about the impact of the miners' strike in the Neath, Swansea and Dulais valleys; and *Swansea Conchie Controversy* (1991), about the peace movement and conscientious objection during the First World War.

Teaching women's history, as opposed to capturing it on film, was especially limited, except in extramural departments and in adult education. The earliest women's studies courses in Wales were organised by the Extra Mural Department at University College Cardiff in the mid-1970s, with classes taught eventually in Cowbridge, Newport and Pontypridd, as well as in the city itself.[2] This provision 'challenged the male-centred learning of the traditional [university] curriculum' and built on older patterns of community-based adult learning tailored to women, in existence since the interwar years.[3] In 1989, Cardiff launched its pioneering part-time postgraduate course in women's studies, covering topics such as feminist theory, gender, the social position of women, history, psychology and social policy. A further postgraduate course was provided at Swansea a few years later. In the 1990s, the collaborative 'Project Grace' initiative launched by the combined extramural departments of the University of

Wales provided for the teaching of women's history in communities across Wales. Learning drew on a ten-volume teaching pack published in 1994, and was conceived of by teaching staff, such as Martin Wright at Aberystwyth, as 'providing students with the methodological tools' with which the 'present generation of Welsh women [can] create their own literate past'.[4]

Apart from the intervention of extramural and adult education, women's studies were generally absent from mainstream Welsh higher education in the 1980s and 1990s. As Angela John recorded in 1991: 'there are *no* women lecturers working on women's history/gender of the nineteenth or twentieth centuries in the University Colleges' History departments and only one (at the Polytechnic of Wales) in higher education in Wales'.[5] Prior to the publication of the Project Grace teaching resources, part of the challenge was the relative paucity of historical research – a point Deirdre Beddoe had made in 1980.[6] A decade later, the appearance of *Our Mothers' Land* (1991), a collection of essays on the history of women in modern Wales edited by Angela John, was heralded as 'the first book' on the subject. The following year Sian Rhiannon Williams's Welsh-language study of women and teaching in Monmouthshire appeared, and Deirdre Beddoe's *Out of the Shadows*, the first monograph detailing the historical experience of women in Wales in the twentieth century, was published in 2000. There has been a notable acceleration of publications on Welsh women's history, particularly in accessible book-length studies, since that time. However, as Martin Wright has cautioned, 'legitimate questions remain regarding the extent to which advances in literate knowledge about Welsh women's history are being distributed'.[7]

There is much less question about the identification and subsequent gathering of archival material and its potential for historical research, although in the 1990s this was also a major concern amongst historians of the Welsh women's movement. In 1995, two years before the foundation of the Women's Archive of Wales, Ursula Masson, then a lecturer at the University of Glamorgan (now the University of South Wales), received funding to document and catalogue the Welsh women's liberation movement. The resulting South Wales Feminist History and Archive Project, undertaken with Avril Rolph as research assistant, established for the first time the extent of the documentary legacy of women's liberation and has ensured its recovery and permanent survival in the archives.[8] Ursula Masson's project recalled her earlier work as an extramural teacher, a member of the Swansea Women's History Group, and a feminist activist, and paved the way not only for the Women's Archive of Wales but also for the creation of the Gender Studies in Wales Centre at the University of Glamorgan. The latter was quickly to become the leading research centre for women's history, literature and gender studies in Wales, and its members would produce several landmark histories, particularly of women's politics.

A university research centre was a long way from the informal study groups established within the women's liberation movement in the 1970s and 1980s. But the principle was the same: knowledge transfer and consciousness raising. In the study groups, women gathered to debate and discuss previously arranged reading material, which itself drew on the books and pamphlets made available by publishers such as Virago and the Women's Press. In Cardiff, women tackled everything from feminist philosophy and history to contemporary fiction: books such as Sheila Rowbotham's bestseller *Beyond the Fragments* (1979) and Antonia White's *Frost in May* (first published in 1933 but republished by Virago as a modern classic in 1978). The group also studied Angela Carter's *The Sadeian Woman and the Ideology of Pornography* (1978), which informed campaigns on pornography and sexual exploitation. The standout work on the group's reading list, in retrospect, was probably Amrit Wilson's prize-winning *Finding A Voice* (1978), which challenged prevailing stereotypes of Asian women as submissive to a patriarchal system which kept them otherwise isolated from society. This was an indication that some members of the Cardiff women's liberation movement were engaging with (what is now considered to be) intersectional thought, although there is no written record of their reaction to Wilson's findings.[9]

The greatest successes of the 1990s and the early decades of the twenty-first century were political – an affirmation of the broad alignment of the women's movement to social democratic party politics. In 1997, Wales's dire parliamentary record was finally overturned, with the selection and election of more women than ever before. It was not a difficult line to cross, given only four women had been elected up to that point, all of them from the Labour Party (although Megan Lloyd George was first elected as a Liberal). Following its creation in 1999, the record of the National Assembly for Wales was significantly better, again with the Labour Party in the vanguard. In 2003, elections to the National Assembly produced a world first: exactly half of the sixty members elected were women. Speaking afterwards, Rhodri Morgan, the First Minister, told a fascinated press that 'I frequently use the high number of women in the assembly to promote Welsh democracy around the world'.[10] It was a point of personal pride. 'The fight for gender equality inside the Labour Party was very familiar to him', observed Kevin Brennan and Mark Drakeford in the foreword of Rhodri Morgan's posthumously published memoir, 'and from close quarters'.[11]

It had been a very long journey, as this book has shown, with significant challenges facing women both within Labour Party circles and without. However, in the nearly twenty years since that high point, the Senedd (as the National Assembly is now known) has retreated into a position in which women are a clear minority of members. Following the 2021 Senedd elections, for example, forty-three per cent of members were women, compared with fifty-seven per cent men. Or, twenty-six seats, compared with thirty-four. The largest cohort of women elected to the sixth Senedd belonged to the Labour Party: they formed the majority of the party's Senedd group, at seventeen seats out of thirty elected, and the overwhelming majority of the cabinet appointed by First Minister Mark Drakeford. At the end of her memoir, *A Woman's Work Is Never Done*, Elizabeth Andrews reflected that in her long career of service to the labour movement she had had 'to try and teach women not to be afraid of freedom' and that readers would 'draw their own conclusions on their debt to the great labour movement with its three paths to power for the people'. Her own judgement was that 'we must encourage [women] not to fear the future', and that the Labour Party's cause, as far as women were concerned, was a worthy one.

In the nearly 200 years since the Chartist movement first campaigned for the vote, for equal rights of citizenship, and for a progressive transformation of the material conditions in which the majority live their lives, the women's movement in Wales – in all its political and organisational diversity – has achieved enormous success. It has taken time for the full extent of that success to be recognised by historians, and for the centrality of women to the labour movement and to social democracy to be understood. (And vice versa.) Women were always integral to the making of Labour Country and have made enduring contributions to its politics, to the creation of the welfare state, to education, to the economy, to health, to local government, and to social and cultural progress. These are facets which go much further than a discrete focus on the suffrage campaign, or notions of national identity and nationhood, and fully justify, I argue, the synonymity of the women's movement with social democracy. The latter was the key to forging a successful Welsh women's movement: these truly were causes in common. The final words I shall leave to the writer Elaine Morgan, a lifelong socialist, who used the arts, the media and evolutionary science to further the status of women in society. 'Once you are embarked on the road to liberation and equality', she told listeners to her radio lecture on the BBC in 1975, 'you cannot get off at whatever stop seems most convenient to you'. We are, all of us, still travelling.

Notes

1. BLSA, C1420/35: Interview conducted with Michele Ryan by Lizzie Thynne, 25 August 2012.
2. Margherita N. Rendel, *Women's Studies in the UK* (London, 1975), p. 13; *Spare Rib*, 2 (November 1976). At its conclusion, members of the Newport class resolved to establish a local branch of women's liberation. Jane Hutt, 'Not Just the Same Old Gang', *Spare Rib*, 59 (June 1977), 23.
3. Beddoe, *Out of the Shadows*, p. 171.
4. Martin Wright, 'Whose Past? Whose Future? An Exploration of Women's History in Wales', *Equal Opportunities International*, 19/2–4 (2000), 25–30, p. 26.
5. John, 'Introduction', in John (ed.), *Our Mothers' Land*, p. 10.
6. Deirdre Beddoe, 'Towards a Welsh Women's History', *Llafur*, 3/2 (1981), 32–8.
7. Wright, 'Whose Past?', 26.
8. Ursula Masson and Avril Rolph, *Guide to Sources for the Women's Liberation Movement in Wales* (Pontypridd, 1997). The *Guide* is split into three volumes. The archival residue of the project is held at the Glamorgan Archives.

9. Although it is worth being cautious in recognising such reading as an indication of a progressive history of engagement, as Say Burgin has argued. See: Say Burgin, 'White Women, Anti-Imperialist Feminism and the Story of Race within the US Women's Liberation Movement', in Scott and Bruley (eds), *Historicising*, p. 70; see also Natalie Thomlinson, *Race, Ethnicity and the Women's Liberation Movement in England, 1968–1993* (Basingstoke, 2016).

10. *The Guardian*, 3 May 2003.

11. Kevin Brennan and Mark Drakeford, 'Foreword', in Rhodri Morgan, *Rhodri: A Political Life in Wales and Westminster* (Cardiff, 2017), p. xiv.

Acknowledgements

This book was first envisaged after I completed writing *Labour Country* (2018) and *A Little Gay History of Wales* (2019). Having sifted through the archival legacy of the labour movement for the former, it was clear to me that the distinct history of the women's labour movement needed to be told on its own terms. Researching and writing the LGBTQ+ history of Wales brought to the fore the need to think through a new, but still archivally focused, methodology appropriate to the recovery of Welsh women's liberation, lesbian liberation, and the struggle of the trans community for recognition and equality. Since I did not quite achieve that in *A Little Gay History of Wales*, although it succeeded in queering Welsh labour history, what readers now possess is the result of my endeavour to bring labour history, women's history and queer history together in the Welsh setting. The two books are designed as companions.

First and foremost, I wish to thank the Rhys Davies Trust, who have supported my work directly since the start of April 2020. The fellowship endowed by the trustees, Sam Adams, Peter Finch and Dai Smith, which is held in partnership with the South Wales Miners' Library and Swansea University, has allowed me the freedom to be inventive and creative as a historian and afforded a once-in-a-lifetime opportunity. At Swansea, it has been my great fortune to work alongside, and learn from, John Spurr and Sian Williams. I wish to thank Kirsti Bohata for prompting me to rethink parts of my earlier work on queer history. At the University of Wales Press, I thank Llion Wigley once more. Immediately supportive of the idea to write a companion volume to accompany *A Little Gay History of Wales*, Llion and the entire UWP team have worked so hard to make these explorations of the Welsh past such a success.

For thoughts, ideas and encouragement, I am grateful to numerous friends and colleagues, but especially (and in no order, save alphabetical) Sue Bruley, Chris Chapman, Vicky Davis, Tom Hulme, Alexander Jackson, Miriam Cohen Kiel, Barbara and David Melksham, Sarah Morse, Mary and Wilf Owen, Lisa Power, Norette Smith, Ceinwen Statter, Duncan Stone, David Toms, Ashley Walsh, Christian Webb, Jeffrey Weeks, Huw Williams, Maria Williams and Ann Wilson. A chance encounter online brought me into contact with Dr Matthew Sweet, voice of BBC Radio Three's *Sound of Cinema* (amongst other things), whose family were mainstays of the Communist Party in the Rhondda during the 1930s. By email and in person, Matthew and I have discussed the Sweets, radical politics and *Doctor Who*, with regular abandon, and I am very grateful to Matthew for encouraging my exploration of his family's fascinating history.

Causes in Common was written entirely in the context of the COVID-19 pandemic and the multiple lockdowns which were imposed to bring the spread of the virus under control. Loss of research opportunities, as frustrating as they can be, pale in comparison to the impact of losing those who passed away as I was writing, and whom I could reach only by the telephone. An earlier version of the text was read by Professor Hywel Francis, who responded to it enthusiastically a few weeks before he died in February 2021. I had spoken with him often about communist women and what they had been up to between the wars, discussions which both of us valued greatly. In the same month, my beloved grandmother, from whom I had learned so much about life growing up as a working-class 'Labour woman' in the twentieth century, also passed away very suddenly – one of the more than 150,000 Britons who died because of the coronavirus. I shall dearly miss them both.

Finally, it is with the pandemic in mind, and in keeping with my desire to recognise the very many sacrifices made by women in education, healthcare, and the service sector, in each successive generation, that I dedicate this book to my sister, Katrina. She spent the entire period working in a primary school in Pontypridd educating and caring for those too young to fully understand what was happening – and yet who knew that these events were strange. This is a small token of appreciation.

Select Bibliography

For reasons of space, the following bibliography details primary sources used in the research for this book and selected secondary works. Full references are otherwise given in the endnotes accompanying each chapter.

PRIMARY SOURCES

(i) UNPUBLISHED SOURCES

Aberdare Library, W. W. Price Collection
Aberdare ILP Records

Bishopsgate Institute, London
Switchboard Records

Cardiff University Special Collections and Archives
Cardiff Trades Council Records
Charlie Swain Papers
Labour Party Archive (microfilm)
Women's Labour League Records (microfilm)

Cathays Library, Local Studies Collection
Community Health Council Annual Reports
Women's Aid Annual Reports

Glamorgan Archives
Aberdare Valley ILP Records (W. W. Price Papers)
Alderman Rose Davies Papers
Barbara Castle (Ynysybwl) Papers
Barry Constituency Labour Party Records
Cardiff and District Fabian Society Records
Cardiff Women's Centre Records
Caroline Joll Papers
Cynon Valley Constituency Labour Party Records
Jennie Cuthbert Papers
Older Lesbian Network Records
Ray T. Davies Papers
South Wales Feminist History Project Records
Ursula Masson Papers
Women's Co-operative Guild, Pontypridd Branch Records
Wales Women's Rights Committee Records

Labour History Archive and Study Centre, Manchester
Communist Party of Great Britain Records
Labour Party Records

London School of Economics Special Collections and Archives
Fabian Society Records
Hall-Carpenter Archive, Campaign for Homosexual Equality
    Records
National Union of Women's Suffrage Societies Records
Suffrage Newspaper and Pamphlet Collection
Women's Franchise League Records
Women's Freedom League Records

National Archives, Kew
Secret Service Personal File for Arthur Horner
Secret Service Personal File for Dora Cox
Secret Service Personal File for Idris Cox
Secret Service Personal File for William Alexander

National Library of Wales
East Glamorgan Labour Women's Advisory Council Records
Labour Party Wales Records

Richard Burton Archives, Swansea University
Aberdare Trades and Labour Council Records
Annie Powell Papers
Caerphilly Labour Party Records
Irene Paynter Papers
Newport Labour Party Records
Women's Co-operative Guild Records

South Wales Miners' Library, Swansea
Annie Powell Collection
Ceridwen Brown Collection
Oral History Collection:
    AUD/216: Interview with Lucy James, 1974
    AUD/233: Interview with Mrs and Mrs Rosser, 1974
    AUD/253: Interview with Lillian Rees, 1974
    AUD/277: Interview with S. A. Harries, 1974
    AUD/342: Interview with Nancy Davies, 1974
    AUD/348: Interview with Mr and Mrs Lewis, 1973
    AUD/385: Interview with Lillian May Price
    AUD/453: Interview with Mrs D. J. Williams, 1973
    AUD/456: Interview with Edna Morgan, 1975
    AUD/476: Interview with Miss Griffiths, 1975
    AUD/477: Interview with Mrs Jones, 1975
    AUD/484: Interview with Mrs Thomas, 1975
    AUD/486: Interview with Elizabeth Morgan, 1975
    AUD/503: Interview with Sian James, 1986
    AUD/505: Interview with Donna Jones, 1986
    AUD/509: Interview with Christine Powell, 1986
    AUD/510: Interview with Hefina Headon, 1986
    AUD/583: Interview with Neath, Swansea and Dulais Valleys
       Women's Support Group, 1984

AUD/584: Interview with Cwm Llantwit Women's Support Group, 1984

AUD/585: Interview with Maerdy Women's Support Group, 1984

AUD/586: Interview with Ferndale Women's Support Group, 1984

AUD/587: Interview with Ammanford Women's Support Group, 1984

AUD/669: Interview with Ystrad Mynach Women's Support Group, 1984

AUD/676: Interview with Oakdale Women's Support Group, 1984

AUD/98: Interview with Mavis Llewellyn, 1974

AUD/442: Interview with Olive Wilson

West Glamorgan Archives, Swansea
Jenny Lynn Papers
Swansea Labour Association Records
Ursula Masson Papers
West Wales Labour Women's Advisory Council Records

(ii) NEWSPAPERS AND MAGAZINES
Aberdare Leader
Aberdare Times
Aberdeen Evening Express
Anti-Bread Tax Circular
Barry Dock News
Barry Herald
Broadsheet (Leeds)
Cambrian
Cardiff People's Paper
Cardiff Times
Cardiff Women's Liberation Newsletter
Carmarthen Journal
Clarion
Colliery Workers' Magazine

Co-operative News
Coventry Evening Telegraph
Daily Herald
Daily Worker
Double Take
Evening Express
Glamorgan County Times
Glamorgan Free Press
Glamorgan Gazette
Illustrated Usk News
Justice
Labour Leader
Labour Woman
League Leaflet
Llais Llafur
Llantrisant Observer
Merthyr Express
Merthyr Pioneer
Merthyr Telegraph
Monmouthshire Merlin
Montgomeryshire Express
Northern Star
North Wales Chronicle
North Wales Weekly News
Planet
Pontypridd Observer
Pontypridd Chronicle
Plebs
Rhondda Clarion
Rhondda Leader
Rhondda Socialist
Rhondda Vanguard
Silurian
Socialist Woman
South Wales Argus
South Wales Daily News

South Wales Daily Post
South Wales Echo
South Wales Gazette
Spare Rib
Star of Gwent
Swansea and District Worker's Journal
Swansea Journal
Tartan Skirt
Transgender Tapestry
Weekly Worker
Western Mail
Western Vindicator
Women Come Together
Women's Dreadnought
Women's Suffrage Journal
Women's Worker
Women's Voice
Worker's Dreadnought
Wrexham Advertiser
Yorkshire Post

SECONDARY SOURCES

Aaron, Jane and Ursula Masson (eds), *The Very Salt of Life: Welsh Women's Political Writings From Chartism to Suffrage* (Dinas Powys, 2007)

Aaron, Jane and Angela V. John (eds), *Our Sisters' Land* (Cardiff, 1994)

Andrews, Elizabeth, *A Woman's Work is Never Done* (Cardiff, 1956)

Beddoe, Deirdre, *Out of the Shadows: A History of Women in Twentieth-Century Wales* (Cardiff, 2000)

Beddoe, Deirdre, 'Women and Politics in Twentieth Century Wales', *National Library of Wales Journal*, 33/3 (2004)

'agini, Eugenio, *Liberty, Retrenchment and Reform: Popular Liberalism in the Age of Gladstone, 1860–1880* (Cambridge, 1992)

Bone, Ian, *Bash the Rich: True-Life Confessions of an Anarchist in the UK* (London, 2006)

Breitenbach, Esther and Pat Thane (eds), *Women and Citizenship in Britain and Ireland in the Twentieth Century: What Difference did the Vote Make?* (London, 2010)

Bruley, Sue, *Leninism, Stalinism, and the Women's Movement in Britain, 1920–1939* (London, 1986)

Bruley, Sue, *Women in Britain Since 1900* (Basingstoke, 1999)

Bruley, Sue, *The Women and Men of 1926: A Gender and Social History of the General Strike and Miners' Lockout in South Wales* (Cardiff, 2010)

Burns, Christine (ed.), *Trans Britain: Our Journey from the Shadows* (London, 2018)

Chase, Malcolm, *Chartism: A New History* (Manchester, 2007)

Clark, Anna, *The Struggle for the Breeches: Gender and the Making of the British Working Class* (Berkeley, 1995)

Collette, Christine, *From Labour and For Women: The Women's Labour League, 1906–1918* (Manchester, 1989)

Davies, Rhys, *Jubilee Blues* (London, 1937)

Delap, Lucy, *Feminisms: A Global History* (London, 2020)

Fisher, Kate, *Birth Control, Sex, and Marriage in Britain, 1918–1960* (Oxford, 2006)

Francis, Hywel and Dai Smith, *The Fed: A History of the South Wales Miners in the Twentieth Century* (London, 1980)

Francis, Hywel, *Miners Against Fascism: Wales and the Spanish Civil War* (London, 1984)

Graves, Pamela, *Labour Women: Women in British Working-Class Politics, 1918–1939* (Cambridge, 1994)

Griffin, Emma, *Liberty's Dawn: A People's History of the Industrial Revolution* (New Haven, CT, 2013)

Griffin, Emma, *Bread Winner: An Intimate History of the Victorian Economy* (New Haven, CT, 2020)

Gurney, Peter, *Co-operative Culture and the Politics of Consumption in England, c.1870–1930* (Manchester, 1996)

Gurney, Peter, *Wanting and Having: Popular Politics and Liberal Consumerism in England, 1830–70* (Manchester, 2015)

Hollis, Patricia, *Ladies Elect: Women in English Local Government, 1865–1914* (Oxford, 1987)

Hopkin, Deian, Duncan Tanner and Chris Williams (eds), *The Labour Party in Wales, 1900–2000* (Cardiff, 2000)

Horner, Arthur, *Incorrigible Rebel* (London, 1960)

John, Angela V. (ed.), *Our Mothers' Land: Chapters in Welsh Women's History, 1830–1939* (Cardiff, 1991)

John, Angela V., *Turning the Tide: The Life of Lady Rhondda* (Cardigan, 2013)

John, Angela V., *Rocking the Boat: Welsh Women Who Championed Equality, 1840–1990* (Cardigan, 2017)

Jolly, Margaretta, *Sisterhood and After: An Oral History of the UK Women's Liberation Movement, 1968–Present* (Oxford, 2019)

Linehan, Thomas, *Communism in Britain, 1920–39: From the Cradle to the Grave* (Manchester, 2007)

Masson, Ursula, '"Political conditions in Wales are quite different ...": Party politics and votes for women in Wales, 1912–15', *Women's History Review*, 9/2 (2000)

Masson, Ursula, *'For Women, for Wales and for Liberalism': Women in Liberal Politics in Wales, 1880–1914* (Cardiff, 2010)

Masson, Ursula and Avril Rolph, *Guide to Sources for the Women's Liberation Movement in Wales* (Pontypridd, 1997)

Morgan, Elaine, *The Descent of Woman* (London, 1972)

Morgan, Elaine, *Women and Society* (Cardiff, 1975)

Oram, Alison, *Women Teachers and Feminist Politics, 1900–1939* (Manchester, 1996)

Phillips, Marion, *Women and the Labour Party* (London, 1918)

Phillips, Marion, *Women and the Miners' Lock Out* (London, 1927)

Pickering, Paul A. and Alex Tyrrell, *The People's Bread: A History of the Anti-Corn Law League* (Leicester, 2000)

Rolph, Avril, 'Too Friendly For Feminism? The Early Years of the Women's Liberation Movement in South Wales', *Planet: The Welsh Internationalist*, 147 (2001), 87–95

Rolph, Avril, 'A movement of its own: the Women's Liberation Movement in south Wales', in Helen Graham et al. (eds), *The Feminist Seventies* (York, 2003)

Smith, Dai (ed.), *A People and A Proletariat* (London, 1980)

Smith, Evan, *British Communism and the Politics of Race* (Chicago, 2018)

Thomlinson, Natalie, *Race, Ethnicity and the Women's Movement in England, 1968–1993* (Basingstoke, 2016)

Thompson, Dorothy, *The Dignity of Chartism* (London, 2015)

Tomaselli, Sylvana, *Wollstonecraft: Philosophy, Passion, and Politics* (Princeton, 2021)

Wallace, Ryland, *Organize! Organize! Organize! A Study of Reform Agitations in Wales, 1840–1886* (Cardiff, 1991)

Wallace, Ryland, *The Women's Suffrage Movement in Wales, 1866–1928* (Cardiff, 2009)

Ward, Stephanie, *Unemployment and the State: The Means Test and Protest in 1930s South Wales and North-East England* (Manchester, 2013)

Williams, Chris, *Democratic Rhondda: Politics and Society, 1885–1951* (Cardiff, 1996)

Worley, Matthew, *Labour Inside the Gate: A History of the British Labour Party Between The Wars* (London, 2005)

THESES AND DISSERTATIONS

Francis, D. Hywel, 'The South Wales Miners and the Spanish Civil War: A Study in Internationalism' (unpublished PhD thesis, University College Swansea, 1979)

Newman, Lowri, 'A Distinctive Brand of Politics: Women in the South Wales Labour Party, 1918–1939' (unpublished MPhil thesis, University of Glamorgan, 2003)

Selway, David, 'Collective Memory in the Mining Communities of South Wales' (unpublished PhD thesis, University of Sussex, 2017)

Index